TOWARDS VISIBLE UNITY

COMMISSION ON FAITH AND ORDER
LIMA 1982

VOLUME II: STUDY PAPERS AND REPORTS

Towards the Common Expression
of the Apostolic Faith Today
and
The Unity of the Church
and the Renewal of Human Community

Edited by Michael Kinnamon

Faith and Order Paper No. 113
World Council of Churches, Geneva

BX
6
. W775
A2
1982
v. 2

Cover design: Carmen Bilbao La Vieja
ISBN No. 2-8254-0726-7
© 1982 World Council of Churches, 150 route de Ferney,
1211 Geneva 20, Switzerland
Printed in Switzerland

Contents

Preface vii
William H. Lazareth

**Part I: Towards the common expression
of the apostolic faith today**

1. PAPERS AND REPORTS FROM THE MEETING
   OF THE FAITH AND ORDER COMMISSION,
   LIMA, PERU, JANUARY 1982

   Staff report 3
   Hans-Georg Link

   Towards the common expression of the apostolic faith
   today 13
   Ulrich Kühn

   Listening to some contemporary statements of faith
   from Latin America 24
   Jaci Maraschin

   Report of the working group 28

   The Community Study and apostolic faith: memorandum from the working group on the Community of
   Women and Men in the Church 47

2. PAPERS FROM A PRELIMINARY CONSULTATION,
   CHAMBÉSY, SWITZERLAND, JULY 1981

   The Roman Catholic Church's fidelity to the "faith of
   the fathers" 51
   Jean M. R. Tillard, OP

In search of an African contribution to a meaningful
contemporary confession of the Christian faith   62
Sigqibo Dwane

The confession of faith in the Lutheran tradition   70
Wolfhart Pannenberg

One confession—many confessions: reflections on the
Second Ecumenical Council of Constantinople (381)   80
Damaskinos Papandreou

3. PAPERS FROM A PRELIMINARY CONSULTATION,
ODESSA, USSR, OCTOBER 1981

The trinitarian understanding of the Christian God in
relation to monotheism and polytheism   93
V. C. Samuel

The transition of the Christian faith from the New Testa-
ment-Jewish context to the Nicene-Hellenistic context ...   101
Ellen Flesseman-van Leer

Affirmations to the Spirit   113
Thomas Hopko

**Part II: The unity of the Church and the renewal
of human community**

1. PAPERS AND REPORTS FROM THE MEETING
OF THE FAITH AND ORDER STANDING COMMISSION,
ANNECY, FRANCE, JANUARY 1981

"That the world may believe": staff discussion paper ...   123
C. S. Song

Working group report   132

2. PAPERS AND REPORTS FROM A PRELIMINARY
CONSULTATION, GENEVA, SWITZERLAND, JUNE 1981

Bases and outline of a study on the unity of the Church
and the renewal of human community   135

— Race, Christian unity and the unity of humankind   144
Gayraud Wilmore

— The Community Study and the unity of the Church and
renewal of human community   153
Mary Tanner

— The unity of the Church and the renewal of human community: a perspective from Africa   166
Amba Oduyoye

3. PAPERS AND REPORTS FROM THE MEETING
OF THE FAITH AND ORDER COMMISSION,
LIMA, PERU, JANUARY 1982

The unity of the Church and the renewal of human com-
munity   184
John Deschner

Working group reports
Creation   198
History   203
Culture   211
Alienation   218
Mission   221
Unity   224

Notes for a study on "The unity of the Church and the
renewal of human community"   229

Preface

At the conclusion of the triennial meeting of the Faith and Order Commission, 2-16 January 1982, in Lima, Peru, the members voted to concentrate their research in the next years on two major studies: (1) "Towards the Common Expression of the Apostolic Faith Today", and (2) "The Unity of the Church and the Renewal of Human Community".

At the same time, it was recognized that the WCC Central Committee had called for the fruitful conclusion of all programmes by the end of 1981, and the holding of no more commission, working or advisory group meetings between then and the WCC assembly in July 1983. This policy would allow each sub-unit to allocate a substantial portion of its regular budget and staff time to a pre-assembly Programme of Visitation and Consultation, along with other needed pre-assembly planning and preparations. Moreover, it was made clear that the newly-constituted Faith and Order Commission would not be named before the summer 1984 meeting of the newly-elected Central Committee, and therefore could not likely be convened before the summer of 1985.

To compensate for this unfortunate 42-month break between the meetings of the two different Commissions, it was decided to attempt some ongoing continuity through the correspondence of two small Steering Committees assigned to guide the activities of the Secretariat on the two major studies.

In support of this procedure, it was further decided that the official reports of the Lima 1982 conference would be published in two volumes: (1) the first would include the minutes of the meeting as well as several of the major plenary addresses; (2) the second could then specialize in materials related to the two major studies and thereby provide both Steering Committees (and others) with a handy reference volume and study guide for their correspondence-limited endeavours. That both explains the purpose and determines the composition of this volume.

"Towards the Common Expression of the Apostolic Faith Today"

In connection with the observance of the 1600th anniversary year of the Second Ecumenical Council, the Secretariat published *Spirit of God, Spirit of Christ*, on settling the controversy over the Creed's wording *(filioque)*, and *Does Chalcedon Divide or Unite?*, on reconciling the interpretation of the christological dogma of the Council (451). Also published were *Towards a Confession of the Common Faith*, an ecumenical prospectus for a long-term research project, and *Confessing our Faith around the World* (Volume I), a collection of contemporary Christian testimonies often made in the face of political oppression.

Building on the theological convergences formulated in the Faith and Order studies on "Giving Account of the Hope" and the "Common Statement of Our Faith", along with the text on "Baptism, Eucharist and Ministry", the Secretariat convened three preliminary consultations—in Chambésy (July 1981), Princeton (September 1981) and Odessa (October 1981)—dealing with various aspects of confessing the Christian faith today.

Then, at Lima itself, delegates integrated the relevant materials into a long-term project model for a common affirmation and current explication of the faith of the apostolic Church. Both the theme and the project model were enthusiastically endorsed by the Commission. Major documents from Chambésy, Odessa and Lima are included in the first part of this volume, as well as the crucial working group report from Lima.

"Unity of the Church and the Renewal of Human Community"

In deciding to pursue anew the earlier study on "Unity of Church—Unity of Humankind", the Faith and Order Standing Commission (January 1981) intentionally wanted to place the classical Faith and Order concern for church unity "on a broadened horizon and to develop its implications for Christian service and mission in the contemporary world".

A preparatory consultation helped to develop some background papers and a tentative outline for the study. At Lima, the delegates listened to a plenary lecture that outlined earlier ecumenical research on this theme. They also developed a series of reports on inter-related aspects of this complex and controversial subject (creation, history, culture, alienation, mission, unity).

Although a draft prospectus for a project model was debated and substantially revised in plenary, it was not officially endorsed. Hence the provisional material collected in the second part of this volume must be considered less mature in its development than that related to the study on apostolic faith. The "Unity and Renewal" study is still in need of clarification and Commission approval.

* * *

Since both of these major themes will now be developed further through the shared correspondence of Commission Steering Committees, the reader is cordially invited to share in this collegial process. Comments, critiques and related contributions should be sent directly to the Faith and Order Secretariat, World Council of Churches, 150 route de Ferney, 1211 Geneva 20, Switzerland.

Finally, as the total Lima report is now published in two separate volumes, I am mandated to convey here, as in Volume I, the deep appreciation for the ongoing work of the Secretariat that was publicly expressed at Lima by the Moderator, other officers and members of the Commission. If the Lima meeting was outstanding, the combined efforts of the entire staff —programme, administrative, coopted and local—helped greatly to contribute to this end.

In this setting, it is also appropriate that a special word of thanks be extended to the Rev. Stephen Cranford, former Faith and Order staff member and current pastor of Douglass Boulevard Christian Church in Louisville, Kentucky (USA), and to Dr Michael Kinnamon, staff Executive Secretary, for their integrated skills as (respectively) conference minutes secretary and editor of this published report.

WILLIAM H. LAZARETH
Director, Commission on Faith and Order
World Council of Churches

Part I

Towards the common expression
of the apostolic faith today

Staff report

HANS-GEORG LINK

Theme of the study

The question of unity in faith has belonged to the main agenda
of the ecumenical movement since the movement's beginnings
(i.e. since the World Missionary Conference in Edinburgh in 1910
and the First World Conference on Faith and Order in Lausanne
in 1927). The theme committee preparing the Lausanne meeting
formulated its first question as: "What degree of unity in faith
will be necessary in a re-united Church?"[1] At the conference
itself, group IV dealt with the theme "The Church's Common
Confession of Faith" on which it produced a short final report.[2]

After the theological basis of the World Council of Churches
was formulated in Amsterdam in 1948 and a further trinitarian
clause was added in New Delhi in 1961, the Fifth Assembly in
Nairobi, 1975, made the following recommendation to the
member churches:

> We ask the churches to undertake a common effort to receive, re-
> appropriate and confess together, as contemporary occasion requires,
> the Christian truth and faith, delivered through the apostles and handed
> down through the centuries. Such common action, arising from free and
> inclusive discussion under the commonly acknowledged authority of

• Rev. Dr HANS-GEORG LINK, Evangelical Church in Germany (Lutheran), is
Executive Secretary in the Faith and Order Secretariat, Geneva, Switzerland.

God's word, must aim both to clarify and to embody the unity and the diversity which are proper to the Church's life and mission.[3]

Following on this recommendation, the Commission on Faith and Order, at its Bangalore meeting in 1978, gave a short report on its first attempt to tackle the question of the common faith:

> The study "Giving Account of the Hope" has raised a new question which will demand detailed study. What way of confessing the apostolic faith is required for the Church to live in visible unity? At Bangalore, the Commission made a first attempt to offer a "common confession of faith". The attempt brought into sharp focus the problems which need to be examined in the coming years, e.g. the role of tradition, and, more particularly, the ancient creeds in the Church, the relationship between the common confession and the doctrinal controversies which arose in the history of the Church, the role of the liturgical confession of faith, etc.[4]

What is at stake today when the Commission on Faith and Order takes up again the theme of 1927 under the formulation "Towards a Common Expression of the Apostolic Faith Today"? The issue points, first, to the need to express the same faith today that was expressed in the New Testament and which has been summarized in the early church confessions; that is what is meant by the expression "apostolic faith". It also points towards the need for a comprehensive "expression" of the faith that includes words as well as deeds. The need, however, is not only for a repetition of the early confessions of faith but also for a new interpretation of the essential content of the Christian faith in the face of contemporary challenges; this is referred to by the addition of "today". The question is also how to find the new expression of the Christian faith in common, not simply individually. The more comprehensive it is, the more authoritative is the expression of "the apostolic faith". This is what is meant by the adjective "common". Finally, we need to approach the issue of confessing the apostolic faith with courage, confidence and concentration; that is why we are "on the way" and not "at the end".

Review of the study process

1. A first colloquium on "Unity in Faith" took place in Venice in June 1978. Its results were submitted to the Joint Working Group between the Roman Catholic Church and the World

Council of Churches and, after further revision, were published in summer 1980 as Faith and Order Paper No. 100, "Towards a Confession of the Common Faith".[5]

2. Two consultations on the question of the *filioque* were held at Schloss Klingenthal near Strasbourg, France, in October 1978 and May 1979. The presentations and recommendations of these meetings are published under the title *Spirit of God, Spirit of Christ*.[6]

3. During the meeting of the Faith and Order Commission in Bangalore, working group 2 dealt with "the common expression of the apostolic faith". This group worked out a "Common Statement of Our Faith" which was approved by the Commission and recommended for further study.[7]

4. At its meeting in Taizé, 1979, the Standing Commission underlined the three requirements for the realization of visible unity which had previously been stated at Bangalore:[8] (a) unity in one faith; (b) consensus on baptism, eucharist and ministry; and (c) common ways of teaching and decision-making.[9]

With regard to unity in faith, the Standing Commission dealt with five areas:[10]

— the place of the ancient creeds in the Church today;
— setting the goal: what can be achieved;
— the relation between corporate and individual renewal of the faith;
— the different interconfessional and intercultural understandings of the authority of scripture and of the gospel;
— the form(s) in which the common faith is to be expressed.

5. In summer 1980, Dr C. S. Song edited a first collection of contemporary confessions of faith from all over the world under the title *Confessing our Faith Around the World*.[11] In his preface, Dr Song distinguishes, with the help of the Petrine confession of Caesarea Philippi (Mark 8:27ff.), between preconfessional, confessing and post-confessional situations.[12]

6. The Standing Commission discussed the study at its meeting in Annecy, January 1981. It was agreed "that any new study of confessions of faith must be done in continuity with baptism, eucharist and ministry and the Account of Hope study".[13] Special attention was given to the close connection between liturgical confessions and the confession of Christ in service and mission, to the diversity of contexts and to the language used in confessions.

According to the minutes: "The Standing Commission affirmed the basic conception of this study. It was agreed that the study should extend well beyond Vancouver." The proposal was made to pursue, during the course of 1981, several "simultaneous small steps and to establish some regionally oriented groups, in order to develop a greater sense of corporate ownership"[14] with regard to this study project.

7. An informal theological discussion group, including members of the Faith and Order Secretariat and the Orthodox Task Force in the Ecumenical Centre in Geneva, came together five times between November 1980 and May 1981 in order to establish closer relationships especially to the Orthodox tradition and to clarify necessary tasks concerning the common expression of the apostolic faith today. The themes dealt with were the following:
— general comments on the subject with special reference to each person's own Christian tradition;
— an article by Msgr Emilianos Timiadis entitled "Common and Uncommon Faith";[15]
— the advantages and disadvantages of the Nicene Creed as a basis for a common expression of the Christian faith;
— the celebration of the 1600th anniversary of the Nicene Creed in the Ecumenical Centre.

8. The worship service concerning the 1600th anniversary of the Niceno-Constantinopolitan Creed, under the responsibility of the Faith and Order Secretariat, took place on 15 June (the Monday after the western Holy Trinity feast and the Orthodox Pentecost feast), in the chapel of the Ecumenical Centre in Geneva. Representatives of Geneva churches and of various Christian world communions were also present. The theme of the service was "We believe in the Holy Spirit, the Lord, the Giver of life". It included the common confession of the Creed (without the *filioque* clause) by all participants, an opening address by Prof. Lazareth, remarks on the Council of Constantinople by Frère Max Thurian, a sermon given by General Secretary Philip Potter, the WCC Pentecost message read by the Honorary President of the WCC, Dr W. A. Visser 't Hooft, and spontaneous words of peace from Protopresbyter V. Borovoi. It seemed to be a meaningful celebration of this anniversary.

9. From 28 June to 3 July 1981, a first preliminary consultation was held at the invitation of the Ecumenical Patriarchate of

Constantinople, at the Orthodox Centre in Chambésy near Geneva. About fifteen theologians from various parts of the world—most of them members of the Faith and Order Commission—met together with Faith and Order staff members responsible for this study, in order to develop a framework for the whole project "Towards the Common Expression of the Apostolic Faith Today". The meeting focused on three areas:

— contemporary challenges which lead to new expressions of the Christian faith in the various parts of the world;
— the role which the early confessions, especially the Nicene Creed, play in the various church traditions;
— previous ecumenical endeavours to express together the Christian faith.

The report of this consultation consists of two papers: Paper A (the main report) deals, first, with the "recognition of the Nicene Creed as the ecumenical symbol of the apostolic faith", second, with the "explication of this ecumenical symbol in the contemporary situations of the churches", and third, with "some implications of common recognition of the ecumenical symbol of faith". Paper B gives a short and general "design of the apostolic faith project". It recommends, among other things, a recognition of both papers A and B as preparatory texts for Lima, and offers suggestions for relating this theme to the Vancouver assembly, developing supporting studies, and possibly preparing a World Conference of Faith and Order on this and other themes. Finally, it recommends a proposal for common recognition of the Nicene Creed to the churches.

10. In May and September 1981 an *ad hoc* working group of about ten American theologians came together in New York and Princeton. As their report says, the group's purpose "was to consider what might be the contribution of the WCC Faith and Order Commission's statements on 'baptism, eucharist and ministry' in their near-final form of January 1981, towards the newly-launched project 'towards the common expression of the apostolic faith today'". The group's strategy was to examine the "baptism, eucharist and ministry" text from the perspective of the main topics traditionally important in dogmatic theology, namely: revelation (and its transmission); Trinity: (a) God, (b) Christ (person and work), (c) Holy Spirit; creation and world; humanity and sin; grace and faith; justification; sanctification; Church; eschatology.

The 50-page report demonstrates how much substantial theological work is already done in the texts on baptism, eucharist and ministry.

11. At the invitation of the Russian Orthodox Church, another Faith and Order consultation, involving about twenty theologians from various parts of the world, took place from 9 to 15 October at the Orthodox seminary and Assumption Monastery in Odessa. Its theme was "The Ecumenical Importance of the Nicene Creed". The participants concentrated on three main aspects of the issue:

— the historical and theological understanding of the Creed, with special regard to the Holy Spirit;
— reactions from various confessional traditions to the Klingenthal Memorandum, "The *Filioque* Clause in Ecumenical Perspective";
— the biblical and credal understanding of God in his Trinity.

The report of this consultation gives, first of all, some impressions about the inspiring spiritual atmosphere of the Orthodox environment in which the participants lived. Then it summarizes the most important insights concerning the ecumenical sufficiency of the Nicene Creed, the relationships between the Bible and the Creed, as well as between the Creed and our contemporary task of common confession of the faith. Finally, it gives some recommendations regarding (a) the pursuit of the apostolic faith theme as "one of the main study projects" of Faith and Order; (b) the continuation, on different levels, of the work on "the ecumenical importance of the Nicene Creed"; and (c) the initiation of further studies, especially on the ways faith was confessed in the scriptures and in various stages of history. They culminate with the recommendation "to ask the WCC member churches, in an appropriate way, whether they would see the possibility of accepting the Nicene Creed as their common ecumenical basis from the time of the ancient Church, understanding this as a first step on the way to the common expression of the apostolic faith today".[16]

12. In Lima one of the working groups focused on the apostolic faith study. Its task was to produce a report—drawing especially on the reports from Chambésy, Princeton and Odessa—which could be accepted (received) by the Plenary Commission as a guide for future work on this project. Their report, which was unanimously accepted by the Commission, starts with

agreements concerning "the importance of this study as an ecumenical project". It develops the "the expression of the apostolic faith" in three stages: (a) common recognition of the expression of faith as formulated in the Nicene Creed; (b) explication in contemporary situations; and (c) confession of the faith today. The final recommendations see the theme "as one of the main study projects of the Faith and Order Commission in the years to come". The recommendations also deal with the contribution of a steering committee, different aspects of the study, methods and levels of the study, publications and next steps in the study project.

Aspects of the study

1. *The Nicene Creed*

As one of the oldest expressions of faith, and as the most widely used confession of faith, the Niceno-Constantinopolitan Creed belongs not to one confessional tradition but rather to the common ecumenical tradition of Christianity from the time of the ancient Church. It represents a kind of vertical ecumenism through the ages and links our present attempts of confessing the faith with their roots in early Christianity. The fact that 1981 was the 1600th anniversary of the Nicene Creed provided a good opportunity for rediscovering this common heritage. It was because of this celebration that we concentrated our efforts during the last year on this issue. Actually, the process of renewed theological recognition of the Nicene Creed began already in 1978-1979 with the two consultations on the *filioque* problem and with the elaboration of the Klingenthal Memorandum, "The *Filioque* Clause in Ecumenical Perspective".[17] The Memorandum provides a solid platform for dealing with this special problem since it makes concrete proposals for interpretation, wording and reception of the Nicene Creed without the *filioque* clause. The question now is: When and how should the churches become officially involved in this process? On the basis of full agreement with the Klingenthal proposals, the Chambésy report recommends the Nicene Creed (without *filioque*) "as the ecumenical symbol" for member churches of the World Council of Churches. This raises a second basic question: Should the common recognition of the Nicene Creed be the framework (as the Chambésy report contends) or a "first step" (as the Odessa report would have it) for our confessing the apostolic faith today? Finally, the Odessa report recommends continuous work on the Nicene Creed on linguistic, hymnological, comparative, theological, catechetical, liturgical and juridical levels. Priorities must be determined for this programme of study and plans must be made for bringing the Odessa proposals to realization.

Therefore, the questions of (a) the *filioque* clause, (b) the various applications of the Creed for today, (c) church involvements in the study process, (d) the Creed as the ecumenical basis for all member churches of the WCC, and (e) priorities for proceeding with work on this study need further clarification.

2. *Contemporary confessions*

The other pole of the project is to take into account the numerous attempts at expressing the faith today in different ways and situations. Starting with the Barmen Declaration of 1934, we seem to have entered a third period for the formulation of confessing texts (the first two being the first four ecumenical councils and the Reformation). There are obviously new challenges to Christian faith that can hardly be answered with traditional confessions; contemporary statements of faith are needed to face contemporary challenges and contexts. Whereas the European and North American churches, by virtue of their history, often concentrate on and are limited by the ancient Nicene and Apostles' creeds, Christians from Africa, Asia and Latin America emphasize more the need for a present contextual expression of the faith.

The Chambésy consultation began with presentations from various parts of the world on "contemporary challenges which lead to new expressions of the Christian faith". There a lot was said about the religious, social and political contexts in which Christian faith must be confessed today. Lima provides a good opportunity for encountering the Latin American context and for dealing with some concrete Latin American confessions of faith. Since we have already begun to collect and publish confessing texts "around the world", we should continue to do so with a special emphasis on confessions from Latin America, Africa and Asia. In this regard it would be helpful to ask each WCC member church to inform the Faith and Order Secretariat about its officially accepted confessions of faith and to send to the Secretariat those contemporary statements of faith, both formal and informal, that are used in the Church. Other tasks would be to analyze these regional materials, perhaps by holding regional consultations (e.g. on "confessing the Christian faith in Latin America, Africa or Asia"). This procedure could help to discover common Christian convictions, accents and questions, as well as the specific regional and cultural aspects of our common faith.

The design of the study project
There is no doubt that the apostolic faith study is a long-term project, extending far beyond the next WCC assembly. It continues the theological work undertaken before, and especially since, the foundation of the World Council of Churches, work that has proceeded in three main stages: (1) the basis of the World Council of Churches 1948-1961, (2) baptism, eucharist and ministry 1967-1982, (3) a common account of hope 1971-1978. With regard to the subject of the study theme itself, at least four steps have already been undertaken:
— Lausanne 1927, Subject IV: The Church's common confession of faith;
— Bangalore 1978, Committee II: The common expression of the apostolic faith;
— Klingenthal 1978-1979: The *filioque* clause in ecumenical perspective;
— Chambésy/Odessa 1981: The ecumenical importance of the Nicene Creed.
Looking forward to the further development of the project, there are at least another four main tasks to be taken into account:
  1. The *biblical roots* of confessing the faith in the Jewish and apostolic traditions need to be explored, especially for clarifying the term "apostolic faith".
  2. We need to continue the work on the ecumenical importance of the *Nicene Creed*.
  3. It would be important to study the *key stages of history* when faith was confessed in a way that remains significant for us today. These include the time of the first four ecumenical councils (325-451), the Reformation (especially during the 1520s and 1530s) and during the period of German fascism (1933-1945) with special emphasis on the so-called "confessing church".

4. We need to continue our collection, publication, analysis and comparison of *contemporary* confessions of faith in the various regions of the world.

It seems that the ecumenical movement has now reached the stage for addressing issues at the very heart of the conciliar fellowship which we seek, including the common expression of the apostolic faith today.

NOTES

[1] Quoted by W. A. Visser 't Hooft in "The 1927 Lausanne Conference in Retrospect", *Lausanne 77*, Faith and Order Paper No. 82, Geneva, WCC, p. 11.

[2] H. N. Bate (ed.), Faith and Order, *Proceedings of the World Conference*, Lausanne, 3-21 August, 1927, pp. 160 ff., 229 ff., 423 ff., 466 f.

[3] D. M. Paton (ed.), *Breaking Barriers, Nairobi 1975*, London, SPCK, and Grand Rapids, Eerdmans, 1976, p. 66

[4] *Minutes*, Bangalore 1978, Faith and Order Paper No. 93, Geneva, WCC, p. 40.

[5] Geneva, WCC.

[6] Ed. Lukas Vischer, Geneva, WCC, and London, SPCK, 1981.

[7] *Sharing in One Hope*, Bangalore 1978, Faith and Order Paper No. 92, Geneva, WCC, pp. 243 ff.

[8] *Minutes*, Bangalore 1978, *op. cit.*, p. 40 f.

[9] *Minutes* of the Meeting of the Standing Commission, Taizé 1979, Faith and Order Paper No. 98, Geneva, WCC, p. 8 f.

[10] *Minutes* of Taizé Standing Commission, *op. cit.*, p. 30 f.

[11] Faith and Order Paper No. 104, Geneva, WCC, I, 1980.

[12] *Ibid*, pp. 1-7.

[13] *Minutes* of the Meeting of the Standing Commission, Annecy 1981, Faith and Order Paper No. 106, Geneva, WCC, p. 50.

[14] *Op. cit.*, p. 5.

[15] *The Ecumenical Review*, Vol. 32, 1980, pp. 396 ff.

[16] In this connection, see *Does Chalcedon Divide or Unite? Towards Convergence in Orthodox Christology*, ed. P. Gregorios, W. Lazareth, N. Nissiotis, Geneva, WCC, 1981.

[17] *Spirit of God, Spirit of Christ*, ed. L. Vischer, Geneva, WCC, 1981, pp. 3-18.

Towards the common expression
of the apostolic faith today
ULRICH KÜHN

The study "Towards the Common Expression of the Apostolic Faith Today" is a response to the request made by the 1975 Nairobi assembly of the World Council of Churches: "We ask the churches to undertake a common effort to receive, reappropriate and confess together, as contemporary occasion requires, the Christian truth and faith, delivered through the Apostles and handed down through the centuries."[1]

This request is part of the search for "the goal of visible unity in one faith and in one eucharistic fellowship".[2] This goal, in recent years defined as "conciliar fellowship", can only be attained when at least three conditions are met: full mutual recognition of each other's baptism, eucharist and ministry by the churches, agreed structures for authoritative teaching and common decision-making, assurance that we stand together on the common ground of one and the same apostolic faith and are able to confess this faith together before God and the world.

In the ecumenical movement, and above all in the Faith and Order movement, the question of the one apostolic faith has been a live issue since the very beginning. At the Lausanne Faith and

---

• Dr ULRICH KÜHN, Federation of Evangelical Churches in the GDR (Lutheran), teaches theology at the Theological Seminary in Leipzig, German Democratic Republic. This paper has been translated from the German by the WCC Language Service.

Order Conference in 1927, it was recognized that "we are united in a common Christian faith which is proclaimed in the holy scriptures and is witnessed to and safeguarded in the ecumenical creed, commonly called the Nicene, and in the Apostles' Creed".[3] In the Basis of the World Council of Churches, adopted in Amsterdam in 1948 after thorough preliminary consultations and revised and enlarged in New Delhi in 1961, all the member churches confess "the Lord Jesus Christ as God and Saviour according to the scriptures" and recognize a common calling which they are seeking "to fulfill together... to the glory of the one God, Father, Son and Holy Spirit". It is no secret that there were serious criticisms of this statement, criticisms questioning, for example, its New Testament basis. For others, however, membership and cooperation in the World Council was considerably eased, and even made possible at all, only by the Basis in this form. In fact, the churches' acceptance of the Basis of the World Council amounted to acceptance of an important christological confession (combined with an appeal to holy scripture) and a doxological formulation of the mystery of the Trinity. In this respect, the WCC Basis goes beyond the more formal Lausanne statements; but it lags behind Lausanne in containing no explicit endorsement of the Nicene Creed (or of the Apostles' Creed), an endorsement which has so far not been forthcoming from the World Council of Churches.

The question of the common faith has been constantly pursued by the Faith and Order Commission. The significance, for example, of the texts on baptism, eucharist and ministry in this connection has been documented in detail in the Princeton Report.[4] The most important item here is the study "Giving Account of the Hope", which was originally planned as an attempt to give "an account of what we have in common in our faith", "to express the gospel we have to offer" and to explore "what is the content and meaning of our life and prayer and proclamation".[5]

Among the efforts of recent years which form the starting point for our present study, mention should at least be made, apart from the draft text presented at the Bangalore meeting of the Commission, of the 1978 consultation in Venice. This was initiated by the Joint Working Group between the WCC and the Vatican, and its report (later published as Faith and Order Paper No. 100) was presented to the Joint Working Group in February 1979. This showed the great interest which the Roman Catholic

Church also took in our work, also illustrated, moreover, by Fr Jean Tillard's important address at the Bangalore meeting.

Efforts and reflections up to the present suggest a choice between two courses, though it is open to question whether we are really faced here with a clear either/or. Should we concentrate on or even limit ourselves to, at least at first, examining and working for a formal reception of the Nicene Creed by the World Council of Churches? Or should we not rather try to produce a new contemporary statement of the apostolic faith? In previous consultations I detect a tendency to regard these two possible courses as successive but inseparable steps and, in my opinion, this in fact is the appropriate direction our further reflection should take.

The significance of the Nicene Creed

Why does it seem to make sense to begin by considering a joint affirmation of the Nicene Creed as a common expression of the one apostolic faith? There are, it seems to me, at least two positive and two negative arguments in favour of doing this.

1. The Nicene Creed is already a contemporary ecumenical bond between many of our churches. It has a very special and central significance in the Orthodox churches. But it is of fundamental importance for the Roman Catholic Church too, and is included among the authoritative confessions of the Lutheran churches. It is also an integral part of the Anglican *Lambeth Quadrilateral*. It is the only ecumenical creed which embraces both west and east, even though it is not recognized in some Protestant churches as authoritative.

2. The Nicene Creed is an official statement of the faith of the still undivided ancient Church. In the "building period" of the Church, it formulated the fundamental mysteries of faith, and therefore has, next to and along with holy scripture, the status and significance of a signpost for all succeeding ages.

3. A more "negative" argument is that we have at present no authority whatever to write a new ecumenical creed; that could only be undertaken by a future ecumenical council.

4. In any case, in view of the extreme pluralism of theological thinking in our churches today, is it not manifestly an illusion to imagine we could produce agreed doctrinal statements?

On the other hand, there are a whole string of serious objections which would need to be overcome if we were actually to envisage a common (new) reception of the Nicene Creed. If I am not much mistaken, these objections are mainly concerning the thought form of the Nicene Creed and its contents.

The problem of the *thought form* of the Nicene Creed arises in the first place, as the Odessa consultation in particular showed, in the light of the biblical message. Questions arise, above all, from the Creed's christology, but also from the doctrine of the Trinity which is expressed in it. Has not the diversity with which the New Testament, against the Old Testament background, speaks of Christ and the Spirit been cut down to suit one single binding form? And does this specific form found in the Nicene Creed not represent an alienation by the Greek mind of a biblical thinking based above all on the Old Testament? Does it not amount to a fatal translation of the functional christological and pneu-matological statements of the New Testament into an ontology operating with essentialist categories? Given these objections, we would certainly need to reflect on the significance of the fact that radical influences of Hellenistic thought are already visible in the New Testament itself. Another question to be raised is whether we can rest content with such a contrast between func-tional and ontological thinking, or whether it is not in fact the case that, in the very nature of things, functional statements already flow naturally into ontological ones. And, conversely, does not even the ontology of the Nicene Creed have to be inter-preted in functional terms? Finally, and above all, do we not also have to understand the ancient Church christology and doctrine of the Trinity as a *defence against* Greek thought (even though making use of Greek thought forms) in which the very notion of God specifically excludes the idea of any counterpart in God or of any entry of God into history?

The thought form of the Nicene Creed also creates problems for our contemporary intellectual presuppositions. Non-European churches and theologians, in particular, question whether it is possible for us *today*, especially in a non-European cultural con-text, to be tied to these fourth-century statements. To be tied in this way would, at first sight, appear to be not only a disastrous "retreat" to obsolete ways of approaching the problem but also a bit of European intellectual imperialism. This objection raises the quite fundamental question of whether the progress of the gospel through history has any significance whatever for our contemporary confession and action or for our self-understanding as churches. We shall certainly need to reflect together on the significance of the fact that the Christian faith is not just an abstract general idea. At the centre of the Christian faith is a historical event which took place at a particular place in a particular cultural context. The cultural context in question was the Semitic-Hellenistic; as the precipitate of the earliest proclamation, the New Testament provides an eloquent testimony of this. Is it possible simply to peel that cultural context off? In our contemporary belief, are we at liberty to ignore the historical *course* taken by the gospel and the Church, especially in their "building period"? We Germans had to learn from bitter experience the consequences of any attempt to abstract Christianity from its unique historical context when an attempt was made in the 1930s to "purify" the Christian message from all "alien" Jewish elements. But salvation *comes from* the Jews (John 4:22) and it was via the Greco-Roman cultural context that the gospel achieved its amazing advance in the world. That is not to say, of course, that the ancient message does not need to be *translated* into our own contemporary context!

At Odessa, the question of the *content* of the Nicene Creed was considered from the standpoint of the "sufficiency" of this creed. Is the Nicene Creed an adequate and complete statement of the Christian faith? To this it was frequently objected, with reason, that the Nicene Creed omits important affirmations of the biblical testimony (particularly with respect to questions of soteriology, but also in the matter of christological potential, as for example, the absence of any reference to the teaching of Jesus, etc.). Many questions which have subsequently arisen in Christendom are naturally not referred to in the Nicene Creed. This also seems to be an argument against a common reception of the Nicene Creed today.

Progress is certainly achieved when a distinction is made, as it was in Odessa, between a quantitative sufficiency and a qualitative sufficiency. But even if we grant the Nicene Creed a *qualitative* sufficiency, does this amount to calling it irreplaceable? It could equally well be said that the primitive Christian confession "Jesus is Lord" is qualitatively sufficient. We Lutherans, moreover, would also consider the Augsburg Confession of 1530 to be qualitatively (if not quantitatively) sufficient.

What then is so distinctive about the Nicene Creed? And why is it important that we should confess it together today? Leaving aside for the moment the question of the thought form of this creed, my answer would be this: it is important because, at a decisive moment in the life of the Church, assisted by other concrete challenges and circumstances, it clearly set forth fundamental truths of the Church's confession of Christ and of the (trinitarian) faith in God. Even in this respect it was not exhaustive. It needed further development and interpretation. But it marked, once and for all, limits and approximate values which must be respected by all future Christian confession and proclamation. To express this in terms of a traditional distinction of European theology, the Nicene Creed has *regulative* significance but not *constitutive* significance, i.e. it is not to be supposed that it states in a once-for-all way *everything* that is essential for the Church. It is in this regulative sense that I would also understand the existing Basis of the World Council of Churches: it marks salient points and guidelines which are jointly recognized, but it does not rule out, within these limits, the diversity of the witness to Christ. This recognition could be extended and strengthened by a common endorsement of the Nicene Creed.

The question of the *filioque* represents a special problem in this context. The report of the Klingenthal consultation recommended a return to the original text of the creed, without abandoning the substantial concern expressed in this additional clause, in the theology, proclamation and faith of the churches. This is another question which will require further discussion in our Commission and, above all, of course, in the churches themselves. As a Lutheran, I would like here to express the hope that insights of the Lutheran tradition, too, will find a greater place in the discussion. As M. Seils pointed out in Odessa, it is a soteriological concern which especially moves Lutherans here. In what we say of the Trinity, the important role of the life-giving Holy Spirit cannot be viewed in isolation from the continuing, forgiving grace of Christ to those who, even as sinners, always remain sinners. Thorough elucidation of any possible official step on the part of the churches would be desirable; the *filioque* question could, indeed, provide an opportunity for us to explain in intelligible language the significance of trinitarian theological statements, which are often extremely complicated, for the life of faith today.

The need for a new common statement of the apostolic faith

An ecumenical reception of the Nicene Creed can *only be an initial step* "on the way to a common expression of the apostolic faith". This became quite clear in the reflections so far. In many respects, the necessary second step—a common contemporary statement of faith—will need to be an *interpretation of the Nicene Creed*; in other respects, however, it will have to go further than the thematic statements of this creed. In the meanwhile, however, a *formal new creed cannot be our goal*, for in fact this could *only be the decision of a future council*. But, in the stage of pre-conciliar partnership in which we find ourselves as churches, theologians and Christians, what Lukas Vischer has called an "anticipatory joint act of confession" seems to me to be mandatory. But can it be done? Despite all the scepticism which is in order here, we have no alternative in my opinion, but to take this certainly-difficult road if we want to obey the summons of the Lord to the visible unity of the Church. It may be that we shall succeed only in formulating a few sentences which will allow us to accept one another's different confessions as Christian and not a hindrance to full communion. In my view, we shall need to look in three directions at least in our efforts:

1. The fact must be squarely faced that a *doctrinal development* has taken place in the *churches of the west*—in the Roman Catholic Church as well as in the Reformation churches (though to a different degree here)—which has led beyond the ancient councils to binding formulations of the apostolic faith in the form of dogmas or confessional documents. Although these doctrinal formulations can be broadly understood as interpretations of the ancient church credo, it is also clear that in essential points (anthropology, justification, eucharist, Mary, doctrine of the ministry) they *go beyond what is stated in the Nicene Creed*. It will be necessary for us to reflect together on the problem of authority which arises here, for some churches more then others, in a way hardly distinguishable from the authority of the Nicene Creed. Another fact to be considered is the largely conflicting nature of these statements, which has subsequently intensified the problem of unity in faith. So far as baptism, eucharist and ministry are concerned, we are on the way to agreement. Is this also true for other important *doctrinal controversies*? Would it also be possible, for example, for the Orthodox churches to endorse with-

out difficulty a Catholic-Protestant consensus on justification?

In this connection, the principle introduced by Jean Tillard in Bangalore, *quod requiritur et sufficit*, deserves close attention. Put in Lutheran terms, what is the relevance of the *satis est ad veram unitatem ecclesiae* of the Augsburg Confession (art. 7) to the themes and particular standpoints of a common expression of the apostolic faith today? For example, could the idea of a "hierarchy of truths", which was used at the Second Vatican Council, dispose the Roman Catholic Church not to require full acceptance by other churches of the *dogmas of 1854, 1870 and 1950*, i.e. to be content with assent to a certain interpretation of these dogmas? From the Lutheran side, an adequate agreed statement on justification and redemption would be desirable also and especially in reference to disputed contemporary problems; but certain details of the teachings of the *Smalkald Articles* or the *Formula of Concord* should certainly not be made a condition for unity in faith.

2. Attention must next be directed to confessional statements in which Christians and churches confess the apostolic faith today in *diverse political, social and cultural contexts*. An early example from our present century is the *Barmen Theological Declaration* (1934), a confession in which the "Confessing Church" in Germany resisted dangerous influences on the Christian faith and proclamation from German fascism. One of its concerns was resistance to a false interpretation of historical events (and racial characteristics) as divine revelations. These were questions which are also in discussion among us, though in a different way. Since 1934 a whole series of confessions of faith has been produced in all parts of Christendom, a first selection of which has been made accessible by C.S. Song in Faith and Order Paper No. 104. The doctrinal status of these confessions varies widely and invites reflection on "contemporary confession" and "authoritative church confession". (Already in respect of the Nicene Creed it would have been necessary to discuss the ecclesial necessity for a confession and the ecclesiological basis for its authoritativeness.) On the way to "the common expression of the apostolic faith today", however, our efforts must, above all, be directed to listening to the utterly diverse and often even contradictory ways of expressing the faith, to a better understanding of them, and to engagement in mutual dialogue. For example, the 1977 Cuban

"Confession of Faith" can only be correctly understood in the light of the social and political situation in Latin America; this necessarily means that quite different aspects of the Christian faith come to the fore here than those dealt with in the traditional confession. Yet the challenge to dialogue is evident. When, for example, the Cuban confession of faith states that "the human being is the centre of all interest", a European reader will at once be reminded of the very dubious influence of this maxim in history. Confronted as we are by the fragmentation of humanity and human life today, are we not compelled to speak more precisely of Jesus of Nazareth as a standard of all that is human? What that statement really means, however, would not be fully explored by that question. We would still have to reflect on how to speak to one another as clearly and unmistakeably as possible in order to be able to accept each other completely! It is my own impression that a real dialogue on the common faith between Christians and churches in Latin America and in Eastern Europe would, in particular, be extremely important. Questions of anthropology and soteriology would be to the forefront in this dialogue, but consideration would also need to be given to questions of the doctrine of creation, ecclesiology and eschatology.

3. On the way to a new contemporary expression of the apostolic faith, we also have, here especially, to take our bearings from the biblical message. Both our traditional church confessions and our contemporary acts of confessing the faith must be exposed by all of us to the pre-eminent word of holy scripture. Is it possible to say what the New Testament means by the "apostolic faith"? It might not be possible for us to come up here with a precise answer; we would be much more likely to be halted by the variety of ways in which the faith is confessed in the apostolic preaching. That cannot be the whole story, however. For all its diversity, the New Testament is still a unity; even its content can be defined, for example, in the confessional formulas of the New Testament.

It is precisely these succinct New Testament formulations of the one faith which challenge us today to say briefly and simply why we believe in Jesus Christ, and to tell what that good news really is which we have to offer to others. Both in a secularized world (such as that in which the author lives) and in a religious context, the authentic and distinctive substance of the Christian faith needs to be stated briefly and intelligibly so that the clear witness for which the world is waiting may be heard. Agreement of this kind, and it alone, also allows and creates space for a legitimate diversity in expressing the Christian faith.

The continuation of the study

From our reflections thus far, certain points have emerged which are of importance for the continuation of our study. Plans need to be made for a long-term timetable and for study at different levels. Three stages could be envisaged:

1. The question of the Nicene Creed calls, first of all, for further clarification. A decision needs to be reached whether we will recommend that the churches undertake a re-reception of this ancient church creed in the form of an addition to the present Basis of the World Council of Churches and as an initial step towards a common expression of the one apostolic faith. A recommendation of this kind would, in any case, call for thorough theological supporting arguments and explanations, including, above all, a discussion of the frequently voiced reservations about this proposed step.

2. Secondly, though not necessarily later in time, preliminary studies would be necessary on the question of a contemporary expression of the one apostolic faith. It would be necessary to study the following:

— the question of what "apostolic faith" really means in accordance with the testimony of holy scripture;

— the question of the importance of the dogmatic tradition of various western churches and the material questions arising therefrom;

— above all, the extremely diverse essays in contemporary confession of the Christian faith must be analyzed and compared, paying attention to their tendencies, contradictions, relationship to tradition, scripture, etc.; regional consultations, and even bilateral meetings in various cultural or social situations, would seem to be essential.

The preliminary studies should consider the maxim *quod requiritur et sufficit*.

3. Finally, an attempt to draft a common text would be needed. This would need to be done in the light of earlier attempts of the Faith and Order Commission, especially "Baptism, Eucharist and

Ministry", "A Common Account of Hope", and the Bangalore text. Would an attempt to say simply and succinctly why we believe in Christ be a possible first step? A common statement would need to be introduced or accompanied by a theological elucidation of the proposed options, dealing with the themes "faith and unity", "confession of faith", "confessing the faith", and "faith and practice in the Christian life". This last point could be of special importance in reference to the Latin American situation.

If we were to embark on this attempt, it would certainly be a step in the direction of the visible unity of the churches.

NOTES

[1] *Breaking Barriers, Nairobi 1975*, London, SPCK and Grand Rapids, Eerdmans, 1976, Sect. II Report 19 a, p. 66.
[2] *WCC Constitution*, III (i).
[3] *Documentary History of the Faith and Order Movement, 1927-1963*, ed. L. Vischer, p. 33.
[4] This report is not yet published.
[5] Faith and Order, Louvain 1971, Report of Committee II, p. 215.

Listening to some contemporary statements of faith from Latin America

JACI MARASCHIN

Like Christians everywhere, Christians in Latin America confess their faith in Jesus Christ in two different ways: (1) as a system of formal dogmatic propositions accepted by reason, or (2) as a cry for the struggle in favour of the oppressed and the poor, the loved ones of God.

Christian faith, confessed as a system of formal dogmatic propositions accepted by reason, tends to rise above the situation in which our peoples are living. Since it refers chiefly to the generic and the universal and abstracts itself from the particular, it can easily become an instrument for the legitimization of the *status quo*. On the other hand, Christian faith, confessed as a cry for the struggle in favour of the oppressed and the poor, the loved ones of God, expresses itself in a fragmentary and particularized form.

In Latin American society, churches are divided according to the divisions of society; the main divisions between the churches are not, in this part of the world, the traditional, denominational divisions, but the divisions between oppressors and oppressed, between rich and poor (though not always at the level of conscience). What is needed, in order to understand the situation in this part of the world, is the development of a serious work of

• Dr JACI MARASCHIN, Episcopal Church in Brazil, teaches theology at the Theological Seminary in Sao Paulo, Brazil.

hermeneutics which can help us grasp the meaning not only of words and logical structures, but of the powers which are behind these words and logical structures. In this situation, theology is so deeply related to ideology that it seems impossible to go ahead with our theological work without trying to dig deeper into our formal heritages and Christian traditions. This is necessary if we are to understand the meaning of interpretation and the ingredients present in the process of understanding.

The history of the Christianization of Latin America is now well known. Christian faith was and is still confessed by the colonizers and the powerful in a way that is formal, dogmatic, authoritarian, infallible and systematic. Believing in Jesus Christ has always meant believing in a series of formal dogmatic propositions. These propositions have given assurance to the powerful of their rights to power, and consolation, through conformity and resignation, to the poor and oppressed.

Such an understanding of the confession of our Christian faith led, until very recently, to a superstitious way of being Christian. After Vatican II (and, more particularly, after Medellin), however, a revolution in Latin American Christianity took place. Confronted by a new reading of the scriptures, by a new listening to the will of the Holy Spirit, by the latinization of the images of Jesus Christ, and by a new sense of pastoral work, Christians could no longer simply keep repeating the traditional formulas inherited from the past without taking a critical position. The new vision of the Christian ethos came through a new theological language and resulted in a new understanding of mission and evangelization. This new theology (which of course is not limited to Latin America) emerged out of conflicts in the social, political and economic order and had to be expressed through the new language which Latin American people could now understand.

So we can say very clearly that Christian faith is not a system, although it has been systematized many times and in many places. It is not a system, although it carries within itself the potential for systematization. Christian faith, we think, is above all a living experience, a mode of being, an atmosphere in which Christians move.

Christian faith is a faith confessed by a living community. In that community each person confesses it individually, together with his neighbour, in such a way that in the other he grows and makes community possible. Christian faith confessed individually is never confessed in isolation.

Christian faith is confessed within the scope of a culture. That is why it is always confessed in a particular way. The confession of the Christian faith which is universal only becomes possible *in my specific place and in my particular time.* It is in this way that the universal gets meaning.

Christian faith is a faith, not a philosophy. It does not depend on rational categories but on the gift of God, full of love, of his Son Jesus Christ nurtured by the power of the Holy Spirit. It does not depend on the wisdom of this world, though the wise ones of this world are not, necessarily, excluded from it.

In the short sample of contemporary statements of faith from Latin America (sent to all Faith and Order members), we notice some very important themes. First, we notice that the hope of the coming of the Lord means the experience of a social life where God is dishonoured by our divisions, pride and disobedience, manifested in our indifference to the cry of the most neglected, oppressed and needy. The hope of the coming of the Lord is a cry for a new earth where the liberation of indigenous people will be a visible sign of the victory of Christ against theft, exploitation and discrimination. This hope is linked to pastoral care, defence of the environment and, very particularly, to solidarity to Nicaragua. Our Latin American confession in God the Father means a confession that God hears the people's cries.

We are asking, in our liturgical assemblies and in our ordinary way of life, where this God of Christian faith is. Is he hidden in some esoteric formulation written by ancient Christian scholars in Nicea and Constantinople? Is he hidden in the suffering of Latin American "campesinos"? Behind the faces of our starving populations? In our hope? The question of our people is not a question about faith and order, but a question of life and death. The question of our people is not, primarily, a question about the unity of the divided denominational churches, but a question about the unity of life.

Much work has been done in the context of this Commission about "The Common Expression of Apostolic Faith Today". We are asking in Latin America what the meaning is of "common expression"? In a very recent encounter among basic communities in Brazil (April 1981), great stress was given to the liturgical celebrations which are understood as a celebration of our faith. During that encounter, the celebrations gave the participants great strength; they discovered the following:

> When we meet to hear the word of God, we cannot but also hear the word of God in the people's cries. When we meet to celebrate the passion, death and resurrection of Jesus in the eucharist, we cannot fail also to celebrate the passion, death and resurrection of our faithful, oppressed people, among whom Jesus, crucified, is present.

The same document, representative of millions of Christians in Brazil, declares that "we must not be circumscribed by old traditions... Christ asks us for a new heart; therefore, he does not want an old Church but a new Church..."

Recent Faith and Order meetings have recommended more detailed studies for developing the ecumenical importance of the Niceno-Constantinopolitan Creed and for arriving at the common expression of the apostolic faith today. These studies should take into consideration the confessing of the faith in the various cultural and social institutions of our twentieth century. We, from this part of the world, ask Faith and Order if it is possible to confess our faith through a "common expression" taking as a base an ancient document built upon a very specific frame of reference and addressed in a very particular language code which in its essence is alien to us in our place and history? The trouble is the word "common". We start with a simple profession of faith:

> We believe that God is Father, that he cares with special affection for the suffering, the little ones, the migrants, the poor, the exploited.
> I believe, Lord,
> but come and increase my faith.
> We believe that Jesus came "to announce the good news to the poor, to give sight to the blind and to set free those who are ill-treated".
> I believe, Lord,
> but come and increase my faith.
> We believe that the Holy Spirit reveals his love to little ones and gives us strength to struggle side by side with our comrades to form a fraternal world in accordance with the will of the Father.
> I believe, Lord,
> but come and increase my faith.
> Amen

1. Papers and reports from the meeting of the Faith and Order
   Commission, Lima, Peru, January 1982

Report of the working group

Introduction: The importance of this study as an ecumenical project

1-2   Relevance and authorization of the study
3-6   Why this study involves the Nicene Creed
7-9   The goal of the study: common recognition, explication
       and confession of the apostolic faith

I. *Towards the common recognition of the apostolic faith as expressed in the ecumenical symbol of that faith: the Nicene Creed*
10-11   Why the Nicene Creed should be recognized in this study
12   Creed and scripture
13   "Sufficiency", adequacy, authority of the Creed
14-15   The specific request to the churches: "to recognize..."
16   Greek text used in this study

II. *Towards the common explication of this apostolic faith in the contemporary situations of the churches*
17-18   The authority of the Creed is manifested in contemporary
        explication
19   The churches' differing use of the Creed in contemporary
        witness
20   Method: inter-relating Creed and contemporary situation

21   Examples of concrete questions for contemporary explication

22-25 Diversity in contemporary explications

III. *Towards a common confession of the apostolic faith today*
26   The need for and meaning of "common confession"
27   The Creed as criterion for a common confession of the apostolic faith
28   On the way to a common confession

Recommendations
I.   The study project
II.   Steering group and issues
III. Levels of study
IV.   Publications
V.   Work in 1982

Introduction: the importance of this study as an ecumenical project

1. In our present divided state, visible unity cannot be restored unless each church becomes aware of the painful situation of our divisions and takes decisions to overcome our disobedience to the will of Christ as expressed in his prayer for unity (John 17:1-26). These decisions will be genuine only to the extent to which they imply a resolve to do what the re-establishment of communion demands: conversion through a constant return to the source which is God as revealed in Jesus Christ through the Holy Spirit. Such a conversion requires an effort to express the content of the faith in such a way that the life of the community is consonant with the word of God.

2. At its Fifth Assembly in Nairobi in December 1975, the World Council of Churches, after its discussion of "conciliar fellowship", adopted the following recommendation:

> We ask the churches to undertake a common effort to receive, reappropriate and confess together, as contemporary occasion requires, the Christian truth and faith, delivered through the apostles and handed down through the centuries. Such common action, arising from free and inclusive discussion under the commonly acknowledged authority of God's word, must aim both to clarify and to embody the unity and the diversity which are proper to the church's life and mission (Section II, 19).

The same assembly, in revising "The Constitution of the World Council of Churches", adopted the following statement as the first of the purposes of the Council:

> (i) To call the churches to the goal of visible unity in one faith and in one eucharistic fellowship expressed in worship and in common life in Christ, and to advance towards that unity in order that the world may believe (Art. III, 1).

The intention of the Faith and Order Commission in formulating the following project is to help the World Council to fulfill its recommendation, and so to advance towards the realization of its first purpose.

3. A primary assumption of this project is the recognition of the special rank and function of the Nicene Creed.* For, together with a growing convergence in our understanding of baptism, eucharist and ministry, the appeal for a common expression of the apostolic faith belongs to the movement towards the unity of the Church. In the attempt to work out such a common expression, it is impossible to disregard the special place of the Nicene Creed. It is the one common creed which is most universally accepted as formulation of the apostolic faith by churches in all parts of the world, where it primarily serves as the confession of faith in the eucharistic liturgy.**

4. The *koinonia* of the eucharistic community, which is united to Christ by baptism, is grounded on the apostolic proclamation of the crucified and risen Christ which is documented in the scriptures, summarized in the creed of the church and is served by the minister who presides over the eucharistic celebration. The common understanding of the apostolic faith was expressed by the ancient Church in the Ecumenical Creed of Nicea (325), com-

---

* Throughout this paper the reference is always to the Creed commonly believed to be of the Second Ecumenical Council at Constantinople in 381 AD, although various customary terms are used, such as "the Nicean Creed", "the Nicene Creed", "the Creed commonly called Nicene", "the Nicene Symbol", "the Ecumenical Creed", etc.

** Thus, the Faith and Order Conference in Lausanne in 1927 referred to its members as "united in a common Christian faith which is proclaimed in the holy scriptures and is witnessed to and safeguarded in the Ecumenical Creed, commonly called Nicene, and in the Apostles' Creed" (Sect. IV).

plemented at Constantinople (381) and solemnly received at Chalcedon (451) as the authentic symbol of the Christian faith, witnessing to the fullness of the Christian faith and life and authoritative for the entire Church.

5. The eucharist builds up the Church and visibly manifests its unity. The apostolic faith, fruit of the Holy Spirit, is the ground of that unity. The outward expression of this intimate relationship of faith and eucharistic celebration is therefore essential to the visible unity of the Church, so much so that without common recognition of the Nicene Creed as the ecumenical symbol of the apostolic faith, it is difficult if not impossible to understand how we are to advance "to the goal of visible unity in one faith and in one eucharistic fellowship expressed in worship and in common life in Christ... in order that the world may believe" (WCC Constitution III, 1). Thus, together with a growing convergence in our understanding of baptism, eucharist and ministry, the appeal for common expression of the apostolic faith of the one, holy, catholic and apostolic Church as expressed in its Ecumenical Symbol of faith belongs to movement towards the unity of the Church.

6. It should be remembered how well this Creed has served millions of Christians, with whom we are also bound together in the unity of the Church, in the past. Its brief statement of the essential faith has provided at least formally a thread of unity down through the centuries. In one form or another, this Creed has been used by the Orthodox churches, by the Roman Catholic and Anglican churches, and by most of the churches of the Protestant Reformation, and in all parts of the world. It has helped the churches to affirm their fundamental belief in God, in the Lord Jesus Christ and his saving action, in the Holy Spirit and the Church, and in the life of the kingdom to come. Some have used it as a baptismal confession, others as a central standard of doctrine. It has been read and sung at the eucharist and other liturgical services and has been used as a statement of belief at the ordination of church ministers. As the product of a council received by the churches in a time of great confusion and strife, it has stood as a model of ecumenical confession, both in the method of its formulation and in the content of its definition. As such, it has inspired theologians, hymn writers, preachers and

artists in all ages. It seems appropriate, therefore, to ask the churches, when they try to express their common understanding of the apostolic faith today, to recognize this Creed from the time of the early Church as the ecumenical expression of the apostolic faith which unites Christians of all ages in all places.

7. Such recognition would call each church to examine its beliefs and actions today in relation to that Ecumenical Creed and so to express and interpret its meaning today theologically, ethically, liturgically, socially in terms understandable in that church's everyday life and in society.

8. We are convinced that any real progress among the divided churches towards the common expression of the apostolic faith today will require a twofold movement, towards unity in faith with the early Church, and towards unity in mission with the Church of the future. The word "towards" is important: both movements are actually, from our present divided situation, movements towards the future. Our hope then is that we can initiate a threefold study project, aiming:

a) to ask the churches to make a common recognition of the apostolic faith as expressed in the Ecumenical Symbol of that faith: the Nicene Creed (Chapter I);

b) to ask the churches how they understand its content today in their own particular situations of worship, fellowship and witness (Chapter II); and

c) to ask the churches "to undertake a common effort to confess together, as contemporary occasion requires, the Christian truth and faith, delivered through the Apostles and handed down through the centuries" (Chapter III).

9. We believe that this project will guide the churches to confess Christ in their life, and lead them towards the common celebration of the eucharist where "we proclaim the Lord's death until he comes" (1 Cor. 11:26).

I. Towards the common recognition of the apostolic faith as expressed in the Ecumenical Symbol of that faith: the Nicene Creed

10. Our hope is that all the churches will recognize the Symbol of Nicea-Constantinople as the common expression of the faith of the Church because:

(a) The Nicene Creed over the centuries has been, and is now very widely acknowledged as, the ecumenical symbol of the apostolic faith, a fact of fundamental significance for an ecumenism which seeks the unity of the Church "in all places and all ages" (New Delhi statement). We therefore plead with those churches that do not acknowledge it, or, while acknowledging it in reality disregard it, that they ask themselves whether for the sake of unity they might agree to reconsider their attitude.

(b) While the act of confessing the contemporary meaning of the apostolic faith has to be done again and again in different situations and in different forms, and this life of contemporary confessing and witness must never be interrupted, nevertheless we consider that designing a new creed, intended to replace the Nicene Creed as the Ecumenical Symbol of the apostolic faith, is not appropriate.

(c) The World Council of Churches is not authorized to propose a new creed.

(d) Proposing an ecumenical symbol of the apostolic faith clearly presupposes the authority of an ecumenical council. Such a council would have as an essential purpose the confession of the apostolic faith on behalf of the whole Church in the situation of its own present day. Among the important preparatory steps for just such an event would be what this project calls for: a wider recognition among the churches of the Ecumenical Symbol of Nicea.

11. The plurality and variety of documents which occur in the act of confessing in particular situations do not imply that each new creed or symbol binds the whole catholic Church. It is true that Christian witness should always aim to express the whole faith of the one Church; but the whole Church is not thereby bound to each particular act of confessing. These various acts and documents of confession rather apply the one apostolic faith to particular situations, and are to be judged, therefore, by the criterion of their consonance with that apostolic faith as confessed in the Ecumenical Creed of the Church.

12. How shall we understand the relation of scripture and the Creed? This, of course, is a principal question to be studied ecumenically in the project we are proposing. Here we can only indicate some points to be considered in that study.

(a) Christian identity is rooted in the acceptance of God's revelation of himself through Jesus Christ and the Holy Spirit. Initiated in creation, witnessed to in the Old Testament, this revelation of God's identity was fully manifested in the mystery of Jesus Christ. Transmitted in the power of the Holy Spirit by the preaching of the apostles, it is the great gift of God to humanity. And the Christian community has the mission to keep it and transmit it to all humankind.

(b) It is this revelation, already understood and lived out in various ways by the first Christian communities, that the scriptures record. It is significant, however, that already in the documents of the New Testament we can see the need for some brief statements in which at least the main elements of the revelation are brought together in such a way that they help the Christian communities to test the consonance of their beliefs with what God did and said in the Holy Spirit by Jesus Christ.

(c) The creeds of the first centuries, in a more elaborated form, tried to continue this service. Their language was, indeed, dependent on the culture, the needs, the situations of their time. But they were intended to convey a summary of the central teaching of the scriptures. Their authority, however, comes from the consonance of their content with the revelation itself. They are instruments for its acceptance by faith, and its proclamation in the life of the Christian community.

13. It is sometimes asked whether the Nicene Creed can be considered "sufficient" to express the Christian faith for contemporary Christians. It is pointed out that some biblical themes and concepts, indispensable for Christian life and thought, are not explicitly treated in the Creed. Again it is noticed that there are many contemporary questions and issues which are urgent for Christian obedience today, but which were simply not actual when the Creed was written.

(a) It is, of course, true that not everything is said explicitly in the Creed, and that certain affirmations came into focus for historical reasons. The Creed is also historically conditioned in its language, its concepts, its thought forms. Moreover, the Creed aims to fulfill particular functions, and its language is sometimes doxological, sometimes dogmatic.

(b) The question of the Creed's "sufficiency", however, leads to the authority of the Creed, and it must be clearly said that the Creed's authority for contemporary Christian life and thought does not lie in the extensiveness with which it treats either the biblical witness or contemporary questions, but in its consonance—claimed and recognized in the Church—with the testimony of the apostles to God's revelation in Jesus Christ. The urgent question for Christian witness is, "Who is Jesus Christ for us today?" This question has been faced and answered in all ages, and the adequacy of any answer, however relevant to its age it may appear to be, ultimately is grounded in its participation in the authority with which the apostles and the early Church bear witness to the revelation of God in Jesus Christ.

(c) But the element of mystery must be noted, both in the Creed and in any attempt to verbalize the Christian faith. When the word was made flesh, the inexpressible became expressed. Words can express the mystery, yet it remains a mystery, and the words used to express it must respect the fullness of it. Every creed and all our attempts to formulate or explicate our faith have their limits before the mystery of what they try to express. In that perspective, it is wrong to expect either too much or too little, also from the Creed.

14. In order to rediscover the unity of faith, therefore, it would be an important step if the churches would remind themselves again of the significance of the Nicene Creed as Ecumenical Symbol of the one, apostolic faith, implying as it does temporal as well as geographical universality. As such it is not merely to be considered as a first stage in the development of definitions of the faith, but also as intimately connected with the unity of the one, holy, catholic and apostolic Church.

15. Therefore, the World Council of Churches might ask the churches to recognize anew that integral unity of the Christian faith expressed in the Symbol of Nicea-Constantinople, to reconsider the status of their own teaching in its light, to affirm its content as the basis of more comprehensive church unity, and to strengthen its place in the liturgical life of the churches wherever necessary and possible under circumstances of pastoral responsibility.

16. In view of research and recent proposals concerning the *filioque* clause in the Faith and Order Commission, we propose for purposes of this study to use the original Greek text of the Nicene Creed, without thereby prejudging in any way the theological views of the churches on this issue,* as follows:

And we believe in the Holy Spirit,
 the Lord and Giver of life,
 who proceeds from the Father,
 who with the Father and the Son together is
 worshipped and glorified,
 who spoke by the prophets.

II. Towards the common explication of this apostolic faith in the contemporary situations of the churches

17. The content of this apostolic faith, although it is the ground in itself for Church unity and contemporary witness, finds its context in the divided state of the Church and the alienation of humankind. This ground can only become effectual as, given time and opportunity, we appropriate it for ourselves in our times, seek to grasp and understand its meaning in our own language and attempt to share and bear its witness in ways which others in turn can understand. Authoritative in itself, it manifests its authority in the midst of that divided state of the Church and that alienation of humankind, as it asks for and empowers contemporary interpretation of its meaning in the countless particular languages, cultures and crises of today.

18. This was already the case, for example, when the Council of Chalcedon (451 AD) reaffirmed the Creed of Nicea, even as it proceeded to formulate its own definition, more than a century afterwards, of the doctrine of Christ. The procedure was repeated as the Reformers reaffirmed the Apostles' Creed and the Creed of Nicea, and in so doing confessed their recognition of the relation between apostolic faith and their context of sixteenth century questions about justification and sanctification. And it appears

---

* See *Spirit of God—Spirit of Christ: Ecumenical Reflections on the Filioque Controversy*, ed. Lukas Vischer, Faith and Order Paper No. 103, London, SPCK, and Geneva, WCC, 1981.

likely that ecumenical renewal today will once again open our eyes to the authority of the Creed and our communion with those who assembled at Nicea. At the same time, it can open our eyes to our vocation to explicate the power and meaning of that faith in the many diverse fields of contemporary Church life and witness.

19. The place of the Creed itself in making such a contemporary interpretation will be matter for study and debate, owing to the differing status it is accorded in different churches. In some traditions, the expression of the faith today is quite inconceivable without giving a central and decisive role to the Creed itself, not only in its substantial contents but even in its wording. Others would see themselves as more or less urgently bound by the substance of the Creed but would be more willing to attempt modern statements of the heart of the faith. Still others might value the Creed above all as a procedural model for a task which needs to be accomplished ever anew, namely the confession of the faith in particular circumstances and with the conceptual and linguistic tools available at the time. Even those churches which do not use the Nicene Creed, or indeed any other creed, are usually ready to acknowledge that the Creed deals with matters that are vital for Christian confession.

20. A common expression of the apostolic faith today will necessarily involve some attempt to relate Creed to contemporary situation and contemporary situation to Creed in such a way that each throws its distinct light on the other. "The unity of the Church is a sign of the coming unity of humankind" (Uppsala, I), and it is the apostolic faith which unites us for the renewal of human community.

21. What kind of questions would such a contemporary explication of the Nicene faith need to address? In the following we offer some tentative examples of such questions. Other clearer formulations of such questions would need to be developed in the study itself. These examples pose questions not only of a social and personal character in the context of our alienation and divisions as women and men but also pose questions of an ecclesial nature in the divided state of the Church.

(a) The Ecumenical Creed confesses faith in one God. How do we explicate that over against tendencies to absolutize today's finite realities, aspirations, historical situations? What does faith in one God mean for human community torn by poverty, militarism, racism?

(b) The Ecumenical Creed confesses faith in the triune God, Father, Son and Holy Spirit. How do we explicate that to those of other faiths or of no faith who charge us with having surrendered the unity of God?

(c) The Ecumenical Creed confesses that this one God created all things. How do we explicate that to persons who consider God to be a human creation, a projection of human wishes and realities?

(d) The Ecumenical Creed confesses faith in one Lord, Jesus Christ. How do we explicate that to contemporaries in a myriad of cultural and religious situations who, venerating Jesus, understand him to be a mere human being? Or who refuse to see his lordship in social, economic, political life?

(e) The Ecumenical Creed confesses Jesus Christ, God's only begotten Son, to be "of one essence" with the Father. How do we explicate today this claim that human salvation and liberation cannot be real without our participation in what is divine and eternal? How are we to understand such a term as "essence" today as a way of speaking about God.

(f) The Ecumenical Creed confesses that God's own Son has become human. How do we explicate to present-day men and women in the many relationships of their lives that it is this incarnation that provides meaning for human life? How does this faith in the incarnate God illumine our understanding of human creation as well as human redemption? Of human community and the cosmos as well as the human self?

(g) The Ecumenical Creed confesses that Jesus Christ was crucified for us under Pontius Pilate. How do we make clear to our contemporaries that salvation has historical character, that it is no mere cosmological speculation, but a matter of divine election and mission to all humanity? How do we proclaim God's coming into human suffering in the cross, strengthening and empowering as well as consoling those who are oppressed by sin and evil?

(h) The Ecumenical Creed confesses that on the third day Jesus Christ arose according to the scriptures. How do we make clear in our twentieth century world that this cross and this resurrection lie at the roots of a new life, liberate and reconcile us, and stand at the centre of all we can say about God's love and justice for God's creatures.

(i) The Ecumenical Creed confesses faith in the Holy Spirit. How can we explain the many ways in which we discern the life, the truth, the communion, the morale in which the Spirit creates the life of God in us in the everydayness of our locations and predicaments? At the same time, how does that same Spirit come to us with prophetic authority? By what means do we recognize that it is the same Spirit who is speaking today who spoke through the prophets? What does the discernment of the Spirit mean for the common recognition of the teaching function of the Church, not only in the church authorities but in the inter-relatedness of the contemporary theological enterprise?

(j) The Ecumenical Creed confesses one, holy, catholic and apostolic Church. How can we bear witness individually, corporately and representatively to the reality of this community of faith as a liberating and reconciling people of God, confessing one faith and one baptism, sharing one table, and hospitable to all, especially to each other's members and ministers?

(k) The Ecumenical Creed confesses one baptism for the forgiveness of sins. How can we strive towards the recognition of that one baptism in each other's churches today? How can we more closely relate baptism and the experience of our forgiveness before God and neighbour? How can we today share in a reconciliation and redemption among women and men, among persons of all races and classes, which is appropriate to the costliness of God's forgiveness of us all in Christ?

(l) The Ecumenical Creed confesses the life of the age to come. How can we explain to twentieth century neighbours an understanding of life which transcends death, yet can be lived now? How can we explicate a Christian hope, rooted and grounded in eternal life with God, which addresses urgent human problems, which illumines human suffering and persecution, which clarifies and judges human utopias in the light of God's coming kingdom? How can we attest the unity in this hope and eternal life which we share with the saints, the ancestors, the church of other ages?

22. It is obvious that such contemporary explication will generate much diversity in confessing the faith. Is that consonant with the common confession of which the WCC recommendation speaks?

23. We believe that it is. We believe that diversity is a necessary feature of any serious attempt to recognize and explicate the one apostolic faith today. The one faith is for all. It is universally relevant. But that means it is for each one, each relationship, each family, each group, each class, each culture, each nation. The Christian gospel entered Greco-Roman culture, and the Church accepted the pluralism which that meant for Christian *koinonia* and witness.

24. Nevertheless, although the Creed of Nicea is widely used by churches all over the world, many Christians are asking legitimately whether confessing the faith of the Creed of Nicea means being bound to ancient Greco-Roman forms of thought and speech. Recognizing this, we nevertheless believe that participation in this project could help all churches to receive their common tradition, and link them with other Christians in other parts of the world and in all time.

25. To speak about "the common expression of the apostolic faith", then, does not necessarily mean a single verbal formulation. Faith may be common even where wordings differ. The immediate task is to move towards mutually recognizable expressions of faith. This does not exclude the possibility that a growing mutual understanding could eventually lead to the widespread acceptance of one expression of faith, without abandoning other congruous forms that exist already or could later be formulated. None of this entails the replacement of the Nicene Creed as the Ecumenical Symbol of the apostolic faith.

III. Towards a common confession of the apostolic faith today

26. *The need for and meaning of "common confession":*
(a) Interpreting the Creed of the church is not the same thing as actually confessing the faith expressed in the Creed. The act of confession is always personal, even if it is done in community. It is personal also in the sense that it finally relates to the person of Jesus Christ and to the personal reality of the triune God. It means taking sides with Jesus (Luke 12:9) for the truth and love he proclaimed. This also involves assertions concerning who Jesus is, but those assertions are subservient to the intention of acclaiming Jesus as Lord and of joining in his mission to humanity and in his proclamation of the kingdom to come.

(b) Confessing Jesus Christ is a communal event, because after Easter it is the apostolic Church in which Jesus is present and which proclaims who Jesus is. To confess Jesus Christ now means to share in the Church's acclamation of Jesus as Lord (Rom. 10:9) through the Holy Spirit (1 Cor. 12:3), and in the profession of the apostolic faith (1 John 4:2-3). Therefore the personal confession of individual Christians is embedded in the community of the Church, even when it occurs in particular situations and is expressed in specific ways. In his or her personal confession, the individual Christian is supported and encouraged by the confessing community. The common confession of the Church does not preclude individual modifications according to specific situations, provided that it is the same faith that comes to expression. Unity is not uniformity. In fact, uniform repetition of the Creed of the Church can become a device in evading a personal confession to Jesus Christ in an actual situation.

(c) The normal place for confessing the Creed in the life of the Church is its liturgy. Here all Christians are united in praise and glorification of their Lord. Thus they devote themselves to the Lord so that they may share communion with him in the eucharistic meal.

(d) This common confession in the liturgy is expressed in a language of glorification of Jesus Christ and of the triune God and of hope for participation in that glory. It also includes narrative elements that serve to identify the Jesus of history and his relation to the Father and to the Spirit. It is based on repentance, because a conversion to God is required, turning to God from bondage to a world that separated itself from God. Only by way of such conversion can Christians share in God's salvation.

(e) If confession means participation in the unity of the body of Christ by joining the acclamation of Jesus as Lord, it must overcome the inherited divisions among the faithful. Therefore the element of repentance and conversion in the act of confession also applies to the separation and division of the churches. Our separations are against the will of the Lord. It is important for the apostolic faith to be confessed by the churches as one and the same faith, so that when the individual shares in the liturgical confession of the Church, he or she will be assured of turning to the one Jesus Christ. The very fact that the act of confession is communal, therefore, obliges the churches to overcome their divisions and to seek a common confession of the apostolic faith that would enable them to enter again into conciliar fellowship.

(f) A common confession of faith is also required in view of the challenges arising from contemporary experience which extend to all Christian churches alike, although their focus may be different in different situations. As every form of confession to Jesus Christ involves repentance, conversion and renewal on the part of the confessing person, so also a common confession of the churches responding to the challenges of the time must involve conversion and renewal in the human community. This applies in the first place to community within the Church and among churches, a community of women and men across all barriers of races, classes and cultures. But it also extends to the human community at large, to its economic and political conflicts in the national as well as international context, because the Church witnesses to the kingdom of God, the goal of all human community. The Church is called to be a symbol of that eschatological community of justice and peace. But it lives up to this function only to the degree that the community of the Church itself is truly united through the love of Christ.

27. *The Creed as criterion for a common confession of the apostolic faith:*

(a) The challenges of the present world, as well as a widespread feeling that these challenges are not answered in the wording of the traditional creeds and other confessional documents of the churches, have given rise to a wide range of contemporary statements of the Christian faith. They come from entire churches as well as from individuals and groups. Besides, there are confessional documents of the past that are cherished by particular churches as expressing the faith of their fathers. How is this variety of confessional documents and traditions related to the unity of the Christian faith and to the task of a common confession of that faith? The unity of the apostolic faith is expressed in the Ecumenical Creed, proclaimed on behalf of the entire Church as a summary of the central teaching of the scripture and therefore serving as a criterion for the unity of other statements of faith with the teaching of the Church. In relation to the Ecumenical Creed later confessing documents, including those from the present age, will be evaluated as to their witness to the same Lord, expressing the same Spirit that unites the Church in the same faith. But the Creed will also be read with different eyes in new situations so that its assertions may reveal new insights.

(b) When on the basis of the Ecumenical Creed later confessional documents are evaluated, the churches may also rediscover in that Creed the basic unity of the faith which they have in common in spite of their separation. The more they come to evaluate their particular confessional traditions in the light of the Creed, the more they may learn to understand other traditions as expressing the same faith under different circumstances and in different situations. While each church should be ready to interpret its own confessional heritage in the light of the apostolic faith as summarized in the Ecumenical Creed, it might also be able to accept other churches and their confessional heritage on the same basis.

(c) In such a process of interpreting the confessional positions of one's own church on this basis, it might become possible to overcome condemnations (anathemas) that have been formulated and understood in the past to exclude the teaching of other churches. Without necessarily dissociating themselves from these judgments as such, the churches might discover that they do not apply to those other churches as they are at present. Perhaps particular condemnations never applied to the basic intentions of those positions that occasioned them. This is not to say that the Church can always avoid condemning false teaching and disciplining its adherents. This expresses an element which is essential to the act of confession as taking sides with Jesus in situations where his claim is disputed. But whether this condemnation actually applies to a particular opponent remains open to reconsideration.

28. *On the way to a common confession:*

(a) A specific challenge that requires the confession of the Church to Jesus Christ and to the triune God emerges in the encounter with other faiths and ideologies, especially as they influence the mind of the Christian people. But other faiths and ideologies are not simply opposed to Jesus Christ. They can contain many elements of truth which the Christian Church should acknowledge and even appropriate to its own life and understanding. Even explicit rejection of the Christian proclamation may often be conditioned by partial misrepresentations of the truth of the gospel by the churches themselves.

(b) Elements of a common confession to Jesus Christ and the triune God are implicit in many documents of ecumenical dialogue, especially in "Baptism, Eucharist and Ministry", but also in many bilateral agreements between particular churches. They should be taken into consideration when the churches move towards confessing together the apostolic faith in the context of the challenges of the contemporary world and on the basis of their common heritage.

(c) A common confession of the apostolic faith today will exhibit the potential of the Creed as a summary of the apostolic teaching to illumine the experience of Christians and of their churches in a secularized world and in the particular context of their different cultures. It will help to transform those experiences through the power of the life-giving Spirit by responding to the challenges of the time and thus reassuring the Christian conscience of the truth of the apostolic faith.

Recommendations

I. We recommend the pursuit of the theme "Towards the Common Expression of the Apostolic Faith Today" as one of the main study projects of the Faith and Order Commission in the years to come.

II. We recommend the constitution of a steering group, to be appointed by the Standing Commission, which would be responsible for the performance and coordination of the different aspects of the study, such as:

A. Concerning the recognition of the Nicene Creed
1) To get information from the churches about the place the Nicene Creed has in their specific tradition and present life.
2) To work on the implementation of the Klingenthal recommendations on the *filioque* clause.
3) To work for a common wording of the Creed in the various languages, so that all churches using the same language should also employ the same wording of the Creed.
4) To make concrete proposals for the use of the Creed in liturgy, especially in the celebration of baptism, in the eucharist, in catechesis and spirituality, and in hymnology.
5) To clarify the relation of the Nicene Creed to other creeds in

widespread liturgical use, such as the so-called "Apostles' Creed".

6) To study the authority, reception and use of the Nicene Creed in the course of the centuries and its role for the unity of the Church.

B. *Concerning the contemporary explication of the apostolic faith*

1) To work towards a substantial theological interpretation and explanation of the Nicene Creed, e.g. with regard to its trinitarian theology, christology, anthropology and the doctrine of the Spirit.

2) To work towards integrating into that explication the relevant issues of the study on the Community of Women and Men in the Church.

3) To clarify the relation of modern confessions of faith to the apostolic faith as expressed in the Nicene Creed.

4) To clarify the meaning of the term "apostolic faith" in relation to the scriptures and to the early Church.

C. *Concerning the common confession of the apostolic faith today*

1) To get information from the churches about contemporary statements of faith which they use officially or unofficially.

2) To relate to this study the results of the study on "Giving Account of the Hope" (Louvain-Bangalore 1971-78).

3) To consider the results of the New York/Princeton consultation on "Baptism, Eucharist and Ministry" and the implied statements of faith of the "Baptism, Eucharist and Ministry" document.

4) To study the confessions of faith which arose in key stages of church history, e.g. the fourth, sixteenth, nineteenth, and twentieth centuries.

5) To consider the use of the Nicene Creed and such biblical summaries of the faith as Ephesians 1:3-14 in ecumenical gatherings.

6) To get information from the churches about mutual recognition of confessions of faith.

III. We recommend, with regard to methods and levels of the study:

A. The preparation and distribution to the churches of sufficient information about this new Faith and Order study, and asking them for participation in it as a long-term study.

B. The cooperation with regional bodies and ecumenical institutes, e.g. the Societas Œcumenica, and with the bilateral dialogues.

C. The formation of regional working groups in Asia, Africa, Latin America, Europe and North America for the different aspects of the study on the Nicene Creed and on contemporary confessions of faith.

D. The preparation of input on this theme for the Vancouver Assembly of 1983.

E. The preparation of a 1987 Faith and Order World Conference involving this theme.

IV. We recommend the following publications among others in connection with the study:

A. "The Ecumenical Importance of the Nicene Creed."

B. Continuation of the series: "Confessing our Faith around the World."

C. "Towards the Common Expression of the Apostolic Faith Today." A handbook for this study with texts from Lausanne 1927 to Lima 1982, and outlines for further study.

V. Work to be done until the first meeting of the Steering Group:

A. To take steps to inform the churches and the organs of the World Council of Churches about the Lima decision concerning the apostolic faith study and to ask them for participation in the project.

B. Publication work as mentioned under IV.

C. If financially possible, to prepare a consultation on "The Apostolic Faith in the Scriptures and in the Early Church".

The Community Study and apostolic faith: memorandum from the working group on the Community of Women and Men in the Church

Preamble

Both the provenance of the historical creeds and the contemporary confessions of faith have in some way to do with threats to the community of faith. One of the intentions of creeds is to enable the community to be maintained in the face of threats, whether from heresy or from other ideologies. Thus, community is a basic notion in understanding the function of credal confessions; there would be no need for creeds apart from the need to maintain the community in the truth. We need to ask, therefore, what role the creeds play—through their language, thought patterns and images—in uniting and keeping together the community of men and women in the Church. Are the language, thought and imagery of the Nicene Creed sufficiently inclusive to keep together the community of women and men, a community whose members are created and redeemed in the image of God? The study on apostolic faith should consider the picture of a renewed community of women and men which has been articulated by the Community of Women and Men in the Church study as a contribution to understanding the context in which their investigations need to be carried out.

In its work on the Nicene Creed, the study will inevitably deal with the relation of the Nicene Creed to scripture, "Tradition and traditions", both in the sense of traditions within the confessional families as well as the various cultural traditions. Already the Community Study has provided insights in these areas which deserve consideration at the relevant points in the discussion (as various papers and reports from the Sheffield consultation demonstrate). The Community Study has had much to say on the place of the inclusive community in the interpretation of scripture and tradition. This should be taken seriously in the formation of any working groups in this project. No meetings should be held without the adequate representation of women, so that the community of women and men can become a part of the groups that explicate the Nicene Creed and contribute towards the answering of the question posed by the study: Is it possible for churches to accept the Creed? The question might be rephrased: Is it possible for the community of women and men, the earthly form of the body of Christ, to accept the Nicene Creed?

Reflections on the contents of the Nicene Creed

The Community Study has direct implications for every item of the Nicene Creed. In particular we ask that special attention should be given to the following:

1. The notion of God as Creator needs further work, especially the understanding of this in relation to the creation of women and men as set forth in the two Genesis accounts of creation and interpreted in the preaching and teaching of the Church.

2. The trinitarian language of the Creed needs particularly careful investigation. How far are the terms Father, Son and Holy Ghost/Spirit, which safeguard the distinctiveness of persons, still adequate today to describe the Trinity? How far should the contention of many women that this language excludes them from the community of the body of Christ be taken seriously and lead us towards discussing new terms for confessing our belief in the Holy Trinity?

3. The confession that Jesus became man *(anthropos)* needs to be investigated to explicate the relation between the Jewish man Jesus and the risen, ascended, glorified Christ. Is maleness central to our perception of Christ? Many women are suggesting that the implication that maleness has been taken into the Godhead profoundly affects their understanding of their redemption. If the incarnation is thought of, as one speaker in Lima expressed it, as "enmalement" and not "enfleshment", then the implications of

a male saviour are impossible for women to bear. An investigation also needs to be made on the way this affects our understanding of the representation of Jesus Christ by the celebrant of the eucharist.

4. The phrase "born of the Virgin Mary" raises important questions about the place and role of Mary in the life of the community today. Should we seek ways of discovering a new and truly catholic Mariology which is neither a foreign imposition on evangelical thought nor an intolerable break in the continuity of Roman Catholic and Orthodox thought? What significance can we give to the fact that these churches which affirm and venerate Mary are the churches that do not ordain women, while those who do ordain women have little or no place for Mary in their spirituality?

5. What is the meaning of being men and women in the kingdom of God beyond time? Is there a new reality which transcends biological and sexual distinction? This is a complex area and needs to be investigated sensitively.

6. How does an eschatological vision of the community of women and men affect our ecclesiology today?

Exploration of contemporary confessions of faith in relation to Nicea

Particular attention should be taken to note the ways in which contemporary confessions of faith challenge Nicea's understanding of Creator, Trinity, incarnation, the place of Mary, eschatology, ecclesiology, pneumatology. At those places where they do offer a challenge to the understanding of Nicea, what criteria do we use to evaluate such a challenge? Would it be sufficient that, while not going directly through Nicea, they were consonant with one of the New Testament traditions or New Testament "trajectories"? In this case, how important is the judgment of the community of women and men in affirming such beliefs?

Recommendations to the Steering Committee on apostolic faith

1. That they take seriously the picture of a renewed community of women and men articulated by the Community Study.

2. That they use as background materials the insights of the Community Study on scripture, "Tradition and tradition".

3. That women play a full part in the study process and make their contribution to answering the question of the possibility of the churches' common recognition of the Nicene Creed.

4. That in the reflective process of this study we hope that the understanding of the tradition that emerges will, in its turn, interact with the insights which have come through the Community study.

The Roman Catholic Church's fidelity to the "faith of the fathers"

JEAN M.R. TILLARD, OP

"How is the Roman Catholic Church, taken as a whole, faithful to the faith of the fathers?" At first sight the answer seems simple. On further consideration, however, it turns out to be highly complex. It involves a judgment not only on the way in which the Church "receives" that faith today but also on the way in which it views that faith in the overall context of the "revealed datum". Obviously, the expression "faith of the fathers" is not synonymous with the "revealed datum".

Approaches to the apostolic faith

The Catholic Church's approach to the faith of the fathers is basically one of "reception". Indeed this is one of the main distinguishing features of the Roman Catholic tradition—as of all other catholic traditions. Moreover, the Catholic Church does not merely "receive" that faith; it uses it as the standard for judging its own orthodoxy and faithfulness to the revelation.

But what precisely is meant by the "faith of the fathers"—an expression that contains a wealth of meaning. A review of its use in different contexts shows that it embraces five "registers" of the

• Rev. Fr JEAN M.R. TILLARD, OP, Roman Catholic Church, teaches in the Dominican Faculty of Theology, Ottawa, Canada. This paper has been translated from the French by Maurice Chapman.

early Church's approach to the apostolic faith which can be set out as follows: the register of the faith *proclaimed* (1 Cor. 11:26) in the liturgy, the register of the faith *taught ex cathedra* by the bishops in communion with the bishops of neighbouring sees, the register of faith doctrinally *defined* in the formal statements of the great councils (especially Nicea in 325, Constantinople in 381, Ephesus in 431 and Chalcedon in 451), the register of faith *expressed* in certain disciplinary rules relating in particular to church order, and the register of faith *bearing witness* of its source in martyrdom. There is osmotic interaction between the five registers.

Since the Catholic Church "receives" the faith of the fathers, it goes without saying that it sees itself today as in communion—not only in doctrine but also in prayer, teaching, church order and witness—with the Church of the early centuries which the document *Towards a Common Confession of Faith* (published by Faith and Order in 1980) regards as the "building period" of the living tradition. Hence, when the Church speaks of fidelity to the faith of the fathers in its official documents, it is usually referring to this totality. This is often overlooked, even in commentaries bearing the signature of theologians with prestigious names. In texts emanating from Rome, the aim is rarely a purely speculative or doctrinal one in the modern sense. The Catholic Church "receives" the faith of the fathers in order to accept as they did the *whole* mystery of salvation.

Obviously, the Catholic Church refuses to depart in any substantial respect from the faith of the fathers as outlined in the registers just mentioned. A few examples will confirm this. The general councils held in the west after the breach with the east (Trent, Vatican I and II) base their decisions on the teaching of the great councils of the undivided Church: the decree *Pastor aeternus* of Vatican I refers to it in its central section. In their dogmatic definitions on the Immaculate Conception and Mary's Assumption, Pius IX and Pius XII explicitly invoke the great tradition and the faith of the fathers. When (in 810) Leo III refused to insert the *filioque* in the Creed, he claimed to be conforming to the faith of the fathers, i.e., that which he inscribed on two silver plaques placed at the entrance to the *Confessio* of the Basilica of Saint Peter. If the Roman See opposes the ordination of women today, it does so relying on the need to avoid a break with the Church of the fathers. In its view, the latter position is inseparable both from fidelity to the *Credo in Unam, Sanctam, Apostolicam Ecclesiam* in the Creed and from communion in the eucharist of the fathers. The aim of the liturgical reform carried out at Vatican II was none other than that of bringing the rites of today into greater conformity with the liturgy of the fathers.

Hence, when the Catholic Church holds the Creed of Nicea-Constantinople and the major conciliar definitions to be documents whose tenor remains inviolable, it is because it sees them in this broad context of faith and always in relation to it. By the term "tenor" it means the underlying meaning that the fathers intended to convey in words which they themselves knew to be often inadequate. For the Church, it is impossible to remain faithful to the revealed truth—at least as regards the decisive and essential elements of it—without being in communion with the dogmatic clarifications that the leaders of the Church felt constrained to give for safeguarding the faith and which were "received" by the Church as a whole before its drastic split into two blocks. Indeed, it believes that, in the crucial and even decisive circumstances leading to these definitions, the promise of the assistance of the Spirit was fulfilled. Although they are conditioned by historical contingencies, formulated in a way that bears the mark of the philosophy of the period and expressed in terms that cannot in themselves adequately express the mystery, they constitute a rule of faith because of this guarantee of the Spirit. They are therefore indispensable. Nevertheless, the weight which they have acquired in no way sets them apart from the ecclesial fabric which alone enables them to be read and understood in accordance with the minds and intention of the fathers. Outside the liturgy, neither Nicea-Constantinople nor Chalcedon yield their true sense.

It would be a mistake to suspect timid conservatism in this attachment to the faith of the fathers as embodied in the dogmatic formulations and the creeds. It is a matter of trusting in the word of the Lord—"I am with you for ever until the end of the world" (Matt. 28:20)—and in the promise of the Spirit. Moreover, the meaning is more important than the words, and the aim more important than the formulation. We hold on to the words because they are the vehicle of an *intentio* which transcends them. In its decisions on dogma, the faith of the fathers transmits "what the

Spirit is saying to the churches" in the verbal formulations in use in a particular epoch and culture but which still remain valid.

This "reception" of the faith of the fathers—in its tradition on liturgy and church order as well as in its formulation of dogma—does not mean that we must today merely repeat the latter. Fidelity is not equivalent to psittacism. The Catholic Church believes in the virtue of dogmatic development. This is indeed one of the key positions in its conception of the living tradition.

How is the expression "dogmatic development" to be understood? Catholic theology has not given sufficient attention to analysis of the concept, limiting itself to a quasi-quantitative view. Development has therefore tended to be seen as a process of laying bare the riches of the datum of faith by adding new propositions. The dogmas of the Immaculate Conception and Mary's Assumption are presented as a dogmatic advance by revealing the sense of the definition at Ephesus in 431. By officially adding them to what it hitherto professed as "defined dogmas", the Catholic Church does not feel that it is going against its attachment to the faith of the fathers as the norm of its existence, even though it realizes that several of the fathers would probably have had no idea of the content of the 1854 dogma. It holds that it has merely given fuller expression to that faith.

Here again, it gives the assistance of the Holy Spirit as a ground for rendering the traditional faith more explicit. But in this case it is no longer a matter of assistance guaranteeing the validity of an ecumenical council's decrees (owing to circumstances that were extremely serious for the faith). The whole context is different. We rely on a guarantee regarding the truth of certain judgments of the Bishop of Rome when given in certain conditions in close relation to the liturgy, the teaching of the episcopate and, above all, the *sensus fidelium*. And even if there is still emphasis on the tradition of the undivided Church, there is no expectation of any "reception" by the churches of east and west as a whole. The whole procedure suggests that the Catholic Church henceforth believes that the "ecumenical faith" is manifested by it alone.

It is obvious that any such conception of dogmatic development raises problems for the other churches. However, certain points should be noted here. The first is that the definitions in this case are not aimed at safeguarding the faith—as at Nicea, Constantinople, Ephesus and Chalcedon. They do not affect any matter in which the faith of the fathers would otherwise be compromised. While they certainly relate to the substance of the Christian message, the atmosphere is no longer that of the "gospels for children" or of kerygmatic utterances. And what is confessed in these dogmas bears the same relationship to the eastern faith as the first chapter of Matthew and Luke do to the resurrection. They do not add to the fundamental truths; they contribute to the *splendor veritatis*.

The recent dogmas are doxological, aimed at promoting recognition of major implications in the revelation, to the greater glory of the Father. In other words, they are not intended to replace the kerygmas, creeds and major dogmas of the undivided Church. Without the latter, we could not know of the way opened by God for our salvation: God's offer in the Son transmitted through the power of the Spirit. On this level nothing can be added, even by an infallible judgment of the Bishop of Rome. The recent "dogmas" have a different purpose, i.e. doxological recognition of the profundity of the grace of God. On this view of dogmatic development the addition of *new* "dogmas" does not imply that the faith of the fathers needs any supplementation.

Another view of dogmatic development is possible. This would be qualitative rather than quantitative. The aim would no longer be one of adding propositions but of progressively clarifying the meaning and purpose of the propositions of the faith of the fathers. Development would become a matter of hermeneutics rather than definition of dogma.

Current research on language has clearly revealed the different influences operating on anyone drafting a text with an aim similar to that of the fathers of the great councils. The things that the position against which one is intervening does not highlight, the things that it concedes, the things that it exaggerates, the competence of those supporting or attacking the position in question, the adverse effects that it has so far had—all these things together (and other factors as well) affect the tenor of the document issued. Hence, the doctrinal and historical background in the fourth and fifth centuries has left its mark on the definitions at Nicea, Constantinople, Ephesus and Chalcedon. It also influences the way in which the churches "receive" them. Advances in our knowledge of the historical context and doctrinal problems are allowing us to get closer to the meaning of the definitions themselves.

This represents genuine progress in our understanding of the dogmas of the faith. While the Catholic Church holds the declarations of the faith of the fathers "received" by the undivided Church to be sacrosanct, its position is less outright than is often thought. What is sacrosanct is the meaning which the fathers, assisted by the Spirit, attached to them, and the meaning which the churches, enlightened by the same Spirit, found in them. Nevertheless, this meaning is not necessarily identical on all points with that read into the text in the centuries that followed. The dissension surrounding Chalcedon is an indication of this: the ways in which this has been interpreted are all subject to review.

When seeking the true meaning of the definitions in which the fathers gave dogmatic expression to the faith embodied in all the "registers" of ecclesial life, it is necessary to consider how they read and understood scripture, since their formal statements were designed to keep the Church in the revealed faith and not to replace that faith. Biblical hermeneutics is one of the main tools to be used as a guide in improving our understanding of the intention of those who formulated the conciliar definitions. Here the liturgy—which is pre-eminently the place for ecclesial reading of scripture—assumes its full function again.

In cases where there may seem to be a discrepancy between reliable findings of modern exegesis and the statements of conciliar dogmas, the Catholic tradition does not usually consider that a choice must be made. It believes that the Holy Spirit guarantees the existence of a genuine link between these statements and the real sense of the revealed datum. It therefore tries to discover the intention of the fathers in a new way on revised assumptions and not to set their judgment aside. This is clear, for example, in the discussions on Chalcedon. Its profound conviction is that Chalcedon states the faith, and it makes use of the resources of exegesis, historical research, liturgical studies and linguistics in order to discover what the Spirit really guaranteed at Chalcedon. It does not object to the challenge from modern science or contemporary ways of thinking, and refuses to limit its view to one or other of the past readings of Chalcedon. However, its aim is to discern with increasing clarity what the fathers of the council really meant. If there must be research, it can only be within the framework of the Chalcedon faith. We do not have to opt for or against this. We are, *a priori*, for it. We do not rule out, however, the possibility that new light may be shed on this faith leading to conclusions that are not exactly in line with those of past theological traditions.

Expressing the faith in different cultures

Holding fast to the faith of the fathers in all the "registers" mentioned earlier, the Catholic Church knows that it has also been sent into the world to announce the gospel and build up the communion on earth. It believes that the faith of the fathers (and not any other faith) is intended for all men and all women, whatever their station, culture, race or religious tradition. The content of the Creed and dogmatic definitions must accordingly be presented or expressed in such a way that they can be seen to be in harmony with the search for truth that—with differences of emphasis and in different forms—runs through the infinite multiplicity of human situations.

Perhaps the Catholic tradition has not been sufficiently awake to the effects of the present desire of certain churches to express and live their faith within their own culture and ancestral tradition. In Asia and Africa this desire is being expressed with growing insistence. It would be a serious mistake to regard this simply as "a protest phenomenon that is merely an extension of strong anti-colonialist feelings into the religious sphere". Something much more important is involved: we are probably on the verge of a new stage in the living tradition. Previously, many peoples evangelized through western missionary activities had been content to accept the faith and live the gospel without having the means of "translating" the content and implications of Christianity into their own scheme of things. The western churches gave rise to Christianities of the western tradition in Africa and Asia. They could hardly do otherwise. Moreover, the cultural awakening in a number of these regions had not yet occurred. And the dominant ecclesiology confused unity with uniformity, catholicity with copying the rites or ways of doing things in the Latin church. The furthest one could go was to make minor adaptations. Now, the renewed interest in and revaluation of indigenous cultures in which the religious and ritual dimension plays a very important part, and the new emphasis on communion ecclesiology, have changed the position. From now on, there is the prospect for Christians in Africa and Asia of giving concrete form to the faith in such a way as to produce an African and an Asian tradition with their own rites, customs and way of professing and expressing the unique apostolic faith. In the churches of India—which have of course an inexhaustible store of cultural and religious riches—significant steps have already been taken in this direction.

If the faith of the fathers is to continue to be a saving faith, it will therefore have to be increasingly embodied in human traditions and ways of thought that are very remote from our western ethos. The process, which I feel to be essential, will take a long time and require much patience—similar to that of the fathers when centuries of trial and error, hard thinking and painful debate to find suitable language followed the first announcement of the faith in Asia Minor. However, the context is now very different. It is a question of incorporating a faith already possessing its own pattern and structure into religious traditions that have fashioned the thinking of other nations. If we are to avoid syncretism, we must identify both the underlying concordances and the irreducible contradictions between these two worlds of thought. This cannot be done as a purely intellectual exercise—a complex of other factors is involved.

Take the case of the African religions. To disregard their cult of ancestors, and the role that these religions assign to ancestors in their relations with the "wholly other God", would be extremely serious. There are parallels not only with the dogma of the communion of saints but also with the mediating function of Christ's humanity as presented in the epistles to the Romans (the new Adam) and Hebrews (the brother who truly became one of our stock, forever close to the Father but for us). Similarly, their view of the human person as necessarily bound up with the human community—and as, so to speak, its "product"—ties in with the initial substratum of the mystery of the Church. These are not issues to which the Christian faith must be adapted but contexts in which it can flourish while fully remaining itself, even if the rites, myths, images and concepts employed are no longer those of the western tradition or even of the great tradition as such. It will of course be necessary to ensure that the essential elements of the tradition are not obscured or distorted by the local values. This can only be done through fraternal dialogue between churches, guided not by a shabby policy of concessions or toleration but by a broad view of the catholicity of the Church of God.

What was said earlier regarding the different "registers" of the faith of the fathers is of vital importance in this connection. Western Christianity has given pride of place to verbal expression of the faith, the register which I have called "the faith which is *defined* doctrinally in formal declarations". This is because conceptual thinking has played a key role in the culture of the west. It cannot be the same in all cultures. Anyone who is fairly familiar with Africa or Asia knows that the liturgy "register"—with its combination of symbols, images, music and ritual gestures—is more important in those regions than is the register of texts and normative statements. We shall have to agree that faith will no longer be judged exclusively in terms of concepts. The countries concerned will probably have to proceed for a long time by trial and error before they find the "dogmatic" language that expresses the content of the "definitions" of Nicea and Chalcedon with all their nuances. Will doubts still be cast on their fidelity to the faith of the fathers when their liturgy succeeds in its own fashion in expressing the authentic content of that faith? Obviously we must take the adage *lex orandi lex credendi* more seriously. We have certainly underestimated its importance.

In this context, another "register" of faith in action that has been undermined by the ecclesiology of recent centuries will have to be restored to its traditional place. The teaching of the bishops—in communion with each other and with the Roman See—is normally the standard for judging the conformity of their churches with the faith of the fathers. For this, the catholic mentality which tends to regard the bishops as administrators rather than as (to use the expression in *Lumen Gentium*) the authentic *vicarii et legati Christi* for their people would have to be changed. If, by virtue of their office, they have the gift of the Spirit and a magistral function, this is to enable the Church of God, which is by its very nature catholic, to take root in the human soil of the regions placed under their care. They have the main responsibility for the transmission of the faith, not by a mere repetition of words that originated in another culture altogether, but by distilling their meaning and translating this into the patterns of thought and life in their areas. They will find models for this in the courage of the great bishops of the first centuries in their efforts to transpose into the Greco-Latin culture of their time a revelation consummated in a Semitic environment. After the renewed emphasis on the episcopal function during Vatican II, and the affirmation concerning the assistance and guarantee by the Holy Spirit, it is strange that there should still be such timidity (and in some cases reluctance) regarding the decisions taken by certain episcopates after mature consideration with a view to the acculturation of the faith, since these were taken with the stated intention of remaining in full communion with the Roman See. The argument that supposes the existence of "a world culture eliminating all frontiers" is unsustainable today; the growth of nationalism and the movements in favour of respecting native languages and customs show how fallacious this is.

Finally, we should give particular consideration to martyrdom as the ultimate form of witness. Under regimes of all kinds—in Latin America, in the socialist bloc in eastern Europe, in Vietnam—Christians are being called upon to give their lives in witness to their faith. However, while they unanimously confess Christ as the source of their commitment, the commitment itself differs greatly according to the socio-political context. Some are impelled by the gospel to change the social order so as to repel the spectre of poverty that leads to injustice and inequality; others, in the name of the same gospel, revolt against a situation where essential goods can only be obtained by sacrificing the spiritual freedoms. Moreover, some are Orthodox, others are Catholic or Protestant, and they are separated by differing interpretations of major points in the faith. We have a great deal to learn from this reconciliation through martyrdom of differences in doctrine and *praxis*. It shows that, as Thomas Aquinus so admirably perceived, the faith (of the apostles and fathers) relates to God and leads directly to communion with God's essence in the mystery. If it is genuine, it is not concerned with forms of words, however solemnly declared and guaranteed by the Spirit, or with other commitments accepted even in the name of Christ. Its absolute is the absolute of God, immeasurably transcending all formulations and explaining all commitments without being identified with any of them. This alone is the *res*, the *reality* of the faith.

Thus, when judging the fidelity of the churches to the revealed datum, the nature of the faith does not allow us to limit ourselves to the "register" of verbal expression. Can our western tradition become convinced of this need? On this point we are suffering from a sort of atavism reaching far back into history and bound up with our culture. The attention we give to the other "registers", including that of the liturgy, often looks like a momentary concession: as soon as an important matter is involved, we put our trust in the words and treat everything else as secondary. Since the ultimate decision-making bodies are in the west (and this applies to the churches of the Protestant tradition as well as to the others), the emergence of authentically African or Asian ecclesial traditions will not occur without disagreements. Nevertheless, everything suggests that the movement just beginning is irreversible. And the future of the faith depends upon it.

Conclusion

The present-day Catholic attitude towards the faith of the fathers seems to me to be characterized by two things. It sees in that faith, as experienced and "defined", the authentic link between itself and the revelation. Hence, it resists anything that might weaken the impact or corrupt the content of that faith. On the other hand, like all the other churches, it recognizes the urgent need to communicate this faith in cultures and situations that are no longer those of the early centuries. We are starting on a new stage in the living tradition. It is possible that in some regions of the world the Catholic Church will give greater emphasis to other "registers" than the *formulae* or "declarations" by which (especially in the west) it judges fidelity to the faith of the fathers. However, as the fathers themselves bear witness, the faith is greater than the *formulae*.

In search of an African contribution to a meaningful contemporary confession of the Christian faith

SIGQIBO DWANE

In African tribal life, religion is the expression of the people's awareness of and reverence for the supernatural. The fundamental religious presupposition is that, behind all forms of life in the universe, there is the Supreme Being who is the Giver of life. Through the ancestral spirits, this Being preserves and sustains life. He upholds and defends those values which have to do with human dignity, and which create and sustain the community. It is therefore not true, as Peter Bolink points out,[1] that God in African religion is a *Deus otiosus*. God in the African tradition may be so utterly transcendent as to be unapproachable, but he is believed to be at work in and behind all that happens. The ancestral spirits are not the final court of appeal, but mediators between this world and the next. Religion, therefore, is the celebration of the common life expressed through friendships, family ties, the mystical bonds of love, mutual care and support between those in this life and those in the next, and the ultimate dependence of all upon God the Giver of life. It is first and foremost a corporate attitude towards life. In this context, religious festivals are the worshipful acts of the community in which young and old, male and female, living and departed mingle with one another and interact in a creative way.

• The Rev. Dr SIGQIBO DWANE, Anglican, is Principal of St Peter's College, Imbali/Natal, South Africa.

The environment in which African religion has developed, and to which it is to a large extent still tied, is rural and pastoral. But there has been a significant shift in many African people's attitudes to the supernatural, and a consequent modification of the values associated with the traditional beliefs in the supernatural. This is due to the influence of the urban, western climate since the colonization and evangelization of Africa. What is therefore described as the African religious heritage is not a monolithic and unchanging corpus of beliefs, ideas, and practices, but something much more piecemeal and fragile (though it is perhaps true to say that it has remained constant in its essentials). One would be guilty of oversimplification and falsification of the state of affairs if one were to create the impression that those forces which have to do with the arrival of Christianity in Africa—e.g. education and the urban and industrial revolution—have left African religion untouched. While one has to say that there is a sympathetic tendency towards the supernatural in the hearts and minds of many African city-dwellers, a tendency which testifies to the powerful influence which the past exerts upon the present, yet one has to be careful not to underestimate the secularizing and individualizing effect of urban industrial life upon African society.

Creative factors in African traditional religion

1. *A creed to live by*
African belief in the supernatural is, in many instances, not clearly articulated and developed into a complete, well-rounded system. In Africa, religion is not primarily a set of ideas for reason to speculate on, but a way of life. It is a living force which permeates and integrates all aspects of human life. The health, prosperity, and wellbeing of the community have a common focal point in the equilibrium between the living and the departed, a point of contact which has consequences for humanity's ultimate destiny. Equally true is the fact that ill-health, misfortune, disaster and death are attributed to a breakdown in human relationships, and raise, in the final analysis, religious questions. Kofi Appiah-Kubi has this to say on the subject: "Most Africans think that health is symptomatic of a correct relationship between people and their environment, which includes their fellow beings; the natural as well as the supernatural world. Health is associated

with good, blessing and beauty—all that is positively valued in life. Illness, on the other hand, shows that one has fallen out of this delicate balance."[2] Gabriel Setiloane[3] maintains that among the Sotho-Tswana the word "disease" means much more than is conveyed by the English word "illness". It implies, he says, a breakdown in the harmony of one's relationships with other living centres of activity, from the supreme being down to inanimate objects. John Taylor has this to say about the tendency in African thinking to attribute all things to a personal cause: "But for the man who assumes a personal causation in every event there is no such thing as accident. Any occurrence may be significant for his wellbeing and therefore needs to be accounted for in terms of some personal will either of the living or of the dead."[4]

It seems to me that the purpose of the search for a meaningful expression of the Christian faith in the contemporary world is to enable those who are inside the theological circle to affirm their faith with honesty and integrity, and to remove the obstacles which prevent those who are outside or on the fringes from giving it their serious consideration. In Africa one of these obstacles is the fact that, unlike traditional religion, Christianity appears to have little or nothing to say to people faced with the crises of sickness, misfortune, and the struggle against evil and mysterious powers. To some extent, the Zionist movement, with its emphasis upon healing through prayer and the laying on of hands, as well as through traditional means, is the attempt to minister to this crying need. A confession of faith, to be relevant in the African context, will have to reflect God's concern as is expressed in the ministry of Jesus to the spiritual and material needs of humanity. Christianity in Africa will have to release Christ from docetic fetters, and itself from the gnostic tendency to denigrate material and physical being. It will have to find ways and means of drawing attention to the resources made available in Jesus the Christ for the healing of human brokenness, and for the satisfaction of humanity's hunger and thirst for God, for life in all its fullness, and for the realization of human community. The God who is presented through many of the Church's catechisms is the God of the classroom and of examinations, a God who is forgotten as soon as confirmation is attained. God so presented is nothing more than an item of a conceptual scheme whose connection with life on this planet is tenuous and theoretical.

In Africa there has to be a different approach altogether. God must be presented as a living person who has created and now controls the personal destiny of the universe to be accomplished in the full realization of *koinonia* in the kingdom.

2. *God and the ancestors*

In our continent God is revered as the wholly-other. As the English say that familiarity breeds contempt, so in Africa mortals shun intimacy with deity. The awe with which humans regard deity makes direct contact with God inconceivable. This emphasis upon the utter transcendence of divine being has led some non-African observers to the conclusion that "God no longer takes interest in the affairs of his creation". What they fail to understand is that there is what John Taylor describes in *The Primal Vision* as "the tender bridge" which more than adequately compensates for what is lost by too much stress on transcendence. It is just as well that in African religions God is believed to be radically different from the creature, and maintains a safe distance between himself and creation. For, if it had been otherwise, the suspicion that the ancestors are "worshipped" would have been buttressed by the confusion as to whether God is just another, though perhaps a more exalted, super-ancestor. But in our view God is God, and humanity is humanity. Mortals may not address him directly, but must approach him indirectly through the mediation of the ancestral spirits. There is therefore no room in Africa for religious individualism, the "me and my God" sort of attitude. The clamour for a direct access to God which is characteristic of western Protestantism very often appears to non-westerners to betray a desire "to go it alone", a very sick and dangerous obsession with the self, and a disastrous preoccupation with the delusion that one is the ultimate norm. Our Lord warns us against the temptation to strain after what is by divine wisdom unattainable for us mortals when he says that no one has ascended to heaven, therefore no one except the Son has seen the Father.

What is given to us is the knowledge of the Father's plan through him who is our Brother. And him we know not in isolation, but only as members of the community which he has founded upon earth.

It is interesting to note, though perhaps a little confusing to non-Africans, that in some of the Southern African languages at

least one of the words which designate the ancestors is by extension a title of the Supreme Being. For example in Sotho-Tswana
the *Badimo* are the ancestors and *Modimo* is God himself. In
Xhosa and Zulu the ancestors are known variously as *amanyange*
and *amakhosi*. And God is the *Inyange Lamanyange*, the "ancient of ancients", or in Zulu the *Inkosi Yamakhosi*, the "king of
kings". What this indicates is that the ancestral realm leans heavily upon the divine realm. The ancestors are spirits who live in the
spiritual domain and are in close proximity to God. They are close
enough to him to be his mediators through whom he sends his
blessings upon those who remain on earth. Bolaji Idowu gives a
very useful account of the distinction between God and the
ancestors, and of the latter's role as go-between:

> Africans make distinction between deity, the divinities, and the
> ancestors. Deity and the divinities are distinctly, out and out, of the
> super-sensible world, while the ancestors are of the living persons' kith
> and kin. The ancestors are related to the living community in a way
> that cannot be claimed for deity or the divinities who are definitely of
> a different order. The ancestors are regarded still as heads and parts of
> the families or communities to which they belonged while they were
> living human beings... The ancestors remain, therefore, spiritual
> superintendents of family affairs and continue to bear their titles of
> relationship like "father" or "mother". Nevertheless it is of impor-
> tance for the assessment of their status to know that they are no longer
> living human beings according to earthly assessment. They have
> become spirits—spirits whose sphere is the spirit world reserved for
> good ancestors and in consequence of which communion with them is
> possible only at spiritual level... To some extent, they are in-
> termediaries between deity or the divinities and their own children: this
> is a continuation of their earthly function whereby they combined the
> headships of the families or communities with the office of family or
> community priest or priestesses.[5]

For reasons which, I hope, are clear from this account of the
role of ancestors in traditional religion, I believe that it is imperative for Jesus, in the African context, to be presented as the
man. This might sound trite in view of the fact that the Church's
orthodox teaching has always insisted on the *vere Deus vere homo*
Chalcedonian definition. However, it is well known that most ex-
positors and teachers of Christian doctrine listen more to Cyril
and the Alexandrian school, and less attentively to the Antiochene
approach. I am coming more to the realization that in Africa

Jesus must be recognized as a man with a genealogy and an ancestry which establishes his human claims firmly and indubitably. Thus understood as our brother, we can look up to him as the New Adam in whom the history of the human race is first of all summed up and then brought to perfection. This man takes up in himself and fulfills the role of the ancestors. As man he is one of the *amanyange*; and, as God's only begotten Son, he is the *Inyange Lamanyange*, the ancient of ancients. Any confession of faith which does not take account of the way in which Christ transforms and perfects the African's ancestry is, in Africa, a currency without value. As Bishop Tutu says: "We Africans cannot ignore the dead who are for us a real cloud of witness. A Christianity that has no place for them speaks in alien tones. It speaks, but not to us."[6]

3. *Religion and community*

One of my favourite expressions is John Mbiti's brilliant twist of the Cartesian *Cogito ergo sum* which swings this dictum round so that self-discovery becomes not the product of introspection, but of one's belonging to others. Mbiti's affirmation is: I belong, therefore I am, or I am because I belong. Tempels argues that Bantu ontology is opposed to the European concept of "individuated" things, that is, things which exist in themselves in isolation from others. Similarly, he says, Bantu psychology cannot conceive of a human being as an individual, a force existing by itself. He says that humans in traditional understanding are not lone beings, but vital forces which interact with, influence, and are influenced by other beings. Setiloane maintains that a person in African society is not a self-directing, self-determining, closed unit, but a magnet, creating with other persons a magnetic field. Harry Sawyer has this to say: "However powerful or, for that matter, insignificant an African may be, he lives his life first, as a member of a community and next, as an individual. His activities may be personal, but hardly individual."[7] John Taylor characterizes the African view of humanity as "the sense of the personal totality of all being, and of a humanity which embraces the living, the dead and the divinities".[8] Religion in Africa is the celebration of the common life of which God is the source, the ancestors its channel, and those who live on earth its recipients. At religious festivals, the ancestors mingle freely with their descendants, and partake of the same food and drink. Old friendships are renewed, bonds of love are strengthened, family and social relationships are affirmed and revitalized.

Christianity began on the day of Pentecost with a flourish. According to the early chapters of the Acts of the Apostles, those who had received the spirit were not able to carry on life as before. They stayed together, and explored the full implications of what had happened on the day of Pentecost. They were so animated by the spirit that they could live a life of complete openness to each other and share God's gifts with one another. The dry bones in them had been transformed into vitality, not of an individualistic kind, but of a life shared with others. In Africa a meaningful confession of the faith will have to incorporate a fully developed exposition of the idea of *communio sanctorum*.

In the Apostles' Creed this article is tucked in as a miscellaneous item at the very end. One would have hoped that, at the very least, it would be recognized by the faithful as the explication of the idea of the holy catholic Church and given more than mere lip service. But I suspect that *communio sanctorum* means little or nothing to most Christian people. If anything at all, its application probably extends only to those with whom one worships God under the same roof. And yet it must surely be the case that where the Church is not understood as a communion of all the saints it is not fully understood. The Church is the enduring and ever-deepening relationship in Christ between all the members of his Church, both far and near, in terms both of distance and of time. The holy catholic Church is nothing more or less than the communion of the saints of the most high, growing in Christ and in mutual love and understanding, sharing his spirit, testifying to his death and resurrection, and waiting for his second coming. The catholic Church in Africa is not the extension of the operations of an exploitative multinational oil or mining company whose directors are in London, New York, or Rome. It is rather the body of Christ living and rooted in Africa, obedient to its Master in the power of whose spirit it proclaims his glorious resurrection and ascension until he comes again in glory. It is linked in its life and witness, in its participation in the one spirit and in the sacramental life, and in its expectation of his return to the Church in other continents. It is also linked to Africa's tribal and religious past and to the roots of her present religious awareness. In Africa, the idea of *communio sanctorum* is not a luxury but the very heart of religion. The African therefore cannot fully belong to the Church until his ancestors are made to belong also. As E.W. Smith puts it:

> The life of the African is essentially social and based on tribal conditions and traditional customs. The interests of the individual are subordinate to the interests of the group... Christian discipleship is not to be realized by man in isolation. The blessing of Pentecost was not vouchsafed to personalities cut off from their fellows, but to a group.[9]

And that group of course includes the family, clan and ancestry.

In conclusion, I would like to make a plea for two things. The first is that any definition or expression of the faith should not so stress the discontinuity between Christianity and culture, or more specifically, primal religion, as to suggest that what God does in creation is radically different from what he does in the unique historical dispensation in the Judeo-Christian revelation.

Secondly, I want to plead that the recognition of the legitimacy of different theological slants arising out of the awareness that there are different perceptions of the one divine reality, and different experiences of his grace, be extended to the developing of theology in non-western idiom. I want to plead that this should be seen not as a regrettable phenomenon to be tolerated for the sake of peace, but as the inevitable and desirable manifestation of the blossoming of the Christian faith in Africa.

NOTES

[1] "God in Traditional African Religion—a deus otiosus?", *Journal of Theology for Southern Africa*, December 1973, No. 5, pp. 19-28.
[2] "The Church's Healing Ministry in Africa", *The Ecumenical Review*, Vol. 27, No. 3, July 1975.
[3] *The Image of God Among the Sotho-Tswana*, Rotterdam, Balkema, 1976, p. 44.
[4] *The Primal Vision*, London, SCM, 1963, p. 79.
[5] *African Traditional Religion*, London, SCM, 1973, p. 184.
[6] Desmond Tutu, "The Ancestor Cult and its Influence on Ethical Issues", *Ministry*, July 1969, Vol. 9, No. 3, pp. 99-104.
[7] In *Presence*, Vol. 5, No. 3, 1972.
[8] *The Primal Vision*, p. 13.
[9] *The Christian Mission in Africa*, New York, The International Missionary Council, 1926, p. 47.

The confession of faith in the Lutheran tradition
WOLFHART PANNENBERG

In the Lutheran churches, special importance is attached to the authority of the confession of faith. The emphasis here is not so much on the duty of confessing the faith in new ways as on faithful adherence to the confession of faith produced by the Lutheran churches at a particular time, at the beginning of the Lutheran reformation. This basic confession of the Lutheran reformation is the Confessio Augustana of 1530. Certainly the collection of Lutheran confessional documents contained in the Book of Concord of 1580 includes other such texts as well. But these subsequently added "confessional documents" are to be seen as an interpretation of the Augsburg Confession and not as an enlargement and completion of its substance. The Book of Concord, in particular, attests to the basic significance of the Augsburg Confession.[1]

In an analogous way, the Augsburg Confession itself emphasizes the authority of the ancient church creeds—the Niceno-Constantinopolitan Creed and the Apostles' Creed. The far-reaching significance of this fact was first fully realized in the course of the studies conducted into the text of the 1530 Augsburg

● Prof. Dr WOLFHART PANNENBERG, Evangelical Church in the Federal Republic of Germany (Lutheran), is Professor of Systematic Theology at the University of Munich, Federal Republic of Germany. This paper has been translated from the German by the WCC Language Service.

Confession in connection with the Jubilee Year 1980.[2] The confession of the Triune God in Article 1 of the Confessio Augustana with its appeal to the Nicene Creed, and the christological statements in Article 3, which follow closely the Apostles' Creed, are not to be interpreted simply as a preamble to the real theme of the Lutheran confession, a theme only broached in the statement in Article 4 on justification. In actual fact, what is stated in Article 3 is an outline tracing in advance the whole organization of part one of the Augsburg Confession down to Article 17,[3] dealing succinctly with the "chief articles" of the Christian faith. As is stated in Melanchthon's concluding remarks, in these articles there is no disagreement with the doctrinal bases of the Catholic Church or, therefore, with those of the Roman Church, whereas the disputed questions dealt with in part two of the Augsburg Confession do not touch the foundations or chief articles of the faith but arise in the main over certain traditions and abuses.[4] The doctrinal articles of the Augsburg Confession (Articles 1-17) are to be understood, therefore, as an exegesis of the ancient church creeds. What is said about justification, ministry, good works, church and sacraments all comes under the control of what is already said in Article 3 about the lordship of the exalted Christ over Christians through his Spirit. It anticipates the return of Christ, which is dealt with in Article 17 and with which the christological affirmations of Article 3 conclude, with an explicit reference to the second article of the Apostles' Creed. The intention of the Lutheran reformation in its confession at Augsburg in 1530 was quite obviously to bring out as clearly as possible the fact that the message proclaimed by the Lutheran preachers was identical with that of the ancient Church and its creeds.

How are we to explain its emphatic insistence on this fact? The explanation is to be found in the situation which gave birth to the Augsburg Confession. The letter of invitation issued by the Emperor Charles V in January 1530, in which he declared his willingness to listen to "every view and opinion" on the doctrinal conflict, prompted the Elector John of Saxony to commission the preparation of an apology for the reforms undertaken in church life and worship in Saxony in disregard of episcopal rights. But the prospects of any such apology being accepted—it would at least have to explain the reasons for radical reforms in respect of priestly celibacy, monastic life and church worship—were slim unless it could be agreed that the Lutherans were not heretics but shared the faith of the ancient Church. Not only were the conciliar decisions of the ancient Church incorporated in the imperial law, but the Emperor himself was also personally interested in the question whether the Protestants agreed with the twelve points of the Apostles' Creed. The Elector John of Saxony hoped that this question could be cleared up before the imperial diet met and, to this end, made sure that the Schwabach Articles, a Lutheran doctrinal summary drafted during the dispute with the Zwinglians, reached the Emperor at Innsbruck on his way to Augsburg. The Emperor did not accept these articles, however, so that the question of the orthodoxy of the Lutherans still remained an open one at the imperial diet. Moreover, this orthodoxy was radically challenged right at the beginning of the diet by Johannes Eck's "Four Hundred and Four Articles". This explains why Melanchthon decided to expand the proposed "apology" for the action of the reformers in the disputed questions by prefacing it with a number of doctrinal articles documenting the orthodoxy of the Lutherans. These constitute the first part of the document which is now labelled a "confession", and not an "apology". This explains the emphatic insistence, in the plan and text of part one of the Augsburg Confession, on the point that the doctrines of the Lutherans are simply an interpretation of the ancient Church creeds and embrace nothing beyond this. But this way of presenting the Lutheran position was certainly not dictated merely by tactical considerations. This is quite clear from other statements of the reformers, and also from the fact that the Lutheran churches have always firmly adhered to this confession of faith as the permanently authoritative statement of the Lutheran understanding of the Christian faith.

The "apology" as originally planned only became the "confession of faith" with the addition of the first part with the main doctrinal articles. The use of the term "confession" in this sense was unusual. The term *confessio* was used by the medieval Latin Church primarily for the confession of sins; for the confession of faith the term used was *confessio fidei*. The term "confession" as used here of the Augustana was obviously derived from Luther himself who had appended to his treatise on the Lord's Supper of 1528 a short summary of his faith and called it "confession", in order "to confess my faith point by point before God and the whole world, that faith in which I hope to continue until death" (WA 26, p. 499). This statement of Luther's, which may be based on the use of the creed or symbol in the eucharistic liturgy (G. Kretschmar), contains a characteristic stress on the definitive and unalterable character of the confession, inextricably bound up with Luther's own death and at the same time, therefore, with the eschatological situation of accountability before the "judgment seat of Christ". This has continued to be decisive for the Lutheran view of the confession of faith: the confession is not something which needs to be completely renewed again and again in changing situations, but something definitive to which the Christian must adhere unswervingly and continue to hold fast,[5] even though the once established confession is certainly in constant need of interpretation. In respect of its content, too, Luther's 1528 "confession" was the springboard for the confession of the Lutheran churches, i.e. for the Schwabach Articles and then for the first part of the Augsburg Confession. The conviction that the confession is not to be altered but maintained explains not only the permanent fundamental importance of the Augsburg Confession for the Lutheran churches but also the adherence of the Augsburg Confession itself to the content and structure of the ancient Church creeds. In this respect, too, Luther was already the pioneer in his confession of 1528.

These two elements—the forensic, in relation both to the world's forum and to that of the coming judge of the world, and the eschatologically definitive and unalterable—provide the Lutheran view of the confession with a very special link with the origin and source of Christian confessing in the confession of faith in the person of Jesus Christ. The need for, and the saving significance of, such confessing is attested by Jesus Christ himself: "Everyone who confesses me before men, the Son of Man will confess before the angels of God" (Luke 12:8f. and parallels). The witness of faith before the world's justice and judgment is already related here to the verdict of the eschatological judge. H. v. Campenhausen has rightly emphasized the fundamental significance and historical influence of this dominical saying in the whole course of Christian witness and confession: "Whenever the christological confession or its corresponding denial appears in primitive Christianity, a direct or indirect influence of this saying of Jesus is always to be assumed in any case of doubt."⁶ The gravity of an ultimate commitment, which is inseparable from such confessing, is also transferred later to the formal confession of faith, the embryo of which is found in the writings of the apostle Paul—not so much in the stylized formulas which, with varying degrees of plausibility, it was for long the exegetical fashion to identify as "confessional formulas" in the Pauline letters, but, above all, in the explicit statement in *Romans*: "... if thou dost confess with thy mouth Jesus as Lord and dost believe in thy heart that God has raised him from the dead, thou shalt be saved" (10:9). The personal act of confession of faith *in* Jesus, when it is his person that is in question (in the sense of Luke 12:8), is developed here into substantive affirmations *about* Jesus, where the individual adopts the liturgical acclamation of the community and its basis in the Easter *kerygma* as his or her own.⁷ The decision for Jesus, when it is his person that is in question, becomes necessarily in the post-Easter situation the decision for the Church which proclaims and calls upon the risen Christ, the decision to participate in the Church's liturgical acclamation of Christ. To describe this change as the substitution of a recited doctrinal confession for a personal confession and commitment is unwarranted. There is no change in the substance itself; only the form of the personal confession of Jesus Christ changes after Good Friday and Easter Day. From now on, this personal confession is only possible in the form of a participation in the confession of the Church. The confession of Jesus Christ is not replaced here by a confession of faith in the Church. On the contrary, it is the confession of Jesus which itself has to be made now by participation in the Church's liturgical invocation of Christ and by the endorsement of the Church's proclamation of Christ. The form taken by the confession of the person of Jesus Christ after Easter is the endorsement of the basic witness of the Church to Christ.

Here again, we are dealing with an eschatologically definitive transaction. This explains the special connection between the confession of faith and baptism, for baptism is the eschatologically definitive deed-of-conveyance transferring the baptized person to Jesus Christ. But the definitive dimension also belongs to the content of the doctrinal statements of the confession of faith: this content is what is fundamental for the whole Christian faith. The act of confessing is always concerned with the whole Christian faith. In the early period of the Church, the *regula fidei*, the trinitarian pattern of the statement of faith, requiring amplification in different ways regionally or individually, served as a general rule of individual confessing with the whole Christian faith as its object.[8] Only at the Council of Nicea in 325 did it become possible for the first time to state the Christian faith in a comprehensive formula binding on the whole of Christendom. For at Nicea in 325 the whole of Christendom was gathered together for the first time in its representatives, the bishops, for the purpose of confessing together the common faith. That it was the whole Christian faith and not just one single dogmatic decision that was at stake here is also shown in particular by the expansion and completion of the Nicene formulas by the Council of Constantinople in 381. The Constantinopolitan fathers of 381 wanted to proclaim "the faith of Nicea" and this in its entirety. It was precisely for this reason that the Nicene formula was supplemented in certain details. The claim thus made was ratified by the Council of Chalcedon in 451 which recognized both formulations as expressing the same identical "faith of Nicea" and, therefore, as binding on the whole Church. In consequence, the Chalcedonian fathers of 451 subordinated their own doctrinal decision to the authority of the "faith of Nicea" and regarded it as an exegesis and application of that faith. In the view of Chalcedon 451, therefore, the faith of Nicea as formulated more completely in the Creed of Constantinople 381 is the definitively authoritative formulation of the whole Christian faith which continues to be binding on the whole Church.

As has already been said, what we have here is not just a single dogmatic decision but the formulation of the whole Christian faith. Subsequently the only area remaining for discussion concerned the interpretation and application of this confession of faith. Those, for example, who wish to replace or supplement it by another confession inevitably expose themselves to the suspicion of wanting either to proclaim some faith other than that of the Church (the "faith of Nicea" as the credal confession of the first representative assembly of the whole Church) or else to deny Nicea's claim to be the expression of the whole Christian faith in a form binding on the whole Church. This unique authority of the Niceno-Constantinopolitan Creed, its claim to be binding on the whole Church, its claim to definitive validity, therefore, reproduces at the level of the representative utterance of the whole Church the dimension of eschatological validity inherent in the Christian act of confession from the very beginning. Whereas, at the individual level, this ultimate validity takes the form of a deliberate, irrevocable personal adherence to Jesus Christ, of a definitive affirmation of the Church's faith for the individual's own life, at the level of the utterance of the whole Church it takes the form of a definitive statement of the faith which claims authority for the whole Church, even for the future as well. What is involved here at the individual level, as well as at the level of the whole Church, is the Christian faith in its entirety. This wholeness and the ultimate, eschatological validity of the act of confession are inseparable. In both cases, of course, it also remains necessary for the confession to be reinterpreted over and over again in changing historical situations. Nevertheless, the publishing of a new interpretation can never be the issue of a completely new confession of the faith, since confession can only concern the one Christ as proclaimed by his Church. Once the question of unity in the confession is raised, the unity in faith and the unity of the Church are also called in question. But it is not just confession, because the confession can only be directed to the one Christ as proclaimed by his Church. When it is a question of the unity of the confession of faith, the unity of faith and the unity of the Church itself are also in question. The question of the unity of the Church and its faith, however, is not posed only in each new present moment but also with respect to the whole history of the Church, beginning with its apostolic origin. The apostolicity of the Church is therefore constitutive for its unity, which can only be unity in the truth of the faith in Christ. This means, however, that even the summary of this faith by the councils of the fourth and fifth centuries, representative of the whole Church, a summary claiming to be binding on the whole Church, cannot be ignored or passed over without destroying the unity of the Church.[9]

It is in the light of these considerations that we must evaluate not only the Lutheran insistence on the final validity and unalterability of the confession of the Church but also the fact that the Augsburg Confession, in its doctrinal articles, claims to be an interpretation of the ancient church creeds and does not claim to be regarded, therefore, as itself a completely new confession of faith. The appeal to the ancient church creeds protects the confession of the Lutherans from the suspicion and accusation of heresy; and it is against the authoritative standard to which appeal is made that its own statements must be examined to see whether they do indeed confess the same faith, and it must also itself be interpreted in line with this intention.[10]

Among the ancient church creeds to which the Augsburg Confession appeals and from whose statements it takes its direction, the Apostles' Creed is, next to the Niceno-Constantinopolitan Creed, the outstanding one. The connection between these two creeds is presented in the Confessio Augustana in such a way that the trinitarian faith of Nicea in Article 1 is referred particularly to God the Creator, and the statements of the Apostles' Creed in Article 3 are referred to the work of redemption; between them comes Article 2 on original sin with its reception of the ancient western Church's condemnation of the Pelagians. The Nicene Creed and the Apostles' Creed are set, therefore, within the framework of an outline of salvation history, itself deriving in turn from the statements found in the creeds and governing the whole pattern of the Augsburg Confession down to Article 17, "On Christ's Return to Judgment". The central guide here, moreover, is clearly the Apostles' Creed, since Article 3, which sketches in advance the arrangement of the succeeding articles, appeals specifically to this creed.

The Apostles' Creed still enjoyed widespread respect in the sixteenth century. It presented a summary of the Christian faith which, as its name suggested, went back to the time of the apostles, even if it was not actually authored by the apostles themselves. Today, however, we regard this creed as one of the local baptismal symbols of early Christianity, the name of which signifies no more than that it provides a summary of the "apostolic" faith. Being the baptismal creed of the Church of Rome, the Apostles' Creed naturally acquired special respect in the west. Its authority today, however, can no longer be that of a document of the apostolic age, behind which stood the authority of the apostles themselves, nor even that of an ecumenical creed which could be compared with the Niceno-Constantinopolitan Creed as an authority for the whole Church. On the contrary, the unique importance of the Niceno-Constantinopolitan Creed, even for the western Church—as the only summary of the Christian faith which can claim to be, and was actually produced to be, binding on the whole of Christendom—has been increasingly recognized today. A contemporary interpretation of the faith of the ancient Church, with its claim to be binding on the whole Church in all succeeding ages, can take its bearings, therefore, in contrast to the Reformation period, *only* from the Niceno-Constantinopolitan Creed. Only in that creed, in its original form moreover, are the churches of all succeeding ages confronted with a summary of the Church's faith which is at the same time an expression of the unity of the Church across all differences of culture and historical period. By this creed, therefore, every church is questioned with particular sharpness as to whether or not its faith is the same as that which was expressed in this ecumenical creed.

The Lutheran view of the definitive character of the confession, and of its fundamental significance for the unity of the Church, can be recognized in a specific sense in the claim of the "faith of Nicea" to ecumenical validity, a claim made at Nicea in 325, at Constantinople in 381, and solemnly ratified by Chalcedon in 451. In view of the fact that others of the now-divided churches of Christendom also interpret their particular doctrinal traditions as an interpretation of the faith of the One Church as confessed in Nicea in 325 and in Constantinople in 381, a fresh study of this common basis could perhaps help us to overcome the divisions which have taken place, without, at the same time, simply abandoning the traditional self-understanding of their own ecclesial tradition. To achieve this, of course, we certainly need an unprejudiced eye for the ecumenical breadth contained in embryo in our own traditions but which is all too easily concealed and stifled by the spirit of narrow and exclusive particularism.

NOTES

[1] Preface to *Concordia* or *Book of Concord, The Symbols of the Evangelical Lutheran Church*, St Louis, Mo., Concordia Publishing House, 1957, pp. 3-8, *passim.*

[2] See V. Pfnür, *Einig in der Rechtfertigungslehre?*, 1970, pp. 97ff. Cf. *Confessio Augustana. Bekenntnis des einen Glaubens. Gemeinsame Untersuchung lutherischer und katholischer Theologen*, 1980, p. 69f.

[3] Articles 18-21 are additions to the original plan.

[4] *Book of Concord*, p. 25f.

[5] Cf. Preface to the *Book of Concord* of 1580 (p. 7 col. 1 at end) where there is also a reference to eschatology, and this indeed in the form of an appeal to the return of Christ as reference point in the process of maintaining the confession.

[6] "Das Bekenntnis im Urchristentum", in *ZNW* 63, 1972, pp. 210-253, citation on p. 214.

[7] In greater detail, cf. my essay on "Konfessionen und Einheit der Christen" (*Ök. Rundschau* 22, 1973) and now in *Ethik und Ekklesiologie: Gesammelte Aufsätze*, 1977, pp. 241ff., esp. 243f.

[8] On this, see H. v. Campenhausen, "Das Bekenntnis Eusebs von Caesarea", in *ZNW* 67, 1976, pp. 123-139.

[9] There is ecumenical importance in the fact that the solemn recognition of the faith of Nicea and Constantinople by the Council of Chalcedon in 451 as basis for its own decisions anticipated the conflict over these decisions and thus also forms a basis for the possible settlement of these disagreements which have continued down to our own day.

[10] It is here assumed that the ancient Church creeds have been shown to be a summary of the authoritative doctrinal content of holy scripture. In an analogous way, the Council of Trent described the *Niceno-Constantinopolitan Creed* as *principium illud in quo omnes qui fidem Christi profitentur, necessario conveniunt, ac fundamentum firmum et unicum (Denz. 1500)*. Does this mean that the decrees of this Council are also understood as an interpretation of the "faith of Nicea" and are intended to be measured by this claim and understood in terms of this intention, which would provide a level of agreement even across the disagreements of the Reformation period?

One confession—many confessions: reflections on the Second Ecumenical Council of Constantinople (381)

DAMASKINOS PAPANDREOU

On the occasion of the 1600th anniversary of the Second Ecumenical Council of Constantinople, the following questions present themselves with regard to the present significance of this Council:
1. The ecumenical validity of this confession of faith of 381.
2. The eventual possibility of a new confession of faith which could have a mutually binding character for the entire Christian world.

1. The ecumenical validity of the confession of faith of the Council of 381

The confession of faith of 381 brings to the surface questions of its origin and validity, as well as questions about the complex and unclear historical and ecclesio-political situation of the late fourth century.

As noted in the Encyclical Letter of the Ecumenical Patriarchate on the 1600th anniversary of the Second Ecumenical Council, the following clear goals were set by the Council: discussion on the christological complications arising from Arianism and other corrosions which undermined the orthodox faithful; rejection and

---

• Metropolitan DAMASKINOS OF TRANOUPOLIS is Representative of the Ecumenical Patriarchate of Constantinople, Chambésy, Switzerland.

purge of the new pneumatomachical heresies of Macedonius; a clear and short formulation and proclamation of the orthodox faith and tradition; condemnation of the condemnable heresies; imposition of the Church's order and discipline through various means, especially through the concrete recognition of the decisions of the Ecumenical Council with regard to the question of faith; restriction and punishment of excessive developments; establishment of the limits of ecclesiastical jurisdictions, and the setting of boundaries of particular jurisdictions; and, finally, through the corresponding canons, the determination and the institutional recognition of the position of the Church of Constantinople in the administrative system of the east.

The Church fathers were called, moreover, "to formulate the teaching of the Church in a wider meaning, and to articulate more specifically on questions outside the domain of the trinitarian problem, e.g. regarding the Church, the sacrament of baptism, the faith in the resurrection of the dead and eternal life, to which issues the First Council of Nicea had not yet taken a position (...)".[1]

Shortcomings in the summoning of the Council and doubts of its recognition intensified to such an extent that the credibility of renowned Church teachers was doubted. Ambrosius, protesting from the west against the ecumenical shortcomings of the Council, complained in one of his letters about the *commutio soluta et dissociata*.[2] Gregory of Nazianzus ostensibly rejected the Creed of the Council as a manipulated form of compromise and, hence, as a betrayal of the Nicean faith: "The sweet and beautiful source of the old faith which has brought to unity the venerable nature of the Trinity, upon which the endeavours of Nicea once aimed, I saw these being miserably spoiled through the salty floods of the undecided people."[3]

The confession of faith of 381 had not obtained unconditional ecumenical validity through its original authority. After a prolonged silence the Creed of the Second Ecumenical Council was taken up by the Council of Chalcedon. It was solemnly read along with the Creed of 325, and it was confirmed as "the holy faith which the 150 holy fathers had formulated in harmony with the faith of the holy and great Council of Nicea..."[4] This is how the Creed was recorded in the acts of the Council of 451. This also means especially that the process of acceptance, which has continued through the centuries, had this as its starting point. The Creed of 381—of the fathers of Nicea and Constantinople—which was to be seen, as it were, as two "statements of faith", fulfilling and elucidating each other,[5] was later named "Niceno-Constantinopolitan", and prevailed over other local confessions. Since the time of the formation of the confessions, it was customary for every local church to have its own confession. It is not surprising then that many confessions of faith could coexist. The plurality of the confessions, however, did not go against the unity of the Creed.

The general dissemination and use of the confession of faith of 381 in ecclesiastical practice continued in the east from the sixth century onward. During this period in the west—for the first time—a gradual acquaintance with this text occurs. Textual changes must be seen together with its reception. In the formulation of the Creed, that which was decisive was the confrontation with the heresies. The Creed of Constantinople had to defend the faith against the Pneumatomachoi. Nicea represents the official conclusion of the Arian controversies. This process regarding the development of the confessions of faith was as valid for the east as it was for the west. The western textual change with the *filioque* follows the same line of thought. It was a deviation vis-à-vis all forms of Priscillianism which, arriving from north Africa through Spain at the end of the fourth century, strove to confuse the faithful in the west.

Controversies arose over changes in the text of the Creed; these changes, necessitated by local needs, claimed a general validity. The claim of validity of the Niceno-Constantinopolitan Creed, in relation to the integrity of the text, exercised a positive influence for its success and propagation. Thus, the exclusive and comprehensive significance which the Creed of 381 had in the east is not surprising. Since the ninth century it is found integrated in the divine liturgy and it also has its place in the sacrament of baptism and catechism.

The process of acceptance ends in the west primarily in the eleventh century. Later on, however, there are other formulas in use along with it such as the Apostles' Creed or the Athanasian Creed. "They manifest a plurality of confessions in the west whose presupposition and criterion, however, is always the unity of the Creed in the continuity of truth... The confession of

381 stands next to various other confessions which, together and separately, are always an expression of unity and communion of the Creed. This is a unity of the Creed in the plurality of the Confessions."[6]

It must not be forgotten that early in the eleventh century the agreement on the teaching between east and west was not always perfect. Nevertheless, these differences, which appeared in every era, should never be regarded as an imposed cause that brought division in the community. It is a general phenomenon that the revealed truth, in both east and west, was received, lived and understood differently. These theological differences are to be understood as consistent with one and the same faith. Moreover, the transcendence of the mystery and the predominant apophatic character received a living meaning, along with its human expression, as it allowed freedom for a legitimate pluralism of theologies within the framework of the same traditional creed. Another contrary movement came into existence on both sides, though more in the west than in the east. This movement tended to identify the faith and its expression with particular theologies to such a degree that it regarded certain aspects of these theologies as absolute.

Regarding the questions which deal with pneumatology, one could assert that the elaborate doctrines of the west must not be interpreted as coming into conflict with the teachings of the east. One can, and must, elucidate the formulas of the Greek fathers as well as the Latin, including the *filioque*, and show their agreement, paying closer attention to their respective originality. The *filioque* was known to the western tradition from the fourth century; however, this was never considered as an impediment to communion, unless this communion was shattered for other reasons.

In any case, a difference here must be noted between the addition of the *filioque* in the Niceno-Constantinopolitan Creed and the various pneumatologies which developed in both east and west.

The return to the standard expression of faith of the Second Ecumenical Council would be the best way to celebrate the 1600th jubilee. Should the various pneumatological developments be of concern, then the Roman Catholic and Orthodox Churches should request each other to refrain from demanding that their individual formulations be rejected as illegitimate. They ought to strengthen their testimony in a way which encourages an awareness of this convergence, a convergence that was started by the official dialogue between the two churches.

Pope John Paul II, in his letter to the Ecumenical Patriarch Demetrius I, points towards these hopeful perspectives when he stresses, among other things, that:

> The teaching of the First Council of Constantinople constitutes to this day the expression of the one common faith of the one Church and of the entire Christianity.
>
> Obviously, I know too well that it has played its role in the course of history between our churches' discussions with regard to the teaching of the Holy Spirit, especially over the eternal relation of the Son and the Spirit.
>
> Like all questions, which have not as yet been made fully clear between our churches, this one must become the subject of our dialogue which, fortunately, has begun, and out of which we all await that it will help bring about speedily the longed-for day in which we, in the light and without reservations, could confess our faith in a common celebration of the divine liturgy.[7]

Although, as already explained, the early confessions of faith were historically and culturally conditioned—they addressed themselves to specific people of their period and to their redemption—they constitute a guarantee of orthodoxy, an expression of universal validity in the trinitarian faith of Christ. These are an absolute experience and not simply an expression of knowledge.

What can these reflections mean for our present Church situation? What is the role of the Niceno-Constantinopolitan confession of faith in our present ecclesiastical state of affairs? Do the conciliar proceedings of Nicea, for example, have any meaning for the present Church communities? A direct comparison is impossible since the First Ecumenical Council took place in a specific historical moment of the Byzantine Empire, while people today find themselves in a variety of different situations.

Nicea (325) and Constantinople (381) occurred in the one undivided Church, while today we find ourselves in a number of church communities which now and then diverge with regard to structure and confession of truth. Can anyone assert that the ecumenicity of these two Councils can presently be confirmed through the recognition of its truth in a process of "reception" which is not to be understood in terms of constitutional obedience nor as a simple brotherly bond?

The reception is much more a matter of good will to reach full agreement of the truth. It is a spiritual event of an *a posteriori* manifestation; it is also the acceptance of the Council's claim to be the voice of the Holy Spirit who becomes active in the entire Church. If his claim, as such, is to have validity for our present time, shouldn't we be speaking of a fuller reception, one which could certainly be very possible?

The claim of the ecumenical councils is valid also today. It is a reality for all churches, especially for those which have expressly committed themselves against the decisions of the councils. Their confessions must be adopted all the more anew!

2. The eventual possibility of a new confession of faith which could have a mutually binding character for the entire Christian world

A future ecumenical creed would make most sense if it expressed the unity in faith—that is, the unity of the Church—which is the goal of ecumenism. It would then have binding doctrinal authority because it would not be just the rational creation of the Church as institution, but would, through its spiritual resonance, take its proper doxological place in the life of the Church as a living expression of the common faith.

Although the ancient creeds were historically and culturally determined—they were addressed to the particular people of their time and were concerned with their redemption—they are a guarantee of orthodoxy, an expression of universal validity in the Christian faith, an absolute experience, not just statements of knowledge. This naturally does not mean that the Church lacks the doctrinal authority to work out a new creed if that is called for by the immediate situation. The Church is the locus of the uninterrupted incarnation of truth through the power of the Holy Spirit.

The Orthodox Church was not involved in the struggles of the Reformation and Counter-Reformation, and was therefore not forced to work out new creeds or to adopt some sort of Tridentine creed. Nor today, in its preconciliar process, does it see the need for a new creed, or indeed for a discussion of dogmatic issues as such. It believes that it would be useless and perhaps even dangerous to discuss, without compelling reasons, issues which do not threaten the Orthodox Church with heresies and schisms. For, apart from a few dogmatic theologians, there are hardly any of the faithful who feel the need for such a formulation. In the first centuries, the councils were convoked, out of necessity and on justified grounds, to prevent a grave split in the community of the Church or to remove divisions.

Regarding an ecumenical creed, I doubt both its possibility and its necessity, for the following reasons:

1. There is no generally accepted, universal teaching authority which could speak with binding force for the whole of Christendom. Such an authority would be conceivable only after the restoration of unity.

2. Even if such a teaching authority did exist, historical experience would point to the impossibility of such a creed. Not even the Roman Catholic Church, with its infallible magisterium and universal ecclesiological structure, has been able to create a new world catechism. It has not found a form of communication suitable for the different situations of nations of diverse cultural, social and psychological origin and constitution. This is not for lack of trying: there was an official Tridentine catechism, and Cardinal Gasparri made another attempt, more recently, under Pius XI. What holds for a catechism holds equally for an ecumenical creed.

3. Moreover, our serious contemporary situation does not cast doubt on a specific Christian doctrine, but on our common Christian faith as a whole; it is the practice and content of this which is being questioned. In this situation, what should any future ecumenical creed (which would have to be short and addressed to all Christians) include, and what should it omit? What would be its main elements? Certainly no creed of the ancient, undivided Church says everything that belongs to the faith, nor was that necessary. When the Creed is treated as life, its content transcends any definition. Life produces life and the Spirit the letter, never the letter the Spirit or death life. Who can express the incomprehensible and inexpressible mystery of God? Who can define the undefinable without running the risk of turning God into an idol? I do not believe that our present condition can be cured by authoritative definitions. The Second Vatican Council rightly made no attempt of this kind.

4. That is not to say that the Church cannot look for different expressions of faith to take the message of salvation into various situations. It would not be useful, but merely comfortable, to seek

a unity without diversity to be expressed in a possible common creed. Unity in diversity and diversity in unity characterize any living Church of Christ which is trying to maintain an organic relation to the world and history and to give the truth of the gospel contemporary flesh without affecting its essential continuity. The historical garb assumed by incarnate truth in every period changes nothing of the essence of truth. The problem of the Church is that some of its members can no longer distinguish between essence and form, with the result that they treat formal aspects as essential (the error of traditionalism) or make the central essence relative (the error of misguided reformism).

In my view, the formulation of an ecumenical creed is not essential. I now put forward some suggestions about the Creed in our ecumenical situation.

A. We must pay serious attention to the ancient and venerable creeds of the undivided Church, in spite of the frequent claims that they are too remote from our modern intellectual situation. We must investigate the place they have or should have in the life and thought of the Church today. How, today, do we profess Christ as the Lord, the Son of the living God? And how do we transmit this testimony about Christ? Through mere formulas which help the non-theologians to stand up for his or her faith in a non-Christian environment? To profess our faith today means thinking of the people of today as they really are: men and women of a scientific and technical age who have lost their bearings and do not know who they are. They seek peace and justice; they want to know what contribution Christianity has to make to humankind and towards world peace. They are the despised and disadvantaged, the people who demand human dignity, the tragically isolated. Our task is the verification of the Christian belief in God in the face of the gulf between God and humanity.

People wonder whether they should not become part of the content of the statement of faith. What is this "I" which proclaims "I believe in one God"? Why should this "I" not become part of the Creed? Many people claim that humanity can be included in the Creed in the same way as God, Christ and the Holy Spirit, but they forget that God's becoming man is inseparably connected with humanity's becoming human. Too little thought is given to the fact that the whole content of the faith presupposes human being, and that christology is essentially soteriology because it bases its legitimacy on an attempt to answer the urgent questions about the nature of human being. We often forget that God became man in Christ so that human nature might be shaped by the humanity of God.

B. Today the Creed is bound up with the question of how theology should be done. For the sake of humanity and the world, we should become theologically more faithful, in the sense of a theology which is inseparable from life and doxology and does not try to defend its content before human reason—a theology which can be harmoniously applied in everyday life. Central to this theology must be the fertile paradox of our faith, the meeting of the horizontal and the vertical which is the originality of Christianity among all religions. It must, in other words, be a theology which can make real for us here and now what we shall experience in the last days, the cohesion of the whole, the harmony of the universe.

If we become more deeply "theological" in the sense that the service of humanity cannot be separated from the service of God in worship, our love of God will lead us to our neighbour and our love of our neighbour will lead us to God. In this way we shall recover the balance between transcendence and immanence.

C. Only in this way will the separated Christians come to a profession of faith in Christ. In spite of the many testimonies to Christ—testimonies determined by time, place and culture—there is only one profession of Christ, just as there is only one indivisible body of Christ. We are on the way towards a creed which will be rediscovered beyond all our divisions and in spite of our different testimonies to Christ, a creed which may even enrich the one Church. There has not been enough investigation, bilateral or multilateral, to see whether our differences in faith really do divide the Church. Unfortunately, there has not been a mutual investigation of the existence of an *ecclesia extra ecclesiam*, which can be recognized in complete fullness where there is unity in the substance of the faith (i.e. the great conciliar creeds) and where the basic structure of the Church (i.e. the apostolic succession) is preserved intact.

We therefore have a common task of seeing whether and to what extent the differences between east and west justify a mutual rejection of communion. We must ask ourselves whether our divisions should not be regarded as different forms of the tradition and not divisions in the one tradition of the faith itself. I believe we must also put the question from the other side: not just "may we have communion with each other?", but also "have we the right to refuse each other communion?" Refusal is only right when the essence of faith and Church order compels it. If it takes place without such a compelling reason, we incur guilt. If we get this far in our awareness, then we can talk about a possible ecumenical creed.

Before the participants in the Third Ecumenical Council proceeded to examine the teachings of Nestorius and Cyril, they first read the Nicene Creed and then raised the following question: Is there disagreement between the teaching of these two teachers and the Creed of Nicea? Christians and the churches in the west and the east must address themselves to this question. Does our faith in Christ agree with the Niceno-Constantinopolitan confession? Nicea addresses itself to the people of that time, and deals with their redemption. Nicea had to prove that the Church of Christ is the place of the uninterrupted incarnation of truth through the Holy Spirit. Because the truth is identical to the incarnate Lord in history, the tradition of the truth is experienced throughout the centuries via this uninterrupted incarnation in any given point in history. Because every period of history is different, the interpretation of tradition—i.e. the incarnation of the truth—should always bear the garb of that particular era.[8]

In practical terms, so that the truth may not be betrayed, it should be incarnated in every historical epoch. It should not be safeguarded like a relic or a museum piece for fear that it will be damaged by history. The Holy Spirit, who always lives in history, renders this incarnation of the truth possible in every era without destroying the essential continuity of the Christian faith. Because of this, we have the common duty to ask whether, and to what extent, the differences between west and east justify the mutual refusal of communion.

The one pistis was always experienced before the one eucharistic table. Every deviation from this truth of faith, which threatened the Church with heretical and schismatic dangers, obliged the Church to employ all possible means in order to safeguard the full communion of the *corpus Christi*.

The desire of the first Councils of the Church was full communion in the sphere of the faith and the sacramental life. Because the holy eucharist was seen in agreement with orthodoxy, and because the eucharistic community presupposed the unity in the revealed faith of Christ, the Councils were obligated—whenever necessary for salvation—to formulate a confession of faith so that misunderstandings and deviations could be avoided. Thus, the concrete boundaries of the Church's constituency were set. An essential criterion by which the truth or error of a teaching could be judged, as a guarantee of orthodoxy, and as an expression of universal validity in Christian faith, is given to us from these confessions of faith of the Councils, which at the same time constitute the first definitions of the Church's teaching office.

Concluding thoughts and reflections

We have celebrated this year the 1600th anniversary of the Second Ecumenical Council which was held in Constantinople in 381.

Ireneus of Lyon associates the assembly of the children of God with the Church which is inseparably united with the Spirit. "God has appointed in the Church the apostles, prophets and all other operations of the Spirit, in which those who do not confess the Church have no part (...). Because there, where the Church (ekklesia) is, there is also God's Spirit; and where God's Spirit is, there is the Church and all grace. And the Spirit is the truth."[9] There is a mutual involvement of Spirit and Church. One can say that where the Spirit is, the Church is; and where the Church is, the Spirit is.[10] This Church, the body of the crucified and risen Christ, which exists through the grace of the Holy Spirit in an uninterrupted way, is the succession of priests in the sacramental believing community of the apostles. This is the Church that Ireneus recognizes as the true Church, which guarantees the continuity of the apostolic faith. It is that Church which the Spirit completes over all and in all. It is the Church of 381 which has given us the common confession of the trinitarian faith, a confession that is lived out to this day in an uninterrupted faith.

The Creed of Constantinople, in its article on the Holy Spirit, presupposes the communion in the one, holy, catholic and apostolic Church. The text says: "And (I believe) in the Holy Spirit, the Lord, the Giver of life, who proceeds from the Father, who together with the Father and the Son is worshipped and glorified, who spoke through the prophets. In one, holy, catholic and apostolic Church..."

All these thoughts, and the fact that we live today our common confession of the trinitarian faith, compel us to a great and pressing task: that is, to restore full communion between the separated churches. When the Church is there where the Spirit is, and when the Spirit is there where the Church is, then we must be ready to seek and acknowledge the presence of the Spirit—i.e. the Church—outside of our particular canonical boundaries, with which we identify the one, holy, catholic and apostolic Church. We can do this without betraying our faith in the *una sancta* if we examine and elucidate our own charisma as much as possible in order to acknowledge the charisma of others. If the communion in the continuity of the apostolic faith is a fruit of the Spirit, then we are obligated to examine, through profound dialogue, whether our differences, expressed in different theological language, are really legitimate expressions of the same mystery of Christ, a mystery which always remains inexpressible. This does not mean that we are to forget the differences of doctrine which have not as yet been reconciled, but we should, however, change our attitude so that we do not see only the difficulties in the present situation but, filled by the Spirit, find possibilities for rapprochement. One must not forget what Gregory of Nazianzus said: "Do not disturb yourselves over questions on words. Let the power of divinity be granted to us [where this power is confessed by the Holy Spirit]. And we will meet you with forbearance in these words."[11]

It cannot be denied that Christianity is painfully divided. We must not accept these divisions as a natural state of affairs, nor explain them incorrectly as Arnold Toynbee has done.

The most crucial mistake of Toynbee's thought lies simply in that he does not take into consideration the tragedy of the Christian division. In reality east and west form no independent unities and consequently they are not "understandable in themselves". They constitute fragments of a single world, a single Christianity which, according to God's will, should not be divided. The tragedy of the division is the greatest and most important problem of Christian history. The attempt to view Christian history as an intelligible whole is already in a certain sense a right step to the road of restoring the broken unity. We could already value as a significant ecumenical success the fact that the "separated Christians" understood that they ought to belong to each other, and, consequently, exist together. Further, we must understand that all Christians have a common history and a common origin.[12]

No one expects from our official bilateral and multilateral dialogues that the other partner ceases to be what he is, but rather that we recognize the other as he really is. Only in this way can we reach a mutual enrichment without demanding others to give up their identity. I do not advocate a "formal tolerance" but a "substantive tolerance"—i.e. a dynamic, living discussion which can lead to a deeper mutual understanding.

Naturally, this is not to be confused with superfluous polemical self-assertions nor with disguised combat in the name of "ecumenism". A beautiful line of Goethe could be instructive for us. "Tolerance", he said, "ought to be only a transitional attitude. Tolerance must lead to recognition. To tolerate means to offend."[13]

NOTES

[1] The 1600th jubilee of the Second Ecumenical Council 381-1981. Patriarchal and Synodal Encyclical Letter, Ecumenical Patriarchate, 5-8 June 1981, 5 (in Greek, French and German).

[2] Epistle 13, 10; P.L. 16, p. 953.

[3] *Poemata Historica*, P.G. 37, 1148A.

[4] Mansi, *Conciliorum amplissima Collectio VI*, pp. 956-957.

[5] Letter of Bishop Flavian of Constantinople to Theodosius, Mansi, *C.a.C.*, VI, p. 541.

[6] Slenczka R., Das Ökumenische Konzil von Konstantinopel und seine ökumenische Geltung heute, *Una Sancta*, 36, 1981, 3, pp. 206-207.

[7] Letter of Pope John Paul II to the Ecumenical Patriarch Demetrius, *Episkepsis*, 12, 1981, 254, 22.

[8] Cf. Metropolitan Meliton of Chalcedon, *Episkepsis*, 1, 1970, 7, 2-6.

[9] *Adv. Haer.* III, 24, 1 (SC, vol. 211, pp. 471-473); P.G. 7, p. 966.

[10] Cf. Congar Y., *Je crois en l'Esprit-Saint*, Vol. 1, Ed. du Cerf, Paris, 1979, p. 101.

[11] In *Laudem Athanasii*, Or. XXI; P.G. 35, 1125B.

[12] Florovsky G., *The Body of the Living Christ*, Thessaloniki, 1972, p. 126 (in Greek).

[13] Cf. "Den anderen anerkennen, wie er ist". Interview with Metropolitan Damaskinos of Tranoupolis, *Luth. Monatshefte*, 8, 1978, pp. 472-474.

The trinitarian understanding
of the Christian God
in relation to monotheism and polytheism

V.C. SAMUEL

In discussing the ecumenical importance of the Nicene Creed, the question of the trinitarian understanding of God has a special relevance. The Nicene Creed, held commonly by Christians of almost all traditions, affirms belief in God the Father, God the Son, and God the Holy Spirit. The New Testament testifies to the fact that baptism was administered by the apostolic Church in the name of the Father and the Son and the Holy Spirit (Matt. 28:19), and St Paul uses the trinitarian formula in concluding his Corinthian letters (2 Cor. 13:14).

This trinitarian understanding of God has continued in the Church ever since the New Testament times. During the second and the third centuries, several attempts were made by Christian leaders and preachers to clarify its meaning. Some of them were rejected by the Church, and some helped the formation of the tradition which lies behind the Nicene Creed and the theological heritage of the fourth, and subsequent, centuries.

How are we to understand the trinitarian affirmation? How can it be related to monotheism and polytheism? These are indeed questions which deserve serious answers. In this paper, a very preliminary attempt to discuss them is made.

• Prof. V.C. SAMUEL, Orthodox Syrian Church in the East, is Professor of Theology at the United Theological College, Bangalore, India.

Polytheism, monotheism and trinity

The trinitarian faith in God held by Christianity is an advancement on Jewish monotheism, which may be noted by referring to the prophet Isaiah. He puts in the mouth of Yahweh the words: "I am Yahweh, and there is no other, besides me there is no God... I make light and create darkness, author alike of prosperity and trouble, I, Yahweh do all these things" (Isa. 45:5-7). We have here a clear presentation of the Jewish monotheistic faith.

The monotheism of the Jews developed within a religious milieu in which Yahweh was looked upon by the Hebrew people as the God of their deliverance, and then as their God exclusively. The existence of other gods was not questioned by them during their early history. But the prophets insisted that the people should accept Yahweh only as their God and sever all connections with the gods of other peoples. The Elijah episode (1 Kings 17f.) does not say that Yahweh alone is God, but that Yahweh alone is the God of the Hebrews, and that he is the most powerful God. However, the Elijah incident may well have paved the way for the evolution of the monotheistic belief which the Second Isaiah uncompromisingly proclaims.

This sixth-century prophet is not simply claiming that Yahweh is the God of the Jews and that he is the most powerful deity, but that Yahweh alone is God. There is no other God, he says categorically. Belief in the only God negates all reality to divine plurality. The position of the Hebrew prophet is not a naive elevation of his god among the many gods as the only divine reality. History, for example, points to the many instances of powerful races or nations imposing their gods and religion on weaker peoples. It is not a case of this kind that we have in Judaism. What we see here is a body of people in their extreme humiliation and dejection as captives in a foreign land discovering the meaning of God anew and proclaiming it. What is important for them is the realization of faith in the only God.

It is from this Jewish monotheism that the Christian understanding of God as triune came to be further clarified. The proclamation concerning Jesus Christ led to it. The one God came to be so understood that the author and revealer of our salvation and the Spirit who guides us to him were believed to be included in him. God was not conceived merely as the logical conclusion of rational speculation on the meaning of the divine. He is affirmed to be one, not simply because an admission of more than one deity is intellectually untenable, but because the religious conviction concerning Jesus Christ commended him to all men and women. "No one ever went up into heaven", writes John, "except the one who came down from heaven, the Son of man whose home is in heaven. This Son of man must be lifted up... so that everyone who has faith in him may in him possess eternal life" (John 3:13f). The saviour who came from heaven communicates life and salvation to those who believe in him. Jesus Christ, and the work which he accomplished through his death on the cross, mean much more than can be grasped empirically. The depth of his reality and the meaning of the salvation which he offers have to be discerned and appropriated by us in the Spirit. So understood, God is one and three. The three-ness does not negate the truth concerning the one, neither is the one opposed to the three.

The Jewish monotheism which lies at the back of the Christian trinity may be compared to the belief in the divine reality conserved in Hinduism. This great religion of India is polytheistic on the one hand, but it includes a strong plea for monotheism on the other. There is, however, a significant difference at this point between Judaism and Hinduism. Whereas the former declares Yahweh alone as God to the exclusion of other gods, the latter does not regard the many gods as unreal. The many are for Hinduism either various names given by different people to the same divinity or manifestations, partial or otherwise, of the one God.

Hinduism also transcends both polytheism and monotheism to trinity. The *thrimurthi* is acknowledged in more popular religious traditions, and *satchidananda* (*sat-chit-ananda*, which means existence, mind and bliss all in one) is recognized at higher levels of religious apprehension.

In both Judaism and Hinduism polytheism is transcended by monotheism, and the Jewish monotheism culminates in the Christian trinity.

The emphases of the Creed

That God is triune constitutes the basic affirmation of the Nicene Creed. As to the Creed, it is a fact that it was not a *de novo* effort of the fourth century to clarify the faith. Creeds have been in use in the Church from the very beginning. Between the apostolic times and the Council of Nicea in 325, different statements of the faith had been current in the Church. This was indeed necessary since the Church was not merely a community of men and women with no character of its own, but a community which lived by holding to a faith and to a life consonant with that faith. Accordingly, to teach the faith and to help the maintenance of the life were of paramount importance for the Church. The Creed was a concrete means to achieve the goal of keeping the faith.

The central point of all the creeds in use was related to Jesus Christ. The New Testament emphasis concerning the uniqueness of his sonship to God does reflect the tradition of the early Church which also acknowledged the special relationship which the Spirit had to him. The trinitarian formula also continued in the Church. This is the context in which the two monistic interpretations of the Trinity came to be offered during the second and the third centuries. That Jesus Christ was the word, a power working eternally in the one God (dynamism), and that he was a mode in which the one God acted uniquely in Jesus Christ (modalism), were both rejected by the Church. These positions were attempts primarily intended to face the question of who Jesus Christ was.

The christological motive is still clearer in the Nicene Creed, both in its original Nicene form and in its more developed form which the Council of Chalcedon ascribed to the Constantinopolitan Council of 381. The former we shall refer to here as N and the latter as C. The immediate reason for adopting a creed at the Council of Nicea in 325 was the Arian assertion that the Son, whose economy was in Jesus Christ, was a creature. Thus the concern behind its composition was christological. Arius and his supporters had insisted that the Son was the perfect creature of the eternally transcendent God. To exclude this view was the basic intention of the N. Later in the fourth century, incorporating all the anti-Arian phrases and ideas and adopting a simpler style, the C was composed. By that time, issues concerning the Holy Spirit had been raised by the *Pneumatomachoi* and those referring to the incarnation from the point of his humanity by Appollinarius. The C sought to be more specific on these points than the N had been. Thus, the second and the longest section of C is very definitely christological, and its section on the Holy Spirit is fuller.

In stating the faith concerning Jesus Christ, both creeds agree in affirming that the Son is very God from very God; he is born of the Father and not made by him; he is *homoousion to Patri* (of the same essence with the Father); it was by him that all things have been made. The Son is not, therefore, a creature but God, one with the Father in the latter's own essence.

The Greek phrase, *homoousion to Patri*, with reference to the Son's relation to the Father, has a deeper meaning than "having the same essence with the Father". It is important to see this in relation to the fourth-century phrases *anomoean, homoean* and *homoiousian*. The first of them was insisted on by strict Arians for whom the Son was a creature and, as such, in himself he is unlike the Father. The second was the position adopted by eastern conservatives who were disinclined to employ the philosophic term *ousia* because it was non-biblical. The third came to be admitted by a small body of eastern conservatives after the middle of the fourth century, following their disillusionment with the manoeuvres of the politically oriented Arian leaders. This last group did in fact pave the way for the ultimate victory of *homoousia*. *Homoousia* however was rejected because it was felt to be inadequate to affirm the unity of the Father and the Son in the same essence. The phrase could affirm, it was believed, that the Father and the Son were only separate members of the same class, a position which was not sufficient to exclude the idea that the Father and the Son were two gods.

Homoousia implies two emphases. Firstly, the Father and the Son have not only the same essence, but are also one in it. In the same essence they are *homos*, not *homoi*. Secondly, being united in the same essence, they are distinct entities. The Father alone is father, and the Son alone is son. They are one, not because the terms "father" and "son" can be used interchangeably. The emphasis is not that they belong to the same *ousia*, understood generically, but that they are one in the same *ousia* or essence. Thus, the unity and the distinctness of the Father and the Son are conserved by the Creed.

The Holy Spirit in the Creed

Though the Creed does not employ the *homoousian* language with reference to the Holy Spirit, the idea implied by the phrase is definitely affirmed by it. The Holy Spirit, it is confessed, is the

Lord who gives life to all things; he proceeds from the Father and is worshipped and glorified with the Father and the Son. In other words, eternally proceeding from the Father and ever worshipped and glorified with the Father and the Son, the Holy Spirit is eternal. The Father who creates all things through the Son brings all things to completion and perfection in the Holy Spirit.

God is. His "is-ness" or essence is eternal. The same "is-ness", which is eternally and fully in the Father, is also eternally in the Son and in the Holy Spirit. The Son derives the essence by generation and the Holy Spirit by procession. God is one, says Gregory Nazianzen: "And when I say God, I mean Father, Son and Holy Spirit." There is one *arche*, he says, and that is God. Here the Nazianzen refers to God in relation to the world. But, within the Godhead, the Father is the *arche* of the Son and the Holy Spirit, who, in relation to the world, are *synarche* or with the *arche*, but not with the created realm of existence.

The issue concerning the procession of the Holy Spirit deserves notice here. The east affirms that the Spirit, who is united in essence with the Father, proceeds from the Father. He is worshipped and glorified with the Father and the Son, with whom he has unity in essence, and is the Spirit of them both. The east sees in the single procession a clear basis for conserving divine unity and excluding tritheism. In the one God there is only one source. God is one and three in a real sense. At the same time, the Father, the Son and the Holy Spirit are not mere names; they signify a differentiation between the Father, the Son and the Holy Spirit in the divine unity. In himself God is Trinity, but the Trinity is triune.

One essence and three persons

That God is *mia ousia kai treis hypostaseis* (one essence and three persons) is the expression hallowed by tradition in the east. Of the different ways in which it can be taken, the following are clearly excluded by the Church.

1. The essence of God, or Godhead, exists by itself like the *Idea* of Plato and makes the reality of the Father, the Son, and the Holy Spirit possible.

Godhead does not exist by itself; it is there eternally and fully in the Father, from whom the Son and the Holy Spirit, each of them, derives it eternally and fully, the Son by generation and the Holy Spirit by procession.

2. The three persons are only three modes in which the one God manifests himself; thus, they are not eternal.

Modalism is believed to have held this view. Its rejection obviously implies the emphasis that the three persons are eternal, each being God in reality.

3. The three persons refer to three powers (dynamies) in the one God.

Dynamism is understood to have taught this idea. The exclusion of dynamism was felt to be necessary because the Father, the Son and the Holy Spirit were believed to be eternally *hypostatic* or personal.

4. The Son and the Holy Spirit are creatures who have been elevated to a level of equality with himself by the transcendent God.

In renouncing Arianism, the Church acknowledged that the Son and the Holy Spirit are not creatures, but are eternally divine *hypostases* or persons.

The one God is also three. They are united in the same essence, nature and will. They coinhere in all that they do. They differ only in that the Father alone is father, the Son alone is son, and the Holy Spirit alone is the Spirit that binds them. The Trinity refers to the eternal harmony of the Father, the Son and the Holy Spirit. The fatherhood, the sonship and the bond of union between them represented in the Holy Spirit are indeed eternal. The love that binds the Father and the Son, a love which has its source in the Father, binds us also to the eternally triune God; and through the same love we are also being bound together in the unity of true fellowship. The Father, the Son and the Holy Spirit are not only eternal, but are also eternally together.

Immanent and economic trinity

The trinitarian understanding of God is the foundation of the Christian view of salvation. Worked out within history by Jesus Christ, the incarnate Son, and completed in the Holy Spirit, salvation is the gift of God the Father. It is to be appropriated by us in faith and through a life consonant with that faith. The emphasis here is that God, who creates the world and all that exists, brings all things to their ultimate destiny in the divine plan.

The saving work accomplished by Jesus Christ is, in fact, a manifestation on the historical plane of the eternal dimension of God's redeeming activity. His dispensation for the salvation of the world is not an afterthought following the fall. Jesus Christ is indeed the Lamb slain before the foundation of the world.

This soteriological view of God can be supported ontologically as well. The Creator and Redeemer God, for example, is perfect and independent in himself. He is not to be perfected or completed by the addition of anything else, neither is he rendered imperfect by the subtraction of anything that does not belong to his being. Everything that exists outside of God is his creation and is dependent on God for its being and existence. The world, for instance, is there because God is there guiding it from an ultimate point of view. The Creator of the world is, in other words, its ground. He is the ground of the universe in its totality just as he is the ground of every part thereof. Therefore, he is one, not in the sense that he is single or solitary, but in that all things find their meaning and coherence in him alone. God who is in himself complete is triune. The Christian understands him as the Father, the Son and the Holy Spirit.

A final comment. Whereas polytheism represents a level of human culture based on a fragmentary conception of the universe and human life, monotheism sees the universe together. In the former, each people have their gods and goddesses. These divinities are either tribal deities or are related to certain aspects of nature or life. Monotheism, on the other hand, views the world as a unity. Its God is the God of all. Independently conceived, the one God of monotheism is not complete in himself without the world, as is the case in Hinduism, or without his word, as is the case in Judaism or Islam. Trinity transcends the unitary God of monotheism. The triune God, perfect in himself, is vitally related to the world as its unshaken ground. The world and all that exists live, move and have their being in the triune God.

The transition of the Christian faith from the New Testament-Jewish context to the Nicene-Hellenistic context

ELLEN FLESSEMAN-VAN LEER

Preliminary remark: the context and thought-forms in which the New Testament is written are not the same as those of the Creed. However, that difference is not merely the difference between Jewish and Hellenistic thinking. At the time of the New Testament writings, Jewish thinking was already strongly Hellenized. Moreover, the situational context was not really Jewish. Though most of the New Testament writers were Jews, their addressees were, in a great many cases, not.

Thesis 1

In the New Testament, no officially accepted and verbally determined confessions of faith are found, but there are short, more or less fixed formulas. These can be described as crystallizations of the transmitted, preached and believed apostolic faith and can be considered as precursors of the later formulated creeds. Their *Sitz im Leben* may have varied: baptism or prebaptismal instruction, worship services with hymns and prayers, rites of exorcism, declarations of loyalty in the face of persecution.[1]

One-clause acclamatory confessions are the most numerous. Jesus (is) *Kurios*, Jesus (is) the Christ, Jesus (is) the Son of God.[2] In using these one-partite christological formulas, belief in the one God was of course presup-

• Dr ELLEN FLESSEMAN-VAN LEER, Netherlands Reformed Church, is a pastor and theologian in Amstelveen, Holland.

posed, so that it might have been superfluous to mention God explicitly. These exclamatory *homologias* could be expanded, as in 1 Cor. 15:3f., Rom. 1:3f., 4:24f., 8:34. Among these more expanded christological formulas are found hymns which are recognizable by their metric form (e.g. 1 Tim. 3:16 and Phil. 2:6-11). These hymns and formulas were, I take it, unselfconscious, more or less spontaneous expressions of the common faith. Their focus was the earthly life of Jesus, especially his crucifixion and his resurrection and exaltation. The hymn of Philippians, and perhaps also the one of 1 Timothy, express moreover some form of pre-existence.

Beside these single clause formulas, there are also bipartite confessional formulations (e.g. 1 Cor. 8:6, 1 Tim. 2:5f., 2 Tim. 4:1). See also the conventional greeting with which Paul opens almost all of his letters, which apparently was a fixed formula: Grace to you and peace from God our Father and the Lord Jesus Christ.

Lastly, though much more sporadic, there are some triadic formulas, notably in the blessing of 2 Cor. 13:14 and the baptismal command of Matt. 28:19.[3]

Thesis 2

The New Testament titles, given to Jesus, notably *Kurios* and Son, are functional predicates which do not say anything about his nature. They express primarily the experience of the early Christians of the sovereignty of their now living Lord and, derived from that experience, the overpowering authority he had already exercised in his earthly life.[4]

Granted that the two- and three-clause formulas existed side by side with the one-clause christological ones and are no later development, the main New Testament emphasis lies understandably on Jesus Christ. He is above all confessed as Lord and Son (of God), "titles" which gradually ousted the more specifically Palestinian titles such as Messiah, Son of man, Son of David.

The title "Son of God" was originally given to the exalted Christ and expressed the honour given to him by God in his resurrection. Later it was also used of Jesus on earth, expressing his special position which God had given him. The title reached full development in John, with his absolute "the Son". There it denoted the intimate tie of the Son with the Father, and the unique and even absolute and divine authority the Father had given the Son. In the New Testament, the title Son of God is never identical with God the Son.

Thesis 3

The New Testament writers are not primarily concerned with the nature of Christ but rather with his function, or, in other words, with what God is doing in Jesus Christ for the salvation of humankind.

This thesis states in more general terms what in thesis 2 was substantiated more in detail about Jesus' main titles. It is questionable whether the New Testament is at all interested in the nature of Jesus Christ. The common presupposition, usually not specifically emphasized, is that he is a man. More thought is given to the observation that he is a man more uniquely and intimately tied to God, in fellowship with God, than any man ever was. He is "from above"—that is, sent or come from God—and as such he stands on God's side over against humanity (John). As the "second Adam" he is pre-eminently man as man is meant to be and as no one ever was (Paul); as such he is representative of all humankind and stands on humanity's side before God.

Thesis 4

The notion of the pre-existence of Jesus Christ, as found in the New Testament, does not entail the thought that before his birth Christ existed as God.

In the early hymn of Philippians 2, but also elsewhere, notably in Hebrews, some form of pre-existence of Christ is expressed. It cannot be decided with certainty what conception this notion carried. We know for sure that pre-existence was a familiar notion in Jewish thinking of that time; several things were thought to have been pre-existent (e.g. the Tora, the temple, the throne of God) which was a way to express their pre-eminent worth in the sight of God. But even if the Bible writers had in mind some real, instead of ideal, pre-existence—and it is not to be taken for granted that all of them had the same conception—the texts which are the most explicit, Philippians 2 and Hebrews 1, did not think that Christ ever was God, for his status after his exaltation is not a reinstatement, but a higher one than he had enjoyed in his pre-existent state.

And the thought that Jesus Christ came from or was sent by God, characteristic of the Johannine gospel (3:31, 5:24, 6:38), was not primarily meant as an ontological assertion, but expressed the uniquely close relation between God and Jesus Christ. Note that "being born not of the will of man but of God" in John 1:13 is asserted not of Jesus but of ordinary believers; and being sent by God applies to John the Baptist (John 1:6, 3:28, 1:33) and to any venerable rabbi (3:2).

Thesis 5

Of the three functions which the New Testament assigns to Jesus Christ—mediatorship of creation, revelation of God and salvation of humankind—the first one is marginal and receives the least attention; it does not necessarily entail the notion of personal pre-existence.

The mediatory function is comparatively little emphasized (Heb. 1:2f., 1 Cor. 8:6, Col. 1:15f.) and it cannot be ascertained with certainty what notion exactly it expressed. Confining us to the biblical context, the Old Testament role of *chokma* in creation (Prov. 8:22f., Ecclus 24:3) may offer an analogy.[5] *Chokma* is not conceived as an existing entity, though it is personalized. It is the deepest signature of creation, its inherent power which holds it together. Analogously, the thought of Jesus Christ as mediator of creation may have the connotation that he expresses the innermost law, intention and destiny of God's creation. Mediatorship, thus understood, does not necessitate a real pre-existent state of Jesus Christ (cf. thesis 4).

In the prologue of John, this mediatorship is assigned to the logos. The many difficulties and uncertainties with which the prologue is beset are well known. In view of the fact that in the Creed the term logos is avoided and that we here are not concerned with the great role which that concept has played in the early development of patristic doctrine, there is no need to go into it. Still, a few remarks are pertinent, in that Christ's pre-existent state as one of the persons of the divine Trinity is traditionally said to be maintained by the prologue.

1. The prologue (1:1, 14) is the only New Testament text where the logos is mentioned. In view of this fact, later extensive speculations about it seem somewhat questionable.

2. There is still ongoing debate about the background of John's logos-understanding. It seems to me most likely that it is the *dabar* of Genesis 1. (Note the identical words of Gen. 1:1 and John 1:1, "In the beginning".) The Old Testament *dabar* of God is not hypostasized into a separately existing entity, and the question is whether there is a compelling reason to regard the logos differently.

3. John's intention is to interpret the logos in the light of Jesus Christ. Therefore, the logos-concept is only of secondary importance. It can be maintained that John has no doctrine of the logos.[6]

Thesis 6

When in the New Testament God is called Father, this appellation does not relate to God's being *per se* nor his activity as Creator, but it expresses his actual and active love-relation with Jesus Christ and his followers.

Primarily, God's fatherhood should be seen against the background of Jesus calling him *Abba*. New Testament scholars are convinced that this Abba-name preserves a true memory of the earthly life of Jesus. In the Old Testament, God is called the Father of Israel, and this people, collectively, is called his son. It is therefore not surprising that Jesus' followers too called upon God as their Father.

Thesis 7

The God of the Old and New Testaments is not an immovable, unchangeable and impassible Deity. Being a God who wants to be in fellowship with human beings (see thesis 6), he is intimately concerned in human affairs, and acts and reacts in response to human actions and attitudes.

In biblical thoughts, humans can gladden and distress God. Repeatedly the Old Testament mentions God's regret, his wrath, his love, his compassion; moreover, he mourns and suffers when his people suffer. In the New Testament, Jesus' parables are especially significant in this respect. Jesus compares God to a father who rejoices when his wayward son returns home, to the owner of a vineyard who is furious when his tenants kill his messengers and even his son, to a judge who gives way when he is pestered long enough. Moreover, the very designation "Father" implies love, concern and care. Apparently, according to the Bible, this anthropomorphic way of speaking is the most adequate way of speaking about God.

Of course, this "changeableness" of God does not imply fickleness. In his love and faithfulness, he is steadfast and unchangeable.

Thesis 8

The biblical conviction that there is only one God is not identical with the philosophical concept of monotheism. In the Bible the *monarchia* of God implies the denial that humankind is subservient to any other god or power, or has anything to fear from them.

In biblical thinking, the assertion of only one God is an insight which gradually is gained by the experience that this one specific God is so powerful that only he is Lord of humanity. When second Isaiah calls the other gods "nothingnesses",[7] he had not primarily in mind their non-existence—though that conclusion came to be included—but rather the fact that they cannot do anything or help anyone (cf. also 1 Kings 18). Therefore, the non-biblical term *monarchia* of the early fathers is much closer to the Bible than the term monotheism.

Thesis 9

The nature of the *pneuma* in itself is not of any interest to the New Testament writers, but its working in the Church and the individual believers is.

> The *pneuma* is not, or certainly not primarily, to be thought of as an entity having a separate existence, but rather as God's or Christ's power working upon and in humans. In the triadic formulas, one may perhaps be inclined to think of the Spirit as an independent being, be it personal or not; but most New Testament texts do not support that view. Even the Johannine *paraklete* should not be conceived as a specific entity which "exists", but rather as metaphorically personalized power.[8] But leaving that question aside, all that the New Testament says about the Spirit is derived from the experiences of the early Christians of the *charismata* they had received and of the pneumatic life of the Church.

Thesis 10

The biblical writers of the Old and New Testaments conceive of salvation in terms of fellowship with God. This fellowship includes knowledge of God and his will, forgiveness of sins and the overcoming of death.

> The main function of Christ is soteriological (see thesis 5). John stresses more the knowledge of God which Christ gives, Paul emphasizes more forgiveness, entailing justification and sanctification. Christ's conquest of death and his resurrection as pledge of the resurrection of his followers is primarily important because death (sheol and hell) irrevocably severs humans from God. Eternal life is a quality of life in closest communion with God.

Thesis 11

The main emphasis in scripture is on God's history of salvation (history of the covenant, *Heilsgeschichte*). That is to say: the focus of scripture is soteriological.

Summing-up thesis

Jewish-biblical thought is functional rather than ontological. It is relational and therefore acknowledges the role of humans and of an experience as recipients of the revelation and working of God, Jesus Christ and the Spirit. This way of thinking is not prone to objectivation; when theological insights are developed, it is rather as a narrative theology than as doctrinal statements.

Statements on the Creed

Thesis A

The Creed is not only the outcome of theological-philosophical controversies, but owes as much to the liturgical life of the Church.

It seems likely that the Creed is an anti-heretical elaboration of an already existing baptismal credal confession in use in one of the Eastern churches; this confession was in substance, if not in exact wording, akin to the Creed promulgated at Nicea in 325.[9] The implication of this observation is that the Creed is not exclusively to be explained by the intricate and sophisticated reasoning of the third and fourth century theologians—leaving aside the non-theological factors as personal animosities and political interests and interferences—but must also be viewed as an expression of the common Christian faith of ordinary believers.

Thesis B

The Creed shows a Hellenizing-philosophical transposition of biblical thoughts.

This thesis can be substantiated on so many points that only a few of them need be mentioned. The Creed is interested in the nature of Jesus Christ and the Spirit and the ontological viewpoint takes precedence over the functional one; God is objectivized and considered *per se*, while the relational and human experiential aspects are not expressed; inner-trinitarian speculations are important; compared to the Bible, undue attention is given to the creational work; behind the term *homoousios* there lies the philosophical notion of a sharing in substance or being *(ousia)* which differs markedly from the relational unity-in-fellowship of the Father and the Son, as expressed in the New Testament.

Thesis C

Side by side with its philosophical-Hellenizing tendency, the Creed also shows de-Hellenizing aspects which bring it closer to biblical thinking.

The term logos and all speculations which went with it in the centuries before are eliminated and the philosophical term *hypostasis* is not used. The very fact that *homoousios* is not defined, and can therefore be interpreted in several ways, offers the opportunity to interpret the relation of the Father and the Son more in a biblical than in a neoplatonic vein; this is all the more true since the words *ek tès ousias tou patros*, found in the Creed of 325, are—be it intentionally or not—left out. To the Johannine *sarkothenta* the term *enanthropèsanta* is added; thus, the thought that Jesus was not merely human but was a specific man [10] is compatible with the wording of the Creed. The formulation of the Creed does not even compel us to consider the Spirit in inter-trinitarian terms as a separate person rather than as God-in-action; the expression that he has spoken through the prophets does not have to be understood as more than a personification, common in the Old and New Testaments, and the attributes "Lord" and "Lifegiver" are, in the Greek text, not substantives but adjectives. [11]

Thesis D

The Creed does do justice to the soteriological concern of the Bible, but its concept of salvation is not identical to the concept which prevails in scripture.

There can be no doubt that the full divinity of Jesus Christ, which became embedded in the Creed, asserted itself amidst the controversies of the early centuries because it was demanded by the soteriological conception of that time. However, that conception is not simply the same as the biblical one. In the Old and New Testaments, salvation is a relational concept, i.e. fellowship with God (thesis 10). In the third and fourth century climate, salvation was conceived of as divinization, [12] i.e. participation in the divine nature or "stuff" *(ousia)*. [13] In that framework of thinking, the Saviour needs to be God, i.e. be of the same "nature" as God, in order to impart that same nature to his followers. When, however, salvation is seen as personal knowledge of God and fellowship with him, the postulate of the divine nature of the Saviour is much less compelling.

Thesis E

It is generally agreed that belief in the trinitarian nature of God, doctrinally called ontological or immanent Trinity, is to be based on God revealing himself as triune, i.e. on the revelatory or economic Trinity.

This thesis is self-evident because nothing can be said about the mystery of God which has not been revealed. Remaining in the compass of biblical thought, it cannot be affirmed nor denied that Jesus Christ is "by nature" God, or that the Spirit is "by nature" God, because those are not the concepts in which the biblical writers thought. If the attempt is made to translate the economic Trinity back into the biblical compass, another kind of language is needed, e.g. that Jesus Christ is the decisive revelation of God, so that in him humankind is confronted with God himself, and that in the Holy Spirit humankind experiences the power of God.

Thesis F

In speaking about God we can never get beyond the *quoad nos*.

It is generally assumed that belief in the economic Trinity implies necessarily the doctrine of the immanent Trinity, because God in himself is as he has revealed himself. This assumption is important, not as a logical deduction, but as an expression of human faith in the trustworthiness of God (there is no God behind or other than the God we know). However, in so far as this assumption entails an attempt to speak about God as he is in himself and is thus an objectivation of God, it is contrary to the biblical climate of thinking. The very theologians who were instrumental in developing the theology behind the Creed frequently stressed their conviction that the divine *ousia*, "nature", is inaccessible and unknowable. This conviction has to be followed through for it would forbid us to speak about God *per se*. That would be basically in concord with today's thinking. We hesitate to speak any more about God apart from our experience of him.[14] That is not to say that God exists only in our experience, or that talking about him is merely talking about our experience, but it means that in whatever we say about God we can never eliminate our experience and disregard our relation to him. We cannot get, in other words, from God *quoad nos* to God's nature in himself.

Thesis G

If the Creed is to be accepted today, it does not have to be understood *e mente auctorum*.

For all practical purposes, that would be impossible since those who subscribed to the Creed differed among themselves in the way they understood it. The very fact that the west added the *filioque* clause and the east spoke of the procession of the Spirit from the Father "alone", proves that difference. Moreover, to understand the Creed as it was understood in its time would tie present believers irrevocably to the Hellenistic-philosophical thinking of the past. A careful study of the thoughts of the Father is dogmatically and historically very important indeed; but, in accepting the Creed, its theological thoughts and reasoning do not have to be taken over (see also thesis E).

Thesis H

If the Creed is to be accepted today, its terminology has to be translated into present-day idioms.

It is self-evident that the terminology of the Creed cannot be taken over. The notion of *homoousios* is so closely bound to the thought-world of the third and fourth century philosophy that lengthy explanations are needed to somehow convey its meaning today. The difficulty is enhanced if the Creed is summarized in the traditional wording of its trinitarian assertion: one substance (or being, essence or God) in three persons. Modern understanding of the word person is quite different from the meaning of *hypostasis* or *persona* in the trinitarian doctrine, and therefore prone to tritheistic misunderstanding.

Thesis I

The Creed addressed itself to problems which Christians, at least in the west, no longer share, and therefore it may be less relevant to them.

The Creed came to be formulated and accepted not only as expression of the common faith of Christians, but also as defence against heresies. Against Sabellianism the difference and separate existence of Father, Son (and Spirit) had to be emphasized. That anti-modalist stance was, in its time, right and even necessary to safeguard the apostolic faith. However, for us today modalism is no danger or even live option; the very thought of God the Father who, in his appearance as Son, was crucified seems to us absurd. Against Arius and Eunomius the uniqueness of Jesus Christ and the unity of God had to be stressed. Today however the thought that Jesus is a *deuteros theos* or a kind of angel-being is no longer held among us and therefore we do not need to refute it. Against various forms of Docetism and Apollinarianism, the full human nature of Jesus Christ had to be formulated. However, we are no longer in danger of thinking of Jesus as an illusionary bodily apparition; the conception of Apollinaris could only be developed on the basis of an anthropology we no longer share. The third clause of the Creed was directed against the Pneumatomachians. Today, however, we no longer have to refute the view that the Spirit is a creature or a spirit because that view is no longer brought forward among us. It should be noted, however, with how much constraint this third clause of the Creed is formulated. The language employed has a scriptural flavour and, though the clause was inserted to convey the thought that the Spirit is consubstantial with the Godhead, the words which express that thought accord with doxological usage rather than strict doctrinal formulation.[15]

The above is not to deny that also today theological opinions are advocated which resemble the formerly refuted heresies. But, because those opinions appear in modern dress and use quite different concepts, they have to be countered in a new way.

Concluding thesis

A reformulation of the Creed for Christians today is not sufficient: We have to do what the Creed did in its time—namely, try to express the common apostolic faith, in view of the heresies and problems with which our faith today is beset, in a language appropriate to our thinking and which does justice to our experienced fellowship with God in Jesus Christ through the Holy Spirit.

The Creed was in its time, given the problems with which the Church was confronted and the syncretistic neoplatonism which was the all-pervading framework of thought, shared by the Church fathers and their opponents alike. The pivotal question is whether Christians today have to take it over.

Its use in worship and liturgy is a valuable expression and symbol of the solidarity of Christians today with the Church of all ages. Therefore, there should be no tampering with its wording. But the Creed as expressing the common credal basis of all Christians and churches is a more debatable matter. Not primarily because its terminology is no longer understood (see thesis H), nor because of the transposition of a biblical into a philosophical context (see thesis B), but because it is questionable whether the relational God in whom we believe can be objectified into a deity *per se* (see thesis F) and because the problems to which the Creed addressed itself, and the terms in which it tried to answer those problems, are no longer ours and have become irrelevant to us (see thesis I). Therefore, the confessional basis of the churches should not be a modern *re*formulation of the Creed, but an attempt should be made to express the apostolic faith in contemporary thought-forms with a view to our modern "heresies".

The main test to decide whether that attempt is successful may be whether it adequately expresses both the soteriological emphasis of scripture and the soteriological needs and expectations of today's believers.

NOTES

[1] J.N.D. Kelly, *Early Christian Creeds*, London, 1960. Ferdinand Hahn, "Bekenntnisformeln im Neuen Testament", in *Studien zur Bekenntnisbildung*, Wiesbaden, 1980.

2 Cf. the Old Testament phrase: Jhwh (is) our God, or the Schema of Deut. 6:4.

3 Perhaps there are still other triadic formulas, as 1 Cor. 12:4f., 1 Pet. 1:2, but their wording does not seem to be very definite. See, besides Kelly and Hahn, also F.J. Schierse in *M.S.* V (ch. II, par. 2.6).

4 See F. Hahn, *Christologische Hoheitstitel*, Göttingen, 1964.

5 See Gerhard von Rad, *Weisheit in Israel*, Neukirchen, 1970, pp. 189-205.

6 T.E. Pollard, *Johannine Christology and the Early Church*, Cambridge, 1970, p. 13. Piet Schoonenberg, *Ein Gott der Menschen*, Zürich, 1968, p. 85.

7 Isa. 41:29. Gerhard von Rad, *Theologie des Alten Testamentes*, München, 1960, p. 257.

8 *ThWNT* VI, 442: pneuma ist für Johannes nichts anderes als die Kraft der Verkündigung Jesu. See also Schierse, *op. cit.*, par. 2.5.

9 Kelly, *op. cit.*, especially 322-331. Alois Grillmeier, *Bekenntnisse der Alten Kirche II - Das Nizäno-Constantinopolitanum*, in *Studien zur Bekenntnisbildung*.

10 Cf. A.T. Robinson, *The Human Face of God*, London, 1977, pp. 36ff.

11 This last observation I owe to P. Schoonenberg SJ, *Berkhof en het Credo*, in *Weerwoord*, Nijkerk, 1974, p. 133.

12 Christ's full humanity, expressed in the Creed too, was equally demanded by soteriology, for what is not assumed is not healed (Gregory Naziensus). Divinization, as ultimate destiny of humanity, is supported by the New Testament, as in 2 Pet. 1:4, but it certainly is no central notion. Cf. H. Berkhof, *Christelijk Geloof*, Nijkerk, 1975, p. 305.

13 Christopher Stead, *Divine Substance*, Oxford, 1977.

14 Maurice Wiles, *The Making of Christian Doctrine*, Cambridge, 1967, pp. 176f.

15 Kelly, *op. cit.*, pp. 339-344.

Affirmations to the Spirit
THOMAS HOPKO

I have been asked to do three things for our discussion:
1) to provide an "exegesis of the affirmations to the Spirit in the third article" of the Nicene Creed;
2) to comment on "the function of the Holy Spirit in the economic and immanent Trinity";
3) to discuss "the special relationship between the Son and the Spirit".

Affirmations to the Spirit in the third article of the Nicene Creed

1. And in the Holy Spirit

The *and* here is of first importance. The Nicene faith is "in one God, the Father Almighty... *and* in one Lord Jesus Christ... *and* in the Holy Spirit..." The one God of the Creed is not the Trinity. The one God is the Father Almighty. The one God has an only-begotten Son and a Holy Spirit. Christians believe in the one God *and* his Son *and* his Spirit. The unity of the one God is the unity of the one Father. Faith in the one Son and one Spirit depends on faith in the one God whose Son and Spirit they are. And *who* the Son and Spirit are, are other than who God is.

• Fr THOMAS HOPKO, Orthodox Church in America, teaches at St Vladimir's Seminary, Crestwood, New York, USA.

2. *The Lord and Giver of life*

The Spirit is not simply "Lord", but "*the* Lord". *Lord* is the divine name, the doxological Septuagint/New Testamental rendering of YHWH. Because the one God is the Lord, so his Son and his Spirit are also each "the Lord". The Spirit is other than *who* God is and *who* God's Son is, yet the Spirit is what God and his Son are, namely, the divine Lord. The affirmation of the Spirit as Lord is an affirmation, in Nicene terms, that he is "of one essence" *(homoousios)* with the Father and the Son.

The English expression "Giver of life" may not be the best translation for *zoopios* which may better be rendered "Creator" or "Fashioner" of life. The meaning of the expression seems to be not so much that the Spirit *gives* or *communicates* life, but that he is its very originator and maker. He is the one whose unique characteristic is to be the very "life-maker" within the Godhead itself, and is, thus, the Spirit of life and existence for all that exists by divine will and action.

3. *Who proceeds from the Father*

This line is exhaustively analyzed in the volume *Spirit of God, Spirit of Christ*[1] which is admirably summarized in the working group paper from the 1981 meeting of the Faith and Order Standing Commission "Towards the Common Expression of the Apostolic Faith Today". There is little doubt that this phrase is originally simply a quotation of John 15:26 which intends to identify the Spirit which Jesus sends to his disciples after his glorification through his crucifixion and resurrection with the *Ru'ah YHWH* of the old covenant, the spirit and breath of the Lord of Abraham, Isaac and Jacob, the God of the law, the psalms and the prophets. This is the same Spirit which descends and remains upon Jesus, anointing him as the Messiah/Christ.

Whatever else the Spirit is, whoever else's Spirit he is, however else he happens to be the Spirit of others, whatever else he happens to be and to do—he is first and foremost the Spirit of God himself. This seems to me to be the credal affirmation of this line from which all further doctrinal affirmations and theological elaborations must proceed with fidelity.

4. *Who with the Father and the Son together is worshipped and glorified*

It might be better to translate this line in English as "who with the Father and the Son is together worshipped and glorified" or "who with the Father and the Son is co-worshipped and co-glorified". The point is not that there is some sort of priority to the worship and glorification of the Father and the Son together to which the worship and glorification of the Spirit is somehow added or attached. The point is rather that as the Father and Son are to be worshipped and glorified, and when they are actually so adored, so is the Holy Spirit, always and of necessity. The worship of the Son and the Spirit, particularly the worship offered to Jesus and accepted by him, as witnessed in the New Testamental writings from the synoptics to the Apocalypse, is the central apostolic testimony to the divinity of the Son and the Spirit affirmed in the Nicene statement.

5. *Who spoke through the prophets*

The intention here seems obviously to be to affirm the identity of the Holy Spirit, known and experienced in the Church of the Messiah, with the breath of YHWH who always accompanies God's word in the Old Testamental dispensation. It appears as an anti-Marcionite statement which retains its power and relevance against the temptation to separate the covenants of the Lord, and to relegate the law, psalms and prophets to something else (and something less) than the inspired word of God.

The function of the Holy Spirit in the economic and immanent Trinity and the special relationship between the Son and the Holy Spirit

1. *Oikonomia and theologia*

We know and say whatever we do about the "immanent" Trinity because of the "economic" Trinity. *Theologia*, in the patristic sense of the term which always refers to the "immanent" Trinity, is only possible because of God's *oikonomia*, i.e. his dispensation in his logos/word and his Holy Spirit in Israel and the Church. We "ascend" to God because of his "condescension" to us. We contemplate God because he has shown himself to us. We make conclusions about God's innermost being and life because he has acted towards us and in us through his word/Son and Spirit.

2. *The relationship between economic and immanent*

God's *oikonomia* is what it is because of what and who God is. In other words, the economic Trinity is a manifestation of the immanent Trinity. The relationship between the persons of the

Godhead—God the Father and his Son and Spirit—are what they are in the *oikonomia* because of what they are in eternity within the uncreated triune divinity. The function of the Holy Spirit in the *oikonomia* reflects and manifests the function of the Holy Spirit within the Godhead. The same is true, evidently, of the Son, and of God the Father as well.

3. *The logos/Son and the Holy Spirit*

In the divine dispensation *(oikonomia)* of creation, redemption and sanctification, God always acts through his word and his Spirit, called by Irenaeos "the two hands of God". The word of God is also God's wisdom, image, radiance, power... and his only-begotten Son who is incarnate as Jesus of Nazareth, the Messiah/Christ of Israel. The word is never present and active without the Spirit of God. And, conversely, the Spirit is never present and active without God's logos/Son. The *Da'bar YHWH* and the *Ru'ah YHWH* are always together from God in the dispensation. This reflects the conviction that they too are always together coming forth from God eternally within the uncreated Godhead.

4. *The interdependence of the word and Spirit*

The logos/Son of God and God's Holy Spirit do not act independently from each other and from God because they have no independent being and life, will and energy. They also exist and act in a manner which might be described as "interdependent" in the sense that one cannot be and act without the other, and one is not "dependent" on the other in a manner which is not (changing the changeable in the relationship) reciprocal.

By this I mean to say that there is no sense in which the Holy Spirit is "dependent" on the Son for his being, life and mission in the *oikonomia* in a manner in which (changing the changeable) the Son is not dependent on the Spirit. Sometimes it is thought that there is some sort of "priority" of the Son in the relationship, both immanently and economically. This is, I believe, incorrect. There is complete reciprocity, mutuality and complementarity in being and action theologically within the Godhead and economically within the dispensation. (If reference is made to the dispensational fact that the Spirit is sent by the Son, or more accurately, is sent on condition of the Son's glorification, it should be remembered that the Son himself is not sent or glorified without the direct presence and action of the Holy Spirit.)

5. *The Spirit's function: Spirit of God and God's Son*

The Spirit's function is to be the Spirit of God and the Spirit of God's Son. His function is to be neither God nor the logos/Son.

While there would be no Spirit of God if there were no God and no Son of God (for the claim is that a God without a Son would not be God since he would not fulfill the conditions of perfection), there also would be no God (and no Son of God) without the Spirit. We usually concentrate our attention on the fact that God the Father is the *principium divinitatis*—the source, cause and principle of the logos/Son and the Spirit—and that, therefore, the Son and Spirit have their existence in a timelessly divine manner "from the Father alone" with the Son's "generation" and the Spirit's "procession" being "dependent" upon each other in a reciprocal manner. But we must dare to insist also that there is a certain "dependence" of the Father on the logos/Son and the Spirit, not in the sense that God derives his being and life from the Son and the Holy Spirit, but in the sense that he never is without them because they belong to his very being as God. This is the meaning of the traditional insistence that the Son's generation and the Spirit's procession are essential *(kat'ousian)* and not volitional or according to God's fancy or good-pleasure *(kat'eudokian)*. The "theological function" of the Spirit is to be quickening spirit and vivifying breath of God himself, and also, therefore, of God's Son whose theological function it is to be God's word, image, wisdom, power, radiance, light, life... The Son is, indeed, the hypostatic actualization of every distinct attribute which belongs essentially to the very being of God. The "economic function" of the Spirit is to be the same quickening and vivifying Spirit in those who are being saved by God through Jesus, and the quickening and vivifying Spirit of Jesus himself, the man whom the logos/Son has become.

6. *A patristic elaboration*

An elaboration of the relationship between the Father, Son and Holy Spirit which reveals the Spirit's "function", both within the immanent Trinity and within the economy, is made in the tradition (for example in the writings of Athanasius and Basil) in the following way:

God is one. His unity is actualized hypostatically in the person of his logos/Son, incarnate in human form as Jesus. The Holy Spirit is the Spirit of unity. This is his function both theologically within the Godhead and within the dispensation of the Trinity in creation.

God is true. His truth is actualized hypostatically in his divine Son, who in his incarnate dispensation realizes the truth in human form. ("I am the truth.") The Holy Spirit is the Spirit of truth. He functions as such within the Godhead and in the *oikonomia*.

God is wise. His Son is his wisdom. The Spirit is the breath of the wisdom of God. He functions as such for the Father and the Son, and for creatures as well.

God is the living God. The Son is life itself. ("I am the life.") The Spirit is the "life-creating" Spirit of God, of God's Son, and of all that exists.

God is the loving God and love itself. He eternally actualizes himself as love in the person of his Son and word. The Spirit of God who is, as such, necessarily the Spirit of God's Son, is the Spirit of love. In the *oikonomia*, God pours his love into our hearts by the Holy Spirit which he gives to us through and in his Son, the human Jesus, the messiah-king of Israel.

7. The Spirit's function: activation of divine being

If the function of God's Son, word and image is to be the "actualization" of every *essential* (as opposed to *hypostatic* or *personal*) attribute of God, as God within the Godhead and as man within the dispensation, so the function of the Holy Spirit is to be the person who activates these attributes. Once again this is both within the immanent Trinity by the Spirit's participation in the eternal generation of the Son (together with the reciprocal action of the Son in his own "spiration" from God) and in the economy where he is the activating person in the incarnation and in all of the word's human activities, including the crucifixion and resurrection. The Spirit is also the one who "forms Christ" in creatures by taking what is his and giving it to us, thereby making us "sons of God" by grace, and his "words" and "images" as well.

8. Summary statement

God always acts in and towards creation by his word/Son and Holy Spirit. And the creation always acts in and towards God by the same word/Son and Spirit. These two actions are in reality one action with two aspects: from the Father through the Son towards creatures in the Spirit; and from creatures in the Spirit through the Son to the Father. Wherever God and creatures interact for there to be love, peace, joy, goodness, purity, kindness, gentleness and every divine virtue which is the Spirit's fruit (whether creatures are aware of it or not) there is an expression of the economic Trinity which is a manifestation of the immanent Trinity. There is the Father with his logos/image/Son and his Holy Spirit being and acting in perfect unity and harmony: the Son personally actualizing and realizing the fullness of God's being and life and activity by the Spirit, and thereby radiating and communicating the Spirit which proceeds from the Father, and the Spirit personally activating all of the divine attributes and virtues in the Son and thereby activating the Son's very birth from the Father as his uncreated image and word, wisdom and power, radiance and glory, truth and life—theologically within the Godhead as well as in the *oikonomia* of salvation. The reciprocity and "interdependence" of the Son and the Spirit in their relationship to each other and to the Father is the guarantee of divine perfection for God himself and for all those who are "becoming god by grace" through his triune activity in the world.

NOTE

[1] Faith and Order Paper No. 103, London, SPCK, and Geneva, WCC, 1981.

Part II

The unity of the Church
and the
renewal of human community

1. Papers and reports from the meeting of the Faith and Order
   Standing Commission, Annecy, France, January 1981

"That the world may believe":
staff discussion paper
C.S. SONG

With deep spiritual insight, John the Evangelist captured one
fundamental challenge in Jesus' valedictory prayer: "May they
all be one... that the world may believe that thou didst send me"
(John 17:21). Who are "they"? Christians, of course. Even at that
"primitive" stage in the development of Christian community,
John already grasped a fundamental truth vital to the Church:
Christian unity would make true to the world its witness to Jesus as
one sent by God. Although John did not go on to say it, the reverse
must also be true: the disunity of Christian community would
discredit its witness in the eyes of the world. John thus placed the
question of unity right at the centre of the life and ministry of the
Church. United, the Church becomes true to Jesus and to itself;
disunited, the Church becomes untrue to Jesus and to itself. The
question of church unity, in the last analysis, is as simple as that.

But this simple truth has been the cause of both agony and inspiration to the Church throughout its history. No period in its
long history has seen the Church free from disunity and division
in its faith, life and ministry. It has always been in danger of being
discredited by the world. What agony could be greater than this

• Dr CHOAN SENG SONG was, until leaving the WCC in August 1982, Programme
Secretary of the Commission on Faith and Order and the staff member responsible
for this study.

for the Church which is expected to live in the world for the saving love of God in Jesus Christ? But such agony has not made the Church moribund. Rather, it has inspired it to search for ways to unity so that "the world may believe". In a very real sense, the history of the Church is the history of a continual search for unity. And in the modern ecumenical movement, this search for church unity has become intensified and deepened.

The ecumenical vision of the Church united, therefore, is a biblical vision profoundly expressed in John's gospel. The Church and the world are closely correlated. The unity of the Church has to do with how humankind lives and what it believes. The vision of unity seen by John the Evangelist and followed by churches and Christians is a "missiological" vision. This is how the World Missionary Conference in Edinburgh (1910) saw it. This is also how the inaugural assembly of the World Council of Churches in Amsterdam (1948) interpreted it. What was said in its report of Section 2, "The Church's Witness to God's Design", was true not only then but now. One finds these words in that report:

> What does the world see, or think it sees, when it looks at the Church? It is a Church divided, and in its separated parts are often found hesitancy, complacency, or the desire to domineer. It is a Church that has largely lost touch with the dominant realities of modern life, and still tries to meet the modern world with language and a technique that may have been appropriate two hundred years ago. It is a Church that, by its failure to speak effectively on the subject of war, has appeared impotent to deal with the realities of the human situation. It is a Church accused by many of having been blind to the movement of God in history, of having sided with the vested interests of society and state, and of having failed to kindle the vision and to purify the wills of people [*men* in the original text] in a changing world. It is a Church under suspicion in many quarters of having used its missionary enterprise to further the foreign policies of states and the imperialistic designs of the powers of the West.[1]

The report goes on to contend that "much in this indictment may be untrue", but it does confess that "the Church is called to deep shame and penitence for its failure to manifest Jesus Christ to people [*men* in the original report] as He really is".[2]

Repentence has been very much at the heart of the ecumenical vision of church unity during the past thirty years. Without this constant call to repentence, the ecumenical movement might have died a premature death. In this repentence of the Church, one cannot emphasize enough the role of the world. The world questions the Church. It challenges the Church's claims to the truth. It tests the Church's faithfulness to Jesus Christ. The correlation between the Church and the world is thus a critical one. The Church exists to bring the message of reconciliation and salvation in Christ to the world, and the world demands that the Church live up to its own message. The world has not been a mere disinterested spectator in the churches' efforts towards unity, nor has it been passively waiting for the Church to bring unity to it. Critical involvement of the world in church unity has to be recognized and appreciated. The slogan that expresses the churches' efforts towards unity in the past few decades—the unity of the Church is a sign for the unity of humankind—cannot be taken at face value. The Church and the world are signs one to the other. It is out of the interaction of these signs that the Church and the world can wrestle with the unity that may manifest God's saving design for the whole of humankind.

Elusive unity

In the meantime, however, unity has continued to be elusive for the Church. The churches have not been idle, allowing disunity to follow its course. On the contrary, they have been diligent. They have been talking to one another bilaterally and multilaterally. Christian fellowship among them has increased both in extent and in depth. Studies and discussions on issues and problems related to the faith and ministry of the Church have produced some notable results, among them the agreed statements on baptism, eucharist and ministry. But the unity that would enable "the world to believe that God did send Jesus" has not been reached. It looks as if church unity will remain on the churches' eschatological agenda indefinitely.

As unity remains elusive, the ecumenical vision that made such a powerful impact on the Church of modern times has become divided. On the one hand, the churches have found themselves under strong pressure to struggle with the people who suffer from socio-political oppression, economic injustice, racism, or sexual discrimination. This is a recovery of prophetic ministry of the churches in the contemporary world. In the message from the fourth assembly of the World Council of Churches in Uppsala

(1968), one hears a strong echo of the prophetic voice in the Bible:

> We heard the cry of those who long for peace; of the hungry and exploited who demand bread and justice; of the victims of discrimination who claim human dignity; and of the increasing millions who seek for the meaning of life. God hears these cries and judges us. He also speaks the liberating word. We hear him say—I go before you. Now that Christ carries away your sinful past, the Spirit frees you to live for others. Anticipate my kingdom in joyful worship and daring acts. The Lord says, "I make all things new."[3]

The agenda of the world has become the agenda of the World Council of Churches. The World Council is quick to respond to cries of refugees of war and people stricken by natural disasters. It moves into sensitive areas of the world torn by racial conflict. It seeks solidarity with the poor and the oppressed.

Through such "prophetic" ministry, the churches have regained credibility in many parts of the world, especially in the third world. This has brought about an organic change in the concept and reality of Church unity. As churches and Christians become engaged in human problems and issues in particular socio-political and cultural-historical contexts, they find themselves in unity that transcends confessional backgrounds and ecclesiastical barriers. By force of circumstances and in exercising "prophetic" ministry, many Christians have come to regard theological and ecclesiological issues that have divided the churches as irrelevant. As a result, basic ecclesial communities have emerged in many parts of the world, enjoying spontaneous unity without, in most cases, the sanction of official churches. But the question of what such unity would mean for church unity in the traditional sense remains unanswered.

Unity resulting from realignments of Christians under socio-political pressures represents a significant trend in the ecumenical movement in recent years. Meanwhile, however, the theological and ecclesiological search for unity has continued with unabated zeal. And it is the Commission on Faith and Order which has carried on the mandate of "visible unity in one eucharistic fellowship". The measure of understanding among the churches which has come about through the efforts of Faith and Order is considerable. The churches have come to have a more profound knowledge of Christian traditions. The study on baptism, eucharist and ministry has revealed that, in fact, they have much in common, that there is less than previously thought which prevents them from becoming "one eucharistic fellowship". The Bangalore Commission meeting in 1978 said, among other things:

> The vision of full visible unity in conciliar fellowship provides the frame for working in concert. The agreements which have emerged or are emerging from multilateral and bilateral dialogues must be taken seriously by all churches and, as far as they are acceptable to each church, translated into practical decisions which affect the relations with other churches. The far-reaching results of dialogues present the churches with the challenge to give new expression to the oneness in Christ for the sake of the gospel and to the glory of God. [4]

The Commission here speaks of "far-reaching results of dialogues". One critical question is how these results can be "translated into practical decisions which affect the relations with other churches". This is one of the challenging questions which will engage the Commission in the coming years.

It must be pointed out, however, that the Commission on Faith and Order, by the very nature of its mandate and by its firm commitment to that mandate, has come to stand for a forceful trend within the ecumenical movement which is parallel to, if not in conflict with, the other trend discussed above. The work of Faith and Order is perceived as strongly theological and ecclesiological, not quite related to issues and problems which face humankind today. Faith and Order is said to be asking questions which no one engaged in the struggles of daily life is asking and giving answers that do not concern the life of the people in today's world. Such an accusation is undoubtedly biased and simplistic, but it points out the need for Faith and Order to re-examine the ways it has gone about its work, re-examine the methods by which it explores the "historical sources" that have theologically and ecclesiologically divided the churches.

The strange thing is that it was in fact Faith and Order which took seriously the challenge enunciated by the Uppsala assembly. The report of the assembly on "The Holy Spirit and the Catholicity of the Church" stated:

> God's gift of catholicity is received in faith and obedience. The Church must express this catholicity in its worship by providing a

home for all sorts and conditions of men and women; and in its
witness and service by working for the realization of genuine humanity. The Church hinders the manifestation of its given catholicity when
it breaks down at any of these points.[5]

This provided the basic impetus for the Commission on Faith
and Order, at its meeting in Louvain in 1971, to begin a study on
"The Unity of the Church and the Unity of Humankind". Out of
that Commission meeting were developed the studies on racism,
the disabled in the Church, and the full programme of the Community of Women and Men in the Church.

Still, the two trends—the Church's solidarity with the world
and Church unity—have not become inter-related. Faith and
Order has not developed ways of dealing with the "ecclesial" implications of its studies on racism, the disabled in the Church or
the community of women and men in the Church. It has become
obvious that a fresh beginning is called for on the subject of the
unity of the Church and the unity of humankind.

An ecumenical vision: a renewed human community

"The Unity of the Church—the Unity of Humankind" expresses in essence an ecumenical vision towards which the Church
and the world can strive together. It is a "catholicity" which embraces both Christians and all other people. The Uppsala
assembly already had such a vision. To quote again from its
report on "The Holy Spirit and the Catholicity of the Church":

Catholicity is... a constant possession and pursuit of the mystery of
faith, the sacramental experience of that incorporation into Christ and
involvement with humankind of which the Church is the form and the
Eucharist the substantial focus. In its deepest sense, liturgy is the
hallowing of all we are for the sake of all that is, that God may be all in
all... Only in the fullness of redeemed humanity shall we experience
the fullness of the Spirit's gifts.[6]

Here is an opening into a full catholicity, a catholicity within
which the unity which the churches pursue and the unity which the
world needs can become interconnected. It also points out the
main areas of concern that must engage our efforts towards an
ecumenical vision of a renewed human community.

First of all, it needs to be stressed that creation constitutes
the common denominator for the Church and the world. It is no

accident that the Bible begins with the story of creation and ends with a vision of a new creation. It is also a fact that all nations and peoples have their own versions of creation. Lives of people, human civilization and community building all bear the power of divine creation. That divine power takes form in pluralistic cultures, becomes embodied in diverse ethical conventions and in different religious beliefs and practices. "In the beginning of creation, when God made heaven and earth..." says Genesis 1:1. How are Christians to understand "theologically" cultures, religions and ethical codes of different nations and peoples in the light of their faith in God as the creator of heaven and earth? God the creator speaks to the world through the Church. But does this God also speak to the Church through the world he has created?

Secondly, the world has not remained good, as God created it in the beginning. God's creation has become corrupted. This is the main background from which the Christian understanding of redemption arises. Regarding this, St Paul has a most insightful thing to say. "Up to the present", he tells us, "we know the whole created universe groans in all its parts as if in the pangs of childbirth" (Rom. 8:22). For many nations and peoples suffering in this created universe is also recognized as a fact of life. If we speak of the catholicity of creation, we can also speak of the catholicity of suffering. The created universe is not what it should be.

"Theological" understanding of the world as God's creation is thus closely followed by "soteriological" insight into the suffering of humankind. And this is the heart of the Christian gospel: the word become flesh. The incarnation is both potentially and actually a powerful impact of God which has sustained humankind in different times and places. The world as well as the Church is being redeemed by God the redeemer. Such thought forces the churches to serve God's mission of the incarnation not "over against" but "in solidarity with" the world. Here we have a basic soteriological ground for the churches' involvement in struggle against the forces that corrupt God's creation—the forces of racism, socio-political oppression, sexual discrimination, human exploitation, or economic injustice. The unity with which people from diverse religious and socio-cultural backgrounds bind themselves in their struggle against forces of evil is deeply soteriological in meaning and significance. The study on "The Unity of the Church—the Unity of Humankind" must explore the implications of such unity for God's redemptive work in the world.

There is a third dimension in the relation between the Church and the world. It is a "missiological" dimension. Christians have emphasized that the Church has a mission to the world—the mission to bring people to God's salvation in Christ. The Church is mission. Mission is the Church's main *raison d'être*. This is true despite the fact that the churches have not always lived up to it. But as we begin to think of the whole creation in the company of those outside the Christian Church, we are compelled to think more seriously about what is said, for example, about Cyrus, king of Persia, in Second Isaiah. As Second Isaiah tells it, God says to Cyrus: "You shall be my shepherd to carry out all my purpose" (Isa. 44:28). Second Isaiah even calls him "God's anointed". In the history of the nations, there must have been many Cyruses. How is the Church to identify them? How do we as Christians reconstruct our mission in the world together with known and unknown Cyruses?

Fourthly, such "missiological" reorientation will lead the Church and humankind to a common quest for a "renewed community". By now it has become clear to us that science and technology, hailed as hope for a future world, have proved to be a threat to the survival of humankind due to ecological problems they have created and the arms race in which they have become deeply involved. Ironically, the future of humankind does not seem to rest with humankind as "rational" beings. This must be the time when human spiritual resources should be mobilized for the emergence of a community in which people become reconciled to one another. There must be a community in which men and women can be in communion with one another, where people can share spiritual and physical resources from God, where a kingdom of God with justice, peace and love may prevail. This, in short, is a vision of a renewed human community on the way to fulfilling God's purpose of creation and redemption for the whole of humanity. What role, then, should the Christian Church play in the coming into being of such a renewed human community? How and where does the vision of a renewed human community interact with the vision of the Church united?

These are some of the important areas to which we must direct our attention in our exploration of the theme "The Unity of the Church—the Unity of Humankind". What we envisage at this critical juncture of human history must not be a Church united in self-defence against the world. The Church must be bold and faithful enough to die to itself, to its own divided past and present, so that it can begin to live for God and for the world in the midst of suffering humanity. What the Church is involved in here is a recovery of its true self as a creative and redemptive part of the whole human community, and a discovery of God's design for the whole of humankind in nature and in history. An ecumenical vision such as this must be at the heart of the theme of the Sixth Assembly of the World Council of Churches to be held in Vancouver in 1983: "Jesus Christ—the Life of the World". What is the shape and content of the life which God has offered to the world in Jesus Christ? How are the churches to commit themselves anew to this life? And in what way could there be ample room in this life to accommodate not only Christians but the rest of humankind? In a word, how could unity and catholicity of the Church serve the unity and catholicity of the life God has given to the whole of humankind in Jesus Christ? Questions such as these may guide the Commission on Faith and Order in its continuing service to the ecumenical movement through its study on the theme "The Unity of the Church—the Unity of Humankind".

NOTES

[1] *Man's Disorder and God's Design*, Vol. II: *The Church's Witness to God's Design*, New York, Harper & Brothers, 1949, pp. 213-4.

[2] *Ibid*, p. 214.

[3] *The Uppsala Report 1968*, ed. Norman Goodall, Geneva, WCC, 1968, p. 5.

[4] *Sharing in One Hope*, Commission on Faith and Order, Bangalore 1978, Faith and Order Paper No. 92, Geneva, WCC, p. 238.

[5] *The Uppsala Report, op. cit.*, p. 14.

[6] *Ibid.*, p. 19.

Working group report

The staff discussion paper prepared by C.S. Song was discussed with critical appreciation. The importance of the issues raised and the potential significance of the theme for our future studies were generally recognized. We asked some questions concerning the theological rationale behind the paper. A strong emphasis on creation and incarnation as the link between Church and humankind is present in the paper; but the Easter message, i.e. the cross of Jesus Christ and his resurrection, was given much less consideration. The underlying concept of the "world" also appeared one-sided to some of us. The concept of "kosmos" in the New Testament refers not only to God's good creation but also to humankind captive in sin. This should be given more consideration in our work.

A particularly intensive discussion concentrated on the concept of unity within our theme. Is it not misleading to use the word "unity" both about the Church and about humankind? What do we mean by the "unity of humankind"? There are dangerous and ambiguous programmes of unity in our world—monolithic political systems and ideologies which so often champion "unity" which hardly present desirable models. A Christian contribution to the unity of humankind cannot be developed in a one-dimensional way, but rather in a "dialectical" way. The unity in Christ and its eschatological vision of the one kingdom is at the same time the fulfilment of our hopes for unity and the judgment on falsified dreams and "realizations" of human unity.

From these deliberations, a proposal for reformulating the theme of the study emerged: "Unity of the Church for Renewal of Human Community". At a later stage in the plenary discussion the Standing Commission adopted this proposal with one modification: "The Unity of the Church and the Renewal of Human Community". This change was introduced and accepted in an attempt to avoid a misunderstanding that unity of the Church be just an instrument of general cosmopolitan or generally humanitarian unity. The unity of the Church is the gift of the Spirit. It has its doxological and sacramental integrity which cannot be measured in terms of its secular efficacity for other goals only. It is the classical task of Faith and Order to stand for this paramount concern of Christian unity, if the suspicion that "the WCC is just a religious sub-section of the UNO" is to be credibly overcome. "It would falsify this theme to assume that commitment to the renewal of human community permits us to ignore or minimize our calling to visible unity in Christ. Through its visible unity the Church becomes a sign to a broken world of God's reconciling purpose for all humanity." And vice-versa: the scandal of its visible disunity jeopardizes the credibility of our churches' witness to Christ. Thus it is in no way the aim of the proposed study to relativize the classical Faith and Order concern, but rather to place it in a broadened horizon and to develop its implications for Christian service and mission in the contemporary world.

Much attention was given to the question of a topical "spreading out" of the study. This was later combined with an attempt to propose thematic areas for working groups at Lima. Finally, the following five areas were recommended and approved:

1. *Cosmological* context of the theme: unity within the one creation as well as humankind's place within, responsibility for, and common destiny with nature (including implications for struggling with "ecological issues").
2. *Historical* challenges to, and the opportunities for, unity in the contemporary world: the divisions between poor and rich, problems of power within human community, tensions between races, classes, nations...

3. *Cultural* dimension: relations between different cultures, religions and ideologies.
4. *Alienation between the generations* in different parts of the world: the disintegration of a "common ground of meaning" between parents and children and the protest and despair of younger people vis-à-vis inherited values and institutions.
5. *Missiological* aspects of our search for renewal of human community ("That the world may believe..."): inter-relatedness between unity of the Church and humankind in the perspective of the kingdom.

These areas are closely related to many concerns represented by manifold activities of the WCC. They are a clear invitation to our colleagues in other departments of ecumenical activity to join in the efforts of this study and to invest in it their wisdom, experiences—and frustrations. This could become particularly important with respect to the preparations for the Vancouver assembly whose theme "Jesus Christ—the Life of the World", in both its inter-related emphases, i.e. in its christological concentration and in its cosmological horizon, provides the focus and the framework in which our study could and should be cooperatively developed.

It will be a special concern of Faith and Order to set the focus of its own study and possibly also of the preparatory process: the centrality of Jesus Christ and the emphasis of the unity of the Church founded in him. For the Lima Commission meeting, which was very much on our mind, this means the obligation to take seriously the relation between the five groups working on the theme with the other groups dealing with other studies of Faith and Order. The unity of the Church has to do with the apostolic faith, with the studies on baptism, eucharist and ministry, with the study on the Community of Women and Men in the Church. "The Unity of the Church and the Renewal of Human Community" is to be understood as one contribution to that common concern—with a specific assignment: to work out the implications of Christian unity in relation to some of the most crucial challenges confronting us in the broken communities of our world.

Bases and outline of a study on the unity of the Church and the renewal of human community

What is the aim of the study?

In the report from the group on "The Unity of the Church and the Renewal of Human Community" at the Faith and Order Standing Commission meeting in January 1981, there are these words:

> The aim of the proposed study is to place it [the Faith and Order concern on the unity of the Church] in a broadened horizon and to develop its implications for Christian service and mission in the contemporary world.

This aim, if carried out faithfully and boldly, must affect the self-understanding of the Church, reinforce the prophetic imperative of the unity it seeks, and strengthen its mission of reconciliation in human community. The unity of the divided Church and the renewal of the broken human community are closely inter-related.

What is the theological method of the study?

We are discovering today new insights about the formation of scripture and traditions which can serve as a paradigm for us as we engage in theological reflection. We are beginning to understand this formation as an ongoing process in which we share, even today, as we reflect on our inherited faith and realities of our life and world.

In the Bible, the Israel of the Old Testament and the community of the New Testament express ever-new insights into the being and action of God, of God's demands upon, and desires for, them and through them for all creation. These insights came as they reflected upon their inherited traditions in the light of their present experience and on their present experience in the light of those inherited traditions. In the Old Testament, the inherited traditions centre around the action of God in calling and covenanting with the people. In the New Testament, the new, decisive and determinative event which judges and affirms all else is the life, death and resurrection of Christ. In both instances there is a *double dynamic* at work in which light is shed on present experience as well as on inherited traditions. The biblical writers testify that such reflection was at the direction of, and under the power they identified as, the hand, the word, the spirit of God.

If we are to be faithful to this biblical paradigm of doing theology, we must engage in the same double dynamic. We must seek to wrestle with our Christian inheritance in the light of our lived experience so that our inheritance speaks to and judges our experience, but also to reflect upon our inheritance in the light of our experience so that in its turn it speaks to and brings alive what we have received. Such reflection must be undertaken under the power and guidance of the Spirit. There must be no theological enterprise which does not attempt to take seriously both what we inherit and also our lived experience.

In our search for the unity of the Church and the renewal of human community, the demands upon us are immense. We have to take account of the multiplicity of secular and ecumenical contexts, with their conflicts and brokenness as well as their joys and signs of renewal. But the multiplicity and diversity of contexts open up new possibilities for enquiry and exchange and hold promise of deeper and richer understandings of God and God's intention for creation, for we believe that God is already there in the midst ahead of us. A global context provides the opportunity to examine our Christian inheritance in the light of our own experience but also the opportunity to listen to and enter upon the lived experience and insights of others. It is a gift we offer one another in the ecumenical movement of opening ourselves to others, of receiving them back, and of becoming identified with one another in sufferings and joys. In such reciprocal involvement we are recreated by our common tradition under the power of the Spirit and together discover new insights in our shared inheritance. Such mutual understanding and identification involves accepting vulnerability, but through it we believe we discover truths about the nature and work of God the creator, redeemer and sustainer and about God's demands upon us. So we become more truly united with each other in the body of Christ and dedicate ourselves to the renewal of human community. There can be no convergence towards the unity of the Church which does not speak to the renewal of human community, and no renewal of human community that does not carry implications for the unity of the Church in its confession of faith, in its sacramental life, in its pastoral care and its mission in the contemporary world. The unity in Christ, and its eschatological vision of the one kingdom, is at the same time the fulfilment of our hopes for unity *and* the judgment on false dreams and realities of human unity.

Already the studies on the issues of racism and on the Community of Women and Men in the Church have sought to use this method of shared reflection and action which we may describe as the *inter-relational method*. Both studies point to the possibilities of enlarging and enriching our understanding of the unity of the Church and the renewal of human community and to the very real connections between and interdependence of the two.

What is the theological focus of the study?

The aim of placing the Faith and Order concern for the unity of the Church in a broadened horizon and of developing its implications for Christian service and mission demands a clear theological focus. It would be wrong, however, to seek this focus by dealing with the relation between "Church" and "human community" in general, abstract concepts. This is not to say that such reflection is unnecessary or undesirable—far from it. The study, however, should suspend such reflection because our subject directs us, first of all, not to theological problems but to situations where Church and human community are part of actual human problems. These situations, therefore, will constitute the primary contexts of our study.

Suspension of a general conceptual reflection is stressed here because such reflection can result, and often has resulted, in either overlooking or escaping the problems posed by the situations in which the urgent need for renewal of the human community presents challenges to the faith and unity of Christians. General theological reflection tends to shy away from rigorous verification in those situations and to become a closed circuit. The very aim of our study requires of us an effort to avoid such a tendency.

The focus on situations mentioned above is determined by the faith that the triune God is involved in human history and that the brokenness of human community is God's concern. Thus, when we look at the Church in situations where it itself is deeply affected by that brokenness, we are confronted not only with deplorable failures on the part of the Church, but with the frontiers of faith and unity that call for new ways of giving witness to God's involvement. Standing at those frontiers of conflicts and tensions often implies judgment and conversion. At the same time, it is through those frontiers that a fresh understanding of God's acts and the mission of the Church may develop. In this sense, the unity of the Church and its witness to the renewal of human community are inseparable. The experience of humanity as being *en route* to the kingdom is inherent to the experience of unity and disunity in the Church.

This amounts to saying that in order to be able to *speak* about the Church we must *see* the ways in which the Church is involved in human history. We cannot talk about the body of Christ except in the face of the brokenness of the human community. In other words, the theological focus of the study is the point at which faith in God's involvement in human history expresses itself as an effort to speak about that involvement on the basis of actual experiences of brokenness and renewal. In this way we, like Israel and the New Testament community, learn again and again what God's creating and renewing action means. This is what has been described as inter-relational method in the previous section.

The history of the Church and manifestations of its unity and division are inseparably related to the situations in which the confession of faith in Christ and the development of Christian community are actually affected by the ruptures and conflicts that beset human community. Realization of this fact keeps challenging Christians to understand the role they play in the existence and perpetuation of brokenness in human community, and to become engaged in costly acts of repentance and renewal. The Church cannot serve the renewal of human community without itself becoming part of that renewal movement out of a deep sense of repentance.

When Christians take up this challenge, their understanding of faith and inherited traditions can be deepened. Experience of suffering, for example, can throw new light on the meaning of redemption; experience of renewal in human community can help grasp the meaning of resurrection, and so on. All theological thinking has its roots in life situations such as these. In order for theology to maintain its integrity, it has to strike root again and again in new life situations. Only then will it become and remain truly incarnational.

There is always a danger of losing sight of this basic inter-relatedness of Church and human community that constitutes our theological focus. The study is an effort to face that inter-relatedness and to stress the incarnational nature of theology and ecclesiology. It may prove to be an exciting exploration. Since the global contexts of pluralism, conflicts and interdependence are "the great fact of our time" constituting an inescapable challenge for Christian faith and theology, our exploration is both timely and necessary.

What is the process of the study?

On the basis of the considerations above, we envision a study process which will occupy Faith and Order for the coming several years. The basic study resources will have to come from a number of groups to be formed in different world contexts. These groups would consist of persons conscious of living in situations of conflict and renewal in which both Church and human community are involved. Their concerns may be related to issues of historical conflict (e.g. racism, the rich-poor struggle, the armament question), alienation (e.g. sexism, generation conflict), cultural diversity, or relation to nature (e.g. ecological problems). The groups will be asked to consider how their intuitive approach to, as well as their conscious reflection on, faith and community are affected by these issues. In many cases the groups may find it necessary to reinterpret certain aspects of the theological thinking they have inherited and to seek new engagement in their situations, a process similar to that which has led some women's groups to reconsider traditional views on creation and anthropology. All these findings will have to be described in the reports submitted by the groups.

It is important to emphasize that the study process should remain focused on local situations. This means, among other things, that reports from the groups must not be regarded as illustrations or derivatives of some general conception of faith and unity. But this does not suggest that the study intends to consider experiences and reflections of the groups as normative for theological thinking on faith and unity. What is important is that the reflections of the groups are respected in their situational integrity as they arise out of the frontiers of Church and human community. They are brought into common discussion neither as normative reflections nor as examples of or, perhaps, deviations from "given" norms. Rather, they are challenges by which all partners in the worldwide Christian community are stimulated to reconsider their own positions and conceptions. This can be foreseen as an ongoing process since there is almost no limit to the variety of situations and to the challenges these situations pose to Christians. Thus, doing theology within the ecumenical movement must face the fact that no Christians, either as individuals or as community, can ultimately ignore the need to relate their own "double dynamic" to that of others.

Towards the final stage of the study, an effort should be made, of course, to draw conclusions, on the basis of reports from the groups, about the ways in which ecumenical theological reflections can profit from taking seriously unity, conflict and renewal experienced in local situations. It is hoped that these conclusions will highlight new insights about the Church and its mission which are developing in a variety of situations and places. Further, they may point to the ways in which Christians may engage themselves in the practice of and reflection on their faith at the frontiers where Church and human community meet.

In this process of study, how does the unity of the Church remain the central concern? The answer is twofold. In the first place, involvement at the "frontiers" will undoubtedly lead to discovery of new aspects of the problems of unity and division and of new insights into the meaning and shape of communion in Christ. Secondly, when the problem of unity is dealt with in a *global* context, the unity of the Church may be perceived not only as reconciliation of traditions of faith, but also as closely related to diverse and varied ways in which renewal of human community is conceived, expressed and attempted.

In this way, the study on "The Unity of the Church and the Renewal of Human Community" has its own special focus and method but also remains closely related to other Faith and Order concerns such as the apostolic faith, agreed statements on baptism, eucharist and ministry, the community of women and men in the Church, and so on. The present study is to be understood as one contribution to the Faith and Order concern for unity with a specific assignment: to explore the implications of Christian unity in relation to some of the most crucial challenges confronting us in this broken community of our world.

Profile of Lima

The Commission meeting in Lima will provide an opportunity for taking up the study and of giving it initial direction and insight. To be faithful to the inter-relational method, as it has been described above, a number of preparatory papers emerging from a variety of situations will be offered. Group members will also bring to the discussions their own experience of conflict and renewal. And all this will happen within the important context of Lima itself. We hope to describe and explore our own lived experiences and to share them with one another.

We hope to discover how such situations challenge our inherited positions on a range of crucial areas of the Christian faith, e.g. creation, history, culture, alienation, mission. And, if the double dynamic is to be effective, we must also reflect on how our understanding of those same basic areas in their turn confirm or judge our own life experience. We are thinking of such areas as the following:

1. Creation

How is creation to be understood as the basis of unity of human community?

How do we understand our responsibility for and our common destiny with nature (e.g. ecological issues)?

Are human conflicts related to God's continuing acts of creation? If so, in what sense and in what way?

2. History

How are we to evaluate historical pluralism theologically?

Within historical pluralism, what place has the Jewish-Christian understanding of history?

What is the alternative, if any, to the Jewish-Christian understanding of history?

How can we speak of the word and judgment of God coming through historical conflicts?

Can a reflection on history have positive impact on intercultural dialogues with other religions?

3. Cultures

How are we to evaluate cultural diversity theologically?

How do we see God's involvement in, for example, American Indian, Asian, or African culture?

What is the meaning of the Judeo-Greco culture in God's dealings with humanity?

What place does western culture play in God's providence?

What place has "secular culture", as illustrated in the life of urban communities deeply influenced by science and technology, in God's providence?

4. Alienation

In view of conflicts within, for example, nature, community and family, how is it possible to believe in the integrity of the human person?

What do conflicts tell us about community and how are situations of renewal to be evaluated in comparison?

In what sense do the conflicts we experience lead us to new understandings of sin and forgiveness, fallenness and redemption?

5. Mission

How are we to understand and reinterpret Jesus' commission to "make disciples of all nations" in the world of conflicts?

In view of the inter-relatedness of Church and human community, what do we see as the major characteristics of the Church as a "missionary community"?

What does our experience of the inter-relatedness of Church and human community tell us about dialogue with people of other faiths? What are the theological and missiological bases of such dialogue?

The areas, and the questions raised under each of them, are not intended to be exhaustive but illustrative. The important thing is how we deal with such questions, namely starting from and working with our lived experiences.

In proceeding in this way, we shall test out the method of the study outlined in the preceding sections. From shared engagement with real situations and in reflection upon them in the light of certain key areas of the Christian faith, the problem of unity will be placed before us and unavoidable challenges will come to the divided churches. We shall begin to capture new possibilities for the unity of the Church in its confessing, sacramental and caring life, and move towards a deeper understanding of the renewal of human community. This must lead to a fresh articulation of the theology of the Church and human community.

Race, Christian unity and the unity of humankind
GAYRAUD WILMORE

No one quite knows what race is. All of us, of course, think we know and the assumption entraps us in a common sense observation that frequently confuses race with nationality, culture, language or geography. Skin colour and physiognomy provide the casual observer with biological categories for differentiating between three basic concentrations of genetic material in the world population. Scientists call these concentrations the Mongoloid, the Negroid and the Caucasoid divisions. But even here fluctuations over time, and the different ways physical characteristics are perceived or preconceived by each group, confuses what is at best only a rough anthropological classification.

Race evades precise definition because of the mixture of humankind over millions of years. Nevertheless, we are faced on the common sense level with an almost universal assumption of the ubiquitous reality of race so that it seems to touch upon every aspect of our existence, consciously and unconsciously. It is taken for granted that everyone must be identified with one race or another. Racial identity thus becomes synonymous with our humanity. It ceases to be an abstraction and, whether or not we choose it to be so, it becomes a factor in our interaction with each other. We cannot

• Prof. GAYRAUD WILMORE, United Presbyterian Church, teaches theology at the Colgate-Rochester Divinity School, Rochester, New York, USA.

take this lightly. As well as I may know what is meant when someone says to me: "I just don't think of you as a *black* person, I just see you as a person", I cannot accept the remark as a realistic assessment of my personhood, my authenticity as a historical being. My blackness is an inseparable part of who I am as a person.

I sometimes think that what we call race is like wetness. When you first plunge into a swimming pool, the water is either too hot or too cold, but in a few minutes it is difficult to tell what it feels like on the surface of your skin. Even wetness loses meaning after a time. But if you are wet in one place, if a waiter spills the water you asked for in your lap, or if you're wearing a wet bathing suit under your clothes at the beach, you can describe the feeling. It is comfortable or uncomfortable, depending on the outside tempe-rature. It is sticky, clammy, moist, semiliquidous or something. Whatever it is, you know you are wet in this place or that.

Race is like that. Immersed in an isolated or genetically homogenous pool of human beings we can accept race as synonymous with our humanity and, therefore, as an abstraction. Race makes little concrete difference in our lives until it clings to some sensitive part of our conscious existence. For example, to our social life when we want to join a private club or consider marriage; to our political life when we are running for public of-fice; to our economic life when we need to join a labour union or want to change careers; to our religious life when some person of another race comes unexpectedly to our Sunday morning worship service. In all of these situations, race suddenly becomes noticeable, salient, something to be reckoned with, whether we like it or not. We are suddenly conscious of and know all about race! In other words, the mystique of race then begins to play its ambiguous role in our conscious lives.

Someday, if the world lasts that long, this may not be the case. Technology may yet break down our relative isolation from other concentrations of human beings and so flatten out our physi-ological and cultural differences that nothing meaningful remains to be classified. Whether or not that is a condition devoutly to be wished is a matter for discussion, but it is certainly conceivable. A thousand years from today, or more likely much sooner, our descendants, travelling near the speed of light at the cost we pay for a subway ride, will shop in Nairobi in the morning and return home for lunch. Their friends in Tokyo will have dinner in Boston and catch a show in Vancouver on the way back to Japan on the same evening.

When that day comes we will truly have one world. Oneness in such a world will be inescapable. It does not take much imagination to picture what a common life-style and the accessibility in that kind of world of now distant peoples will do for international romance and inter-racial marriage. What racial differences will remain under those conditions? One thing seems likely in view of current statistics—they will have to look at photographs and old movies to find out what white people or black people looked like before they were both swallowed up in a mélange of many shades and colours. The prospect of a world of one off-colour race does not intrigue me. I like the sharp contrast between pale white and jet black. I prefer the varying shades of skin colour, hair texture, shape of eye, nose and lip. A garden which has one kind of flower can be pleasing, but more striking and beautiful is a garden with a variety of colours of flowers.

The fact is that the racial problem in the United States and South Africa is not basically about colour but about control. We Americans have been taught some important lessons in race relations since the Brown decision of 1954. Based upon our own experience, we may well suspect that the Afrikaans are not nearly as concerned about their daughters marrying black men as they are about losing those gold mines, diamond mines and uranium deposits—losing control over the gleaming industrial society they have erected over the bodies of millions of non-white peoples. It is not different in the US.

This does not mean that race and colour are not important, but that they mask other less visible considerations related to the will to power, the need to control and dominate others whatever their race or colour might be.

In the meantime, however, we live in a very race-conscious and dangerous world, one that has been dominated by the Caucasian minority since the last outpost of Africanized Islam surrendered in western Europe almost 600 years ago. One hundred and twenty years later, twenty Africans were disembarked on the quays of Jamestown and thirty years after that the Dutch landed in South Africa to begin a history that sounds strangely very much like our own. The history that unravelled in North America and Southern

Africa since those days has given us a world in which invidious racial distinctions, segregation and discrimination have been basic characteristics of the hegemony of white people wherever they have encountered people of other colour. And what about the Church? It is well known that the Christian religion which participated in those conquests on three continents was compromised by the convenient alibi that racial and cultural differences made available for political oppression and economic exploitation.

It seems obvious, in the light of the pervasiveness and tenacity of white racism, the most powerful of the many racisms of this world, that in order to achieve that raceless, yet hopefully variegated human family of the future, Christians and other religionists need an interim strategy that will ensure its coming to pass. For as long as what we have made of race heightens and exacerbates the drive for power in other intergroup conflicts, we can never speak glibly of the "diminishing significance of race", nor avoid the fact that it can fuel the ultimate conflagration that can bring the world to an end long before that amicable future has an opportunity to dawn.

Strategies against genocide

The question of what that strategy should be haunts all of our discussions about the unity of the Church as a desideratum. For unless the gospel can help to effectuate the unity of humankind, and unless the issues thrown up by alienation between racial and ethnic groups can condition in a positive way how we proclaim and demonstrate the gospel, there is little hope that either the Church or the world can avoid a situation in which the temptation to genocide will be irresistable.

Genocide is not something that was abolished from the world after the Nazi holocaust. As Samuel F. Yette reminds us in his frightening book on black survival, *The Choice*, it is a political decision that can be made "any day in the year by a town, city, state, nation or group of nations". Genocide is the ultimate and predictable expression of ordinary racial antipathy. The fact that what is reputedly the most Christian nation in the world for more than thirty years has consistently refused to ratify the United Nations Convention on the prevention of genocide should convince us that the American churches are either in complicity with that decision or have been shamefully negligent of their public responsibility. To give token attention to the issue of racism or to talk about it as an optional, monotonously over-emphasized item on the Faith and Order agenda, leaves one's profession of faith in doubt. In a real way God the Father, incarnate in the Son, Jesus the Jew of Nazareth, suffered ethnic oppression as the prelude to genocide; we saw the re-enactment of this pattern of human depravity at Auschwitz and Dachau, and more recently—with other actors—at Soweto and in the call for compulsory sterilization in the United States. No Christian can regard the struggle against genocide and racism as optional.

The issue of strategy, at least in the United States, has to do with two important tactics: (1) the promotion of the kind of ethnic pluralism which gives recognition and respect to all groups and shares with them the power that is now concentrated in the white community, and (2) the participation of the churches and other private institutions in the struggle for the unity of all peoples in a just world—a world characterized by what my colleague, Prof. Kenneth Smith, calls "structured neighbourliness".

Let us take a moment to look at each of these tactical considerations. First, ethnic pluralism.

The central question of the ecumenical movement today is what is the nature of our unity in the Church with respect to racial and ethnic differences. In the United States, the ontological significance assigned to colour makes any question about Church and race pivot on the question of the existence and will to survive of black people—at least for the foreseeable future. Despite the resurgence of white racism in America and Great Britain today (and I need not recite what the newspapers are reporting everyday), it has become popular in some circles to speak of the irrelevancy of ethnicity in favour of class, and, in any case, to de-emphasize particularities in favour of universals. But if it is necessary to speak more accurately of ethnicity or peoplehood than of race, then it follows that *cultural* differences should be considered as important as cultural similarities and, if handled properly, as potentially enhancing as they may be divisive in any future that will be something more than the creation of the racial group which now dominates the powerful North Atlantic community.

Some scholars who are prepared to concede the value of a cross-cultural perspective for the future of American Christianity are not prepared to include Afro-American culture in this mix. For them the culture of Afro-Americans (which includes the black religious experience) is simply a poor, second-rate carbon copy of the Caucasian original, or at best the culture of poverty which has no intrinsic value when compared with the more authentic inheritance of Hispanics, Asians and Native Americans. The consequence of this thinking in the field of theological education, where the norms of the American churches are dignified and indoctrinated, is to deny the reality of what may be called the black Church in teaching and research. The religious experience of Afro-Americans and their historic contribution to American Christian belief and practice is given only token recognition in the academic disciplines of both the theological seminary and the universities, Protestant and Roman Catholic.

In an enlightening article on the myth or reality of Afro-American culture, the University of California sociologist at Berkeley, Robert Blauner, writes:

> The viewpoint that black culture is only a lower class life-style and Negro Americans have no ethnic traditions to value and defend falls within a liberal frame of reference that I call neo-racism—though its proponents abhor traditional racism... Furthermore, this position is historically tied to past patterns of negating or appropriating the cultural possessions and productions of black people. The racist pattern was to destroy culture, to steal it for profit or to view it contemptuously or with amusement... The denial of Afro-American ethnicity is the more serious form that white appropriation takes today. Through abstract and intellectual analysis, the social scientist (and I would add the theologian) attempts to undermine the claims of black Americans to distinctive ethos and value system.

As long as the white churches and those who have the responsibility for educating their clergy and laity assume that black culture and its religious component are irrelevant to the major Protestant and Roman Catholic traditions, the quest for Christian unity in the United States will be frustrated. As long as the massive presence of Afro-American ethnicity and the condition of the black population is ignored or neglected by the white churches of the United States, any discussion about Christian unity will lack cultural and theological realism—not to mention obedience to the will of God.

Partnership in faith and life

The second consideration has to do with the question of the unity of the Church and the unity of humankind which is the most appropriate context for the discussion of race and Christian unity.

The nature of our unity in Christ is a partnership which expresses both the tensions and harmonies of our interdependent relationship in the world and the Church. Indeed, it is through the strains and stresses of diversity and change that we learn how to communicate and negotiate with each other under conditions that will not allow the sacramental unity of the Church to spiritualize the contradictions of our historical existence. Conversely, it is through discipleship—the *discipline* of common worship which entails forgiveness, mutual trust and healing, and the *disciplines* of education and collaboration in mission—that we express the reality of the body of Christ which will not allow the contradictions of historical experience to take precedence over our unity in word and sacrament.

Partnership in faith and life which avoids both a spurious universalism and an exaggerated particularity, or a spiritualized sameness and a politicized diversity, is the term which best describes the nature of our unity during this epoch. God is not yet through with his creation or with any of us, and it does not yet appear what we shall be if we take each other's realities and perceptions seriously while we seek the unity to which we are called together with the whole creation.

This is what I take to be the meaning of the paper on the "Unity of the Church—the Unity of Humankind" which was presented by Dr C.S. Song for discussion at the January 1981 meeting of the Standing Commission on Faith and Order (printed above).

> The Church exists to bring the message of reconciliation and salvation in Christ to the world, and the world demands that the Church live up to its own message. The world has not been a mere disinterested spectator in the churches' effort towards unity, nor has it been passively waiting for the churches to bring unity to it. Critical involvement of the world in church unity has to be recognized and appreciated... The Church and the world are signs one to the other.

In other words, the partnership of racial and ethnic groups within the Church, in the context of their respective struggles for survival and liberation in the world, is parallelled by the partnership of the Church and the world in their mutual calling and responsibility to manifest the reign of God until all things are fulfilled in Jesus Christ.

The Church and the world are signs one to the other. It is the partnership which the Church of rich white people enters into with the Church of the poor black people that makes the Church, as God's community of shared suffering and reconciliation, and the world, as the source of the Church's missionary agenda, become signs one to the other.

We cannot seek the unity of the Church without seeking at the same time the unity and the justice of humankind. This is how the dethronement of the powers which separate black from white, one ethnic group from another, become the object of historical projects which have the power to draw us together in a partnership of liberation and reconciliation. And, because of the uncontestable reality of our respective existential situations and our claims upon each other, it becomes a partnership which honours and respects differences while demonstrating that the dividing wall of hostility is broken down and we are indeed one united community of faith and life in Jesus Christ.

Black and white churches in the United States have a mutual responsibility to seek this kind of partnership without benevolent paternalism on the one side or exploitative dependency on the other. Such partnership has to do with the revision of theological education, and Christian education curricula, joint work on hymnbooks and liturgies, joint worship services and intercommunion, and collaboration in evangelism and social ministries.

This kind of partnership cannot be limited in the US to the National Council of Churches and the Consultation on Church Union (COCU). I do not mean to imply that these national agencies are irrelevant to inter-racial partnership in the Church. I am encouraged by the new position which COCU is taking regarding interim steps towards its ultimate goal of organic union. But the ultimate goal must not be permitted so to relativize and overshadow the realities and possibilities that they are not taken with utmost seriousness in the present situation. I believe that it is a mistake for the Consultation to assume that organic union between black and white denominations in the US, as desirable as that may be someday, is the ultimate measure of faithfulness to the gospel today.

I quote from a new COCU document on racism which clearly states the point I wish to make:

> Black Christians and churches, however, have observed or experienced the divisive and demoralizing consequences of merger for the black experience, institutions and community. Many blacks feel that integration or merger causes fundamental and serious disruptions resulting in the elimination of leadership and the loss of black self-control, absorption and the loss of self-reliance. And while some of these are offered up in the body of Christ, it all too often is assumed that they must not be given up in the body of white Christianity. Blacks ask: "If a church is not willing to risk too much of itself prior to union on the scale envisioned by COCU, will it practise equality and representation after union in matters of race, sex and age?"

There are important roles for both the National Council and COCU to play at the national and regional levels. The real question of unity, however, has to be faced at the local level, and at that level I see hope—albeit short of organic union.

Both the National Council and COCU are too far removed from the pastors and people who experience daily the full impact of the forces of the secular society which tear us apart and necessitate reciprocity if we are to solve the problems of our common life. True partnership will always be on the local level, between two or three congregations, or within local councils and federations of churches—close to the resources of our own making, and close to the creative imagination and joy we can share when people and pastors discover the experience with Christ which each group represents.

The Community Study and the unity of the Church and renewal of human community

MARY TANNER

From 1977-1981, many people at local, national, regional and international levels have been drawn into the study of the "Community of Women and Men in the Church". The story of the study is an impressive one and repays studying in detail for the message is closely bound up with the story itself. It shows repeatedly how deeply the issues set out in the original invitation to join the investigation—issues of identity and roles, church structure and ministries, the use and abuse of the Bible and tradition and the language, symbolism and imagery of the Christian tradition—are related to an understanding of the unity of the Church and the renewal of human community. It points to the inter-relation of and interdependency of the Church and the world.

Theological method
The theological method on which the project was based was similar to that planned for the Faith and Order study on "The Unity of the Church and the Renewal of Human Community". It was based on the conviction that our experience of life—whoever we are, wherever we live, whatever church we belong to—is vital raw material for understanding Christian truth and for our vision

• Mrs MARY TANNER, Church of England, Lecturer in Theology at Cambridge at the time of presenting this paper, is now an ecumenical officer for the Church of England in London.

of the community we seek. But such experience has always to be measured against the Christian tradition which has come down to us through the centuries and which is given to us in and through the teaching, life and witness of the Christian communities to which we belong. That inherited tradition must judge and speak to our experience. But, in its turn, reflection upon our experience as women and men in community helps us to perceive ever fresh and creative insights in that tradition we receive in and through the Church to which it is entrusted and in which it is embodied. This theological method of a continual interplay between experience and tradition and between tradition and experience lay at the basis of the Community Study. Here was a double dynamic at work in which, on the one hand, examination of our experience of being women and men, in relationships and in community, put critical questions to the Christian tradition and, on the other, the tradition pointed to new evaluations of our experience. The process was more complex than such a simple analysis would suggest. There was no ordered move from experience to tradition, from tradition to experience, but a continual interplay between the two. The various reports, prayers, creeds, liturgies, recommendations, letters, books, pamphlets which emerged from the study illustrate the complex relation of experience and tradition in the reflective process showing that the text/context/text method lay at the base of the study.

Such a method was seen to be true to the biblical way of doing theology and to reflect that it was just such a task that the writers of both testaments were themselves engaged upon, so they believed and claimed, under the hand, the word, the Spirit of God.

The Community Study was also based upon the conviction that the experience and reflection had to be that of as wide a group of women and men as possible. It was not to be the reflection, as so often in the past, of a group of mostly white western male theologians meeting together to pronounce on renewed community; neither should such a group be replaced by a reflective group of radical feminists. Stemming as it did in part from the Berlin consultation on "Sexism in the Seventies", it was often thought to be a Faith and Order project for women. Indeed, at the end of their time, the women in Berlin issued a statement:

> Together we have found a new community
> and we renewed our commitment to work

for change and to end all those things which
deny our humanity and the creative purposes of God.

And amongst their recommendations came one to launch a major project on women, staffed by women, with an international consultation for women. But later the same year the direction was changed significantly at the Accra meeting of the Faith and Order Commission by a call for a "community study". It was based upon a statement from a small group of women and men trying to give account of their hope:

Called as men and women together to become signs of the power of the kingdom, we hope for a truer and more complete community in Christ.

Some would say that too swift a change was made between a women's study, called for by Berlin, and a community study, implemented by Nairobi, to redress the imbalance of 4,000 years of male-dominated history and theology. But the Community Study does point to the belief that our understanding of renewed community of women and men must engage, in the reflective process, women and men from as widely different contexts and with as widely different experiences of life as is possible. A convincing expression of renewed community must be based on as comprehensive a study of experience in the light of our common tradition as we are able to achieve. However, within this exploration, we must not lose sight of the fact that the reflection has been done for centuries almost entirely by men on behalf of the whole community and it is, therefore, necessary for women, sometimes within the total process, to withdraw and reflect together as women before they can contribute fully to the whole. This is not in order that women should gather strength to attack the past in a negative way, but in order that they may learn to identify and articulate what is the unique experience of women. Many of the groups that contributed to the study were groups of all women; others had a high proportion of women. However, at the European consultation, it was often the men, finding themselves heavily outnumbered by women, in a position so often experienced by women and beginning to understand what it is like to be part of the minority, who called out for more equal representation. The Sheffield consultation included forty men and twice as many women, and it might be argued that in future any consultation particularly on this theme needs equal representation. But the Community Study is not an end in itself; rather, it marks the beginning of a process which encourages women and men together to articulate a renewed vision of the community we seek and to chart ways in the Church and the world for bringing this about.

"Algebraic signs"

The many reports and testimonies emerging from the study are the "algebraic signs with a great depth of well buried meaning behind them" (Philip Potter). They describe the brokenness of community both within the Church and in the wider community which challenges our concepts of unity and all our past attempts at renewal. A few examples may illustrate that, although the descriptions are particular to each situation, the underlying values and assumptions are the same.

From a local group in Uruguay:

> The Christian tradition has taught us, as Latin American women, to be subordinate and prudent... Men always are given greater authority and more liberty, including in the sexual field. What might be a sin for a woman is not for a man. The Church really must reconsider its teaching in this matter.

From the Caribbean:

> In many places in the Caribbean, women and men work side by side in the fields or in their small industries from Monday to Saturday, but on Sunday they go to church to be divided. It is said that for "scriptural reasons" women sit on the left, men on the right.

From India:

> My questionnaire, which I used to get information for this meeting, led to actual combat in an Indian Christian village. The women argued that Jesus spoke to them of liberation, while the men claimed a scriptural warrant to beat the women and silence them in public. Many of us are beginning to realize that Christianity may, in some cases, have made the traditionally low status of women in Indian society even worse because claims of male domination are now "supported" by sacred texts.

From Germany:

> Why are men so little prepared to reconsider their own roles in order to find a new community? Many men simply smile about my deep frustrations and anger when I seek new forms of relating. They do not hear my deep cry for understanding.

Behind such concrete examples of brokenness lie assumptions—sometimes consciously, sometimes unconsciously, held—of an inherent inequality of the sexes. Such a belief has given rise to a pattern of domination and subordination. It is part of the fabric of our lives and is worked out in the way society is founded and ordered in complex and subtle ways. The systematic and continuous subordination of women on the basis of sex alone, "sexism", is an expression which dehumanizes both the oppressed and the oppressor. It is reflected in our family lives, often in the most intimate of relationships, perpetuated in our educational system, in job expectancy and opportunities, in our working and social lives alike. It is no less to be found in the theological expression, the worship and the structuring of our church life.

The uncovering of these deeply embedded assumptions of inherent inequality on which the ordering of society and so much of our lives is based, assumptions which challenge the Church, evokes a mixture of conflicting and contradictory feelings. For some, the revelation is liberating for it holds out promise of a way to a new pattern of equality and partnership. For others, including many women, there is threat bringing fear and insecurity. Attempts are made to justify the traditional pattern, often on the basis of the Christian revelation itself. Often such attempts are made by those who have learned, perhaps unwittingly, to cooperate with the system and to survive in doing so.

Web of oppression

As the study progressed, the brokenness of community caused by sexism was more and more understood, not in isolation but linked together in an insidious and complex web of oppression, "a symphony of groaning". Race, class and sex, instead of being forces which militate against each other, often combine and complicate the discrimination against different groups of people. At Sheffield it was the third world participants who saw most clearly the link between racism and sexism and classism. Black women from South Africa are terribly oppressed: "They cannot breathe." One of the strongest and most often quoted recommendations from Sheffield was that on prostitution and international tourism. Here was a concrete example of the inter-relation of different forms of oppression. Wealthy men from the first world buy package holidays, in the third world, in which a female companion is part of the deal. The women come often from impoverished backgrounds and are forced into prostitution by economic necessity. The uncovering of the inter-relatedness of forms of oppression calls for a combined struggle for liberation, for no one form of freedom can be realized in isolation; even if that were possible, no one form of freedom alone would of itself accomplish a renewed community either of the Church or of the world. Yet each struggle towards freedom, whether against sexism, racism or classism, is a sign of God's intention for renewed creation in which the community is restored. We are not fully set free to be "children of God" until all are free.

Nevertheless, while we continue to explicate the interlocking web of oppression and the relatedness of the struggle for liberation, that struggle will be particular. Different contexts and different situations will demand particular changes. Without denying the critical analysis of the interlocking web of oppression, we each have to take up the struggle for change against oppression that is forced upon us by our situation. So, the black woman from South Africa is oppressed by racism, classism and sexism. Her first struggle will be against racism, although sexism and classism are linked with it. A woman in Guatemala is among those who might be oppressed by imperialism, classism and sexism and while her first struggle might be against imperialism, yet other struggles must go hand in hand. A white middle class woman may struggle against sexism, but her struggle must be linked to one against classism, which in the west reinforces and is reinforced by sexism.

The more steps each of us learns to take in our particular situation, the more we shall see other parts of the web of oppression and come to understand our situation in a global context. We shall be less likely to force our concerns on others or to feel cheated when their struggles lead them to take up different concerns and to act in other ways.

So it was through the describing of actual situations and experiences and in putting questions to them that the underlying assumption of the inequality between the sexes, as well as the inter-relatedness of all forms of oppression, began to be more sharply focused. Together with this came the discovery of the ways in which such brokenness prevents any real unity of the Church or any renewal of community, and implications were drawn for a renewed vision of the unity of the Church. It was seen that the unity of the churches cannot be limited to the coming together of ecclesiastical bodies on the basis of doctrinal agreement alone or in any narrow structural way. Matters of faith and order belong together with life and witness. Agreement reached on doctrine and sacramental expression of baptism, eucharist and ministry is only a part of what a life of unity is about. The unity of the Church has to do profoundly with the quality of our lives together as Christians. Unity must involve breaking down the barriers erected by sexism, classism and racism, realities which are within the Church as well as in the torn and divided world. With the agreed statements on baptism, eucharist and ministry and the new confessing of apostolic faith, there must go hand in hand as part of the consensus process the will to challenge all that divides and separates. The latest WCC statements themselves point in this direction showing that baptismal unity and eucharistic sharing must be outward signs of a life in which all that divides and separates is being broken down. How rich the concept of the unity of the Church becomes when we begin to take seriously the relation between faith and order, life and witness and when all struggles for liberation are seen as related to the sacramental life of the body of Christ and to its structural expression. As we define brokenness more perceptively, and learn to challenge it more effectively, so we shall enrich our understanding of sacramental sharing, the structuring of our lives as Christians and find new ways of confessing the apostolic faith. We can only discover what organic union or conciliar fellowship is as we struggle to live in response to a call for fellowship *(koinonia)* in which women and men, black and white, rich and poor are brought within that fellowship and play their valued parts.

Letty Russell has expressed it in this way:

> In the paradigm of cooperation the unity of the Church is to be sought in trying to reach out to the outsiders in order to discover a more inclusive consensus.

The Community Study suggests many changes which must be made in church life if sexism is to be broken and we are to live the offered life of unity in the power of the Spirit. The mass of recommendations from the international consultation point to concrete areas where change needs to take place. The picture which emerges is not a carefully worked out blueprint of a Church of the future, but the many clues deserve to be studied by anyone concerned with the unity of the Church. They concern an ecclesial community which is more inclusive and which has found ways of valuing and expressing in its life those qualities which have been carried by women but so often undervalued and suppressed.

Scripture in new community

For this to be achieved, it means the Church must learn to take a fresh look at scripture and tradition through the eyes of women. The scriptures are given to the whole community and the whole community must interpret them together, including women. This is not to deny the work of scholarly interpretation, nor professional preaching or teaching, though more women need to be encouraged and equipped to participate at this level as well as every other level. But it is only when the whole community of faith engages together in the task of biblical interpretation that we shall discover the richness and variety which will provide a right basis and inspiration for our unity.

> We are convinced [the Sheffield report says] that the interpretation of scripture must take place within a community of dialogue and that it must incorporate the insights and experiences of women and men interpreters as equal partners. The act of opening the sphere to women adds an essentially new element. Men have dominated biblical interpretation for centuries. Now that women are beginning to reach with their own eyes, bringing their own expertise and experiences, we find that women are able to see things that men have not been able to see, feel or recognize in the texts. By interpreting scripture in the light of women's experiences, women are contributing to a new level of expertise and quality of life to biblical understanding.

The study contains many examples of the part women are learning to play in the interpretation of scripture, pointing to a way in which a church living in unity will value and build its life and witness on the insights of women as well as of men.

Phyllis Trible, an Old Testament scholar who led the Bible studies in Sheffield, re-read the Genesis 2-3 stories, the Song of Songs and the Book of Ruth from a woman's perspective and offered fresh insights into the ancient texts. Her studies, based on a thorough knowledge of the Hebrew text, drew us into new ways of viewing the Old Testament tradition, showing how the context in which we read the Bible allows us to see different and recreative things in scripture and so demands that we shape the community in other ways. Such insights, of course, raise fundamental questions about the nature and authority of scripture, and about the rule, if any, by which we judge new interpretations.

Nor is it only a matter of a new understanding of the Bible that will help to renew and reshape the community in greater unity; there is much also to be reclaimed and revalued within the history of the Church. Philip Potter pointed in this direction in his speech at the opening of the Sheffield consultation:

> We have made a great sacred cow out of our different traditions, but what I find, as a student of history, is an urgent need to rewrite history as the history of women and men in mission and service. Our existing church history is largely a history of men.

He continued to suggest how history might look different if we concentrated on the women in the tradition:

> One of the things this conference ought to do is to send us all back to do our homework, so that we can begin to discover what was the real tradition in the life of the churches and why the churches became so male oriented in the way they did.

So one of the implications of the Community Study is that only a community of faith which returns again and again to its sources, with openness and with the involvement of all, will see new dimensions in the concept of unity and discover there the resources for life.

Authority in new community

A renewed community will be one that has learned to be critical of its structures wherever they are built on an assumption of male superiority; it will be a community that has freed itself from destructive forms of hierarchy and discovered new depths of meaning in authority and power. Many voices in the study agreed in their description of the oppressive way they experience the Church as a pyramid with men at the top exercising power and women at the bottom. No community so organized and so experienced can have a life of unity or hope to be an effective sign to the world.

But living in community necessarily involves authority and power in the ordering of its life together. We are embarrassed and uncomfortable with our inherited notions of authority and power and the ways in which they are worked out; and we are angered by attempts to reinforce and maintain them on the basis of biblical texts. Going back to the scriptures, the Community Study discovered clues in the life, ministry and teaching of Jesus, and in the demands of the kingdom, which run counter to our contemporary views of authority and use of power. Jean Baker Miller, the American psychotherapist, expressed it in different terms:

> Women, historically the powerless, know that their quest is not for power on the male model, but for a new model of power. Thus, even though women and men are talking about the same reality, it holds for them a different meaning.

And the section at Sheffield investigating this area wrote that:

> The traditional male view of power is that it is something very precious, to be defended at all costs, or fought for as if the quality of power in the world were limited. On the other hand, many women experience power, like love, as limitless: the more one's power is shared with others, the more power there is. When persons both contribute and receive power, all are enriched.

Even so, such a view of power and authority cannot remain structureless; but we need to understand that structures preach more loudly than sermons and are signs conveying what we believe about equality and partnership. Our present structures do testify against the equality of the sexes and as such are inappropriate to a church endeavouring to live a life of unity. Emerging from the study, and needing further discussion, are criteria for church structures in order that they may enable and empower the whole community. These include the following:
1) that they provide for maximum participation for people in the life of the Church;
2) that they enable corporate decision-making by the whole people of God;
3) that they fulfil the purposes for which they were created and are still relevant in today's situation;
4) that they should not be imposed importations from another culture or context;
5) that they should have built-in checks and balances against concentration of power in persons and roles of the Church.

As women begin to share power and play an equal part in the leadership of the Church, new styles and models will emerge in which leadership is from below and shared more equally. It was in relation to this discussion that Sheffield recommended to the World Council that 50% of the persons elected to sub-units and committees of the WCC be women. So incredible did this appear to some that it was thought to be absurd. It could be argued, however, that the leadership of a community needs to be representative of its members, in which case the number of women in positions of leadership should far outnumber that of the men. But the intention behind the recommendation was to show that if we are to be united as a community of women and men in the Church, then there should be equal participation of women and men in all areas of church life. The 50% representation is something we cannot enforce at once, but something to which any church seeking real unity must be committed and towards which it must move.

Ministry in new community

Any discussion of shared power and leadership cannot escape questions regarding the Church's set-apart ministry. Throughout the study, the question of ordination of women to the set-apart ministry has been a painful area of investigation, challenging all traditions, Catholic, Orthodox and Protestant alike. One of the most important points to emerge in the debate is the acknowledgment that there can be no real progress towards unity if any one church, state or group within a church seeks to force a change in practice upon another. There is anguish on both sides of the debate, as much for those who long for ordination and are convinced that it is of God as for those who feel that they are being too harshly challenged to give up what they believe as unalterable tradition. To live in unity means finding ways of carrying on the discussion of the ordination of women, both to the diaconate and the presbyterate, within the unique context of the WCC, with a sensitivity to the complexity of the existing situation and the reality of the differences both within and between different churches.

The final recommendations of the study in this area try to encourage and not to prevent continuing dialogue between all branches of the Christian Church, between those who are opposed on grounds of tradition and those who do already ordain women to the presbyterate and even episcopate. Concerned for the convergence process towards consensus, they call for a continuing ecumenical exploration into the possibilities and implications of churches being in communion when they have different practices concerning the ordination of women. They ask also for an exploration of the diaconal dimension of all ministries to which women are attracted and especially of an understanding of the diaconate and the place of women within it.

No one can afford to dismiss the tension which exists in this area between those who believe that the life of unity must include women in every level of the churches' exercise of authority for it to be fully inclusive (and itself a sign of women and men created in the image of God), and those on the other hand who are convinced opponents on the basis of tradition. We cannot retreat in silence on this issue for it does profoundly affect the fellowship of the Church and lived unity. We have to learn new ways of offering our understanding and our experience to one another, ways that uphold and do not deny the other. How far we can be reconciled in diversity at this point is a serious question to our churches; but the very way to discovering an answer may well promote and deepen the unity we long for. It is possible that the Community Study has pointed in the direction of the need for all at least to engage in new ways in the debate and to be open to challenge from one another's perspectives.

So the vision of a renewed community must be one in which the Church has responded to the challenges to the harsh and sometimes destructive concepts of hierarchy, in which the Church lives with new models of leadership, in which sharing power with the powerless becomes a reality, and in which servanthood and the symbol of the wounded healer are dominant.

The life of unity grounded in an interpretation of scripture and tradition which is expressed in its structure and ministries will also involve a more sensitive use of language symbols and imagery. The Church must learn to include and to nurture all of us by the imagery it uses in its God-talk as well as its discussions about the community. Any church which uses exclusively male images and language cannot be united, for this is to perpetuate a form of domination and exclusion and to refuse to listen to the hurt experienced by many women.

Final thoughts

These are just a few of the insights of the Community Study which have implications for the unity of the churches and the renewal of human community. Any authentically renewed community will be one which is not turned in upon itself, which does not exist for itself, but is outward-looking and has become, in and through its own life, a prophetic community around which transformation of the world can take place. In this way the Church, as it moves to new understandings and expressions of unity both in doctrinal statements and in the quality of life, will become a sign of and an agent for the renewal of human community. The vocation of Christ was to reconcile the world to himself; the vocation of his body, the Church, is to be his instrument of reconciliation through the power of the Spirit. The Church can only be an effective instrument if it is itself constantly renewed and expresses this in its outward forms. Those outside the Church will never be won over by the clarity of doctrinal statements, by words of confession or by structures of ministry, but they will be won over by the quality of life of an undivided Christian community, a life lived in the unity of the Spirit.

To talk of the relationship between the Church and the world as "sign" can become triumphalistic and miss the truth that the Church and the world are signs one to another. The Community Study drew upon many insights of those outside the Church who have discovered new ways of understanding the relationship between women and men and created new ways of living lives of equality and partnership. The Church does not have a monopoly of truth and needs to be open to fresh insights and signs in the world in the belief that God is there in the midst ahead of us.

But when all the insights of the Community Study have been analysed and tabulated perhaps the most significant thing is the experience, shared by many, of participating in this investigation. Through their experience they have not only begun to put into words a renewed vision of an ecclesial community, but have, through that participation, experienced a renewed community. So one African delegate addressing Sheffield said: "I am because I participate." Others said: "We experienced and became that renewed community". They have experienced living with others who no longer base their lives on the assumption of the inequality of the sexes and who are committed to struggling against all forms of oppression and who, in so doing, have a foretaste of living in a united and not divided way.

The unity of the Church and the renewal of human community: a perspective from Africa

AMBA ODUYOYE

To a religiously pluralistic world, young in the art of dialogue, and only dimly aware of the unifying power of religion for humanity, it sounds presumptuous to associate the renewal of human community so closely with the unity of the Church. One's first reaction (and a genuine one) is, what does the Church know and experience of community? As far as "unity" goes, the Church (Christianity) is only "one" vis-à-vis other religions; its internal unity is belied by the ever-proliferating manifestations of Christianity. In the African situation, this fact has constituted a stumbling block to the unity of families and whole communities. This fact has set son against father and daughter against mother in the way predicted by Jesus (Luke 12:48-53). What does the Church know of human community when the fire of Christianity's faith has consumed traditional and "natural" alliances and when its effect has been disunity? If it is breaking down old barriers that it might build a new wholeness, then Africa still awaits the fulfilment of this hope.

Africa, as a human community, has its own diversity, disunity, as well as unifying factors. (The Organization of African Unity has an eschatological flavour.) The continent would have had

---

• Mrs AMBA ODUYOYE, Methodist Church, Ibadan, Nigeria, is a member of the Faith and Order Commission and of the Central Committee of the World Council of Churches.

enough of diversity without the arrivals of Christianity and Islam, colonialism and racism, socialism and capitalism. Thus, like the Church, Africa is plagued by intractable challenges of disunity and diversity. It appears that, on both levels, meaningful change will demand a reorientation of values, a revival of tried and tested norms, as well as an evolution of fresh perspectives.

This contribution to the Faith and Order study of "The Unity of the Church and the Renewal of Human Community" is set in Africa and based on the understanding that all human communities, apart from any religio-cultural interaction with the "outside", have been and are being guided by God towards the life that is life indeed. It is my understanding that whatever external influences Africa has had, and continues to experience, are only part of the process of God's upbringing of Africans, and of the human community at large.

The discussion is divided into four parts: (1) the cosmology that underlies African life and thought in so far as it deals with the unity within the one creation; (2) the historical encounter with Europe and how it has affected the theological thinking of Africans; (3) the mission of the Church in relation to the challenges posed by the brokenness of the African community; and (4) the demands of this brokenness on the Church's professed unity.

Unity within the one creation

Traditional cosmology of African peoples, having interacted with those of their "invaders", cannot be said to stand unique and unaffected. The invasion of the world as a whole—by mass media, movements of peoples and the formation of global organs like the UNO and the WCC—has had the effect of challenging African traditional ideas, confirming some and putting others under a question mark. This interaction has had the effect of stimulating attempts to create African regional organizations that aim at unity in Africa, and to encourage those whose specific burning desire is to make manifest how the one God of the cosmos has been revealed in Africa. The coming together of the world does not impinge on Africa alone; primal and traditional worldviews all over the world are under review. African traditional worldviews have demanded that others be reconsidered. The situation is further complicated by the fact that none of the cultural symbols is at a standstill, though it is also a fact that the truths they symbolize have an enduring quality.

What I intend to do, therefore, is to highlight certain concepts which I believe an African would fall back on in the attempt to see the world whole. People who are keenly aware of and affected by the mass media, those who have lived or continue to live *expatriate*, those who have sampled life in human communities other than their own, or make periodic excursions into other human situations, are bound to learn at least one thing: that human-types are to be found all over the globe. My own experience confirms for me the Akan adage that *Nipa nyinaa ye Onyame mme*, or, as Paul says: "He has made of one (blood) all nations" (Acts 17:26). Humanity is one, but is the human community one?

For historical reasons, African politicians of the 1960s needed to promote the idea of the African personality to underline the full personhood of all African peoples which had been subverted by colonialism. There was need to demonstrate not only the full humanity and dignity of each person but also that the whole race on the continent is an inalienable part of the human race, that our heritage is part of the heritage of humanity and as such is not to be despised or subverted. It was an affirmation that the human race is one, having taken its origins from the one Deity. All this seems banal and insipid, but one ought to keep saying it for as long as we have institutionalized racism on this continent and elsewhere. Secondly, Africans, especially those who had been and are closely associated with white culture, have to a greater or lesser degree internalized that culture's attitudes to Africa. They have become paranoid and need mental liberation.

A very high percentage of the people on this continent (Africa) live close to nature and so keep uppermost in their consciousness the traditional assertion that the whole creation is one, that its source is the same one Deity, God. African myths of origins designate God as source of all that is. God is not only the ultimate source of all, but also the creator who is the "living-one", ever active in the world, attentive to our calls upon him and judge of the ways of humanity. Whether by fiat, by direct fashioning or moulding through an agent, it is God who is the reason for the existence of the whole cosmos. All these thoughts, as the scholars of traditional African religion point out, are native to the African soil and people.[1] The language and formulae in which they are communicated may smack of Christianity or Islam, but the thoughts are African. Thus, one can assert that, on the basis of African beliefs, a theology of the dependence upon God of all that exists can be constructed. This African belief in the divine origin of the universe is shared by Christianity and other religions. They originate from the innate feeling of dependence which is manifested in human beings all over the globe. Both human and non-human depend upon God. They are linked together by their common source and, just as Paul says, the delivery of the latter is dependent upon that of the former (Rom. 8:23). So the Akan believes that the pollution of the former results in the pollution of the latter.

Psychological and cultural types are worldwide, but geographical concentration of physical types is also a fact of experience. Most striking of the physical variation of human types is colour. I find the Indian sub-continent very interesting, containing as it does a Caucasian-type that varies in pigmentation from white to black. Does (or should) this fact of pigmentation create a variety of human being? Is a person with black skin and straight hair a different being from one with black skin and woolly hair? Do black dogs and white dogs see themselves as different beings? The question which, however trite, continues to be asked is: should a people's worth depend upon its pigmentation? Secondly, one should ask, is this variety not God-given? To both, the Akan would answer: "All are children of God; it is one's deeds that should condition one's deserts", for *nsem mmone nti na Nyankopon kyee din* (it is the fact of evil-doings which caused God to give each of us a name). In spite of our different physical types, the African will say we all come from the one God. God put us here, either as families or as the offsprings of a primordial couple. Even when we are fashioned or moulded individually by God or God's agent as the Yoruba say, it is God who endows us with our inner-being. The *Okra* (*inner*-being) and its *Nkrabea* (the mapped-out course of one's life—"destiny") are of God. In Igbo, for instance, the words for God and inner-being are related. The inner-being of a person is *Chi* while God is *Chukwu*, "Great Chi". In Yoruba one's *Ori* rules one's life just as God, *Orise*, rules the whole of the cosmos. Thus, inner-being, the reality of the human person, is seen as relating to God. Generally speaking, then, our human be-ing is associated with deity.[2] We exist because God exists; all power and existence derive from God and continue to exist because God permits. In some African myths, God is seen as being in close rapport with humanity—teaching, admonishing, blessing!

On this score there is not much that biblical theology can add; that worldview has simply confirmed what the African already knew, i.e. our creatureliness and our dependence upon deity, the fact that we did not make the cosmos. God is the common "ground" of all reality.

God, then, is the unifying factor of all creation, between human and non-human, between different types of human being whether the distinction is of pigmentation, of psychology or of culture. Moreover, the unity of humanity spans the whole of the race—the dead, the here and now and the not-yet-born.[3] One embodies in one's self both the past and the future of the race and, therefore, holds responsibility for both. The theology emanating out of traditional beliefs and Christianity agree on the basic point that all creation belongs to one scheme whose originator and controller is God.[4] God then is "above" all the divisions of sex, nationality, religion and race which we make so much of. God is not partisan except against that which shows disrespect to deity and contempt to creation.

The place of humanity within nature

There are Akan folk-tales of transmutation which tell of whole villages and groups of people having taken their origin through the transformation of primates into humans, and others telling of humans turning into non-human entities. On the whole, however, humans are seen as specially created, not given dominion over the rest of creation, but allowed to learn from them and to utilize what they can for their survival just as other creatures do. We human beings have no special place, for the rest of nature, too, is imbued with "spirit"; we are, therefore, to respect our co-creatures. Divinities, considered as agents of God, are also associated with natural phenomena. Thunder, to take an example, is a symbol of the anger of God. There is no creature which has no spirit of its own, or which cannot become the symbol of a spirit; trees, rivers and mountains become the habitation of spirits.

This association of unseen powers with nature generated in the African a deep respect for nature which contact with western science and technology is only now beginning to "demythologize". In the history of Christian missions in Africa, we have had controversy over the use of African drums in churches. The drum-maker has to "propitiate" the spirit of the tree, ask it to move elsewhere before he can fell it and use the log for his drum. The missionaries call it "paganism". But having seen a film of how forests in North America were flattened by a devilish chain device while native Americans stood by watching helplessly, I have come to understand why *each* try should be respected. This carnage could never have been perpetrated by Africans in "traditional" Africa, where taboos and customs safeguard social harmony as well as the links between humanity and the rest of nature.

Contrary to the Hebrew myth of origins, we, human beings, have not been given dominion over any part of creation; we are not even designated by God as "stewards". If we have to till the earth, we seek her permission; if we have to fish the seas and rivers, we seek their permission; if we have to fell trees, we do so because we need them. We explain that they will be useful to us, and the rest of creation "graciously" agrees to enable us to survive on them.[5] This makes the masterful, arrogant exploitation of nature by means of technology foreign to traditional African religious beliefs. It is the misinterpretation by theologians of Genesis 1:26, 28-30 which freed Christendom to embark on doctrines that liberated the human spirit from the fear of other spiritual powers that exist with us in God's universe.

It seems to me, however, that the propensity of the human spirit to consider itself the centre of creation is not foreign to African culture. We often tell with great delight the myth of God's departure. In the Akan myths, the women oppressed the sky with their enthusiastic pounding of *fufu*. They refused to heed the warnings of God who inhabited the sky in close proximity to human company. The Deity found this unbearable and moved the sky further up and beyond human reach. Instead of seeing this as a myth expressing the innermost feeling of the religious Akan, that God abhors the wanton exploitation of our physical resources, we tell this tale to show that it is women who have brought separation from God into human experience. One asks the question, for whom were the women pounding the *fufu* or taking chunks from the clouds to put into the soup pot? Or, the even more serious question, where were the men when all this was going on? We, that is men and women, are jointly responsible for the fact of sin, either by omission or commission. The same applies to our joint responsibility as human beings for the care of our environment. There is a lot in the pre-scientific view of our relation to nature that we need to examine and perhaps return to.

Myth and stewardship

It is becoming increasingly clear that western natural sciences can no longer be accepted as the last word in the study and utilization of nature; if they were, the researches into traditional healing methods and medicines would mean nothing and the popularization of acupuncture would not hit the headlines. The return to ecological chaos is evidence that somewhere down the line we humans took a wrong turn; instead of collaborating with God, we now seem determined to return the eco-system to the chaos out of which God rescued it and created us. What then is our place in nature? A little lower than the *elohim*? In traditional religion, both human beings and the *elohim*, who are the messengers of God, are dependent upon God. Both we and they share in a "community of spiritual being".

Thus, we can even interact in such a way that we "order" them to do things for us or to carry messages to God. We and they are both dependent upon the physical world. For some of the *elohim*, their "abode" is in something physical, while we humans develop our technology on the basis of our ability to utilize the physical world. In the last resort, humans, the *elohim* and physical nature depend upon God. Human beings are *part* of the ecological system and swim or sink with it.

Some of the coastal peoples of Ghana have yearly festivals built around the necessity to dredge the lagoons to allow their waters to flow into the sea, thus giving them renewed life. If this is neglected, the lagoon simply rots away and the fish with it. Several of the agricultural festivals have the effect of regulating planting and harvesting. Among the Akans, rest days are provided weekly for rivers, seas and the earth to give their spirits some peace at least once a week. This provides mutual rest for both human beings and nature. Here once again is the Pauline doctrine of our common destiny with the rest of nature (Rom. 8:23).

To the Akan, our relation to creation, and our place within it, are humble, but that does not diminish our responsible stewardship of nature; indeed it heightens it, for the God who knows the fall of each sparrow is the same who knows the number of hairs on our heads (Matt. 10:29, Luke 12:6), the one who, according to the Akan, also calls each of us by name. It is through the spirit of nature that prayer and praise and thanksgiving go up to God, although nothing prevents a direct cry to God in African traditional religion. Our exegesis of "the beginnings" will be incomplete without this respect for the rest of creation. We must seek nature's cooperation to survive, but we cannot exploit it ruthlessly and then hope to survive. The taboos and customs relating to our utilization of nature's resources, and the yearly festivals and sacrifices associated with them, serve as memorials of our dependence on nature and, beyond nature, God.

The living-together and interdependence of all created things indicate an indispensable "covenant" which is honoured in traditional Africa. If anything has "changed", it is the relation between humans and God. We have begun to take God for granted, interpreting his ever-nearness and tolerance of us as weakness until, according to the Akan, God has had to move "beyond our reach", though still near enough to hear when called. It is the same refusal to observe "limits" that caused God to drive human beings out of the primordial garden (Gen. 3:1-6). Both the Hebrew and the Akan myths could do with the truth of the Christian "Emmanual myth", God living among us once again. This, perhaps, is one of the un-expressed attractions of Christianity as against Akan traditional beliefs. In that traditional worldview, an impasse had been reached which calls for a "new beginning".

History and theology

We have seen how the human community as a unit in creation is closely related to, and interacts with, the rest of creation. As a human community, in spite of the variety of our physical make-up and the environments we inhabit, we have declared ourselves children of the one God. This "article of faith", however, is not transparent in human relations. We have not only exploited and disturbed the eco-system, we have exploited, and continue to exploit, those who are "different", often with the same type of disruptive effect as we have had on nature. Take any human society made up of the same physical type—Nigeria, for example, where all citizens are more or less "black", where there are few immigrants and few with "mixed blood". Take the smallest village, where it is possible to eliminate all "mixtures", and you find human relations that have arisen from the acceptance of hierarchical principles or ascribed positions. Take South Africa and you have a microcosm of human relations that has repudiated the belief in one human being.

In contemporary Africa (and, by extension, the world) the division between rich and poor is a painful fact. We discuss the problem with good intention, but acts of sharing are most difficult to come by. Perhaps we could return to the abandoned theology of sacrifice. I believe, for instance, that the acceptance by African women of a lot of what some western women decry is the outcome of an ethic based on the traditional belief in the benefit to the community of sacrifice. Sacrifice, however, should not be the prerogative of a sector of the human community. Taken seriously, a theology of sacrifice could lead to a number of reforms in the style of life of individuals as well as whole societies. A style that is less wasteful and more mindful of humanity's stewardship of life and ultimate dependence upon God might be evolved. The theology which centres on the cross of Christ has in African Christianity become a liability. It either breeds a Christianity devoid of the ethical demands of building up the community or one that sacralizes imposed suffering as the will of God. Voluntary poverty and consciously accepted limitations, arising out of the acceptance of the life-style of Christ, become a pretext for asking *others* to accept in inhuman conditions.

African traditional religion, too, places a high premium on sacrifice as a means of rectifying damage done. I believe, therefore, that the core of the matter is: do we or do we not accept that the existence of rich and poor is an anomalous situation that ought to be corrected? A Nigerian adage which has it that all fingers are not equal, enables people to conclude that inequalities are normal, inevitable and need not be challenged. Yet few will boldly and openly espouse a political theory based on this popular saying. In fact, the traditional assumption and practice is that the stronger will aid and protect the weaker. Provisions for ensuring this are woven into the fabric of society. All should have enough of the basics of food, shelter and clothing through sharing. The problem is that this sense of communal responsibility has been eroded or neutralized by changes in the society. Increased plurality and mobility, the very fact of the increase in the variety, quality and nature of people's requirements has rendered traditional solutions ineffective. Transferred to the international scene, the problems become so complicated as to defy solution, not to talk of a relevant theology. All in all, solutions based on individual conversion seem to stand less chance of being effective than those based on a communal approach. Individuals will share goods, maybe skills, but not power.

In the development of Christian social teaching we have tried a variety of theological bases, "charity" (misinterpreted as almsgiving), "justice" (righteous living before God), "stewardship" (based on the thesis that all we claim properly belongs to God), etc. A theology of the cross as a symbol of the power of powerlessness and sacrificial love may be in order. It is my view that the time has come to try "sacrifice". "Greater love has no one than to let go of life, that the other might live" (John 15:13). This is asking those who have economic power to voluntarily share power, prestige, privilege, to die a little that others might live a little more fully; it raises the whole question of power in society. At the moment many would rather be corrupted absolutely by power than divest themselves of an ounce of it. A more realistic approach, I believe, would be to question the purpose of its use. Traditional African religions would affirm the belief that God hates injustice and exploitation among mortals. The Akans would say "beneficience" is the core of the good life, and yet these lofty ideas remain unattainable dreams.

Another theological parameter for attempting to arrive at some ethical base for dealing with socio-economic problems may be the concept of covenant relations, both on the interpersonal as well as on the political level. Covenants and oaths play a very significant role in Africa, just as they do in biblical theology. Strictly speaking, absolute political power is foreign to traditional Akan society, for between the ruler and the ruled there is always a reciprocal oath-taking.[6] This is not to say that the Akan and others who share this covenant-based politics have not produced their share of the world's despots. What I am suggesting is that there are a lot of existing international, commercial and economic agreements which ought to be re-examined. There are others that call for implementation. "Covenants" between some African nations and the multinational corporations that exploit their resources leave a lot to be desired. The terms of the "covenants" between employee and employer need to be re-enacted to reflect our renewed awareness of the humanity of the "other". Between the rich and the poor there ought to be a covenant of partnership, not that between the powerful and the powerless, for we now understand the dynamics of the creation of poverty a bit more.

The dynamism of symbols

The eucharist among other things is a covenant meal, a symbol of our acceptance of communal responsibility and sharing. In traditional Africa, an ordinary meal eaten by hand from one earthenware bowl by relations and friends is a common sight. In rural Ghana, strangers who all are invited to eat, but genuinely do not need to eat, decline politely with the words "our hands are in it". In other parts of Africa, what is shared may be colanuts; those who do not wish to eat them will still symbolically touch them. Even in the refusal to literally partake is woven a meaning of participation, a sign of accompanying the primary actors.[7]

That is what the eucharist means for me, a family meal to which even "strangers" are invited and from which none is expected to abstain unless he or she does not wish the family well. The holy communion should function as a symbol of Christian unity and Christian responsibility towards the world. It is for me not only a symbol of the relationship between the individual Christian and God but also the relationship of one Christian to another. It can be, moreover, a symbol of the unity of all humanity if we believe that Christ is significant for all peoples. In this way the eucharist becomes a symbol of the hope that we shall experience this unity even here on earth, and that all will come to recognize the sovereignty of God over all creation.

Those who have dipped fingers into the same bowl, have shared the same colanut, have "broken bread" together, or are made to drink of one Spirit (1 Cor. 12:13) are united by a common bond. Christians condemn the actions of Judas as revolting and in traditional Africa those who have drunk the same spirit dare not indulge in acts of betrayal.[8] The oaths we take at international meetings by voting and signing conventions we often do not honour, yet all human beings share the one human spirit that is of God. These symbols seem to have lost their dynamism, though we have not given up on their meaning. The tensions within races, classes, ethnic groups and nations may be seen as resulting from the struggle to survive versus the struggle to maintain the highest possible standards of life and comfort in this process. We seem unable to operate as those whose destinies are bound together. Life among traditional Akan is understood primarily as life-in-community. Hence the concept of individual success or failure is alien or at best secondary. This makes one's sense of belonging a very important factor in one's self-estimation. But this does not mean that the society was or is tension-free. Tensions, both inter- and intra-group, are facts of human life. What is important is that tension is recognized as negating unity, community and also our common humanity. Among the Akan, therefore, long processes of negotiation, diplomatic language, compensation for wrongs sustained, etc. are devised for the management of tension. It seems to me that, in our perplexity concerning the brokenness of the human community, we have not paid enough attention to the search for means for the creative management of the various tensions that plague our human community.

Viewed from this particular cultural perspective, one could delineate various sources of brokenness. From a global perspective, the kaleidoscope becomes bewildering. History and environment have joined together to bring about a variety of worldviews and styles of life. These manifest themselves in beliefs and practices, some of which are quite peculiar to the various peoples and localities, others of which are more or less universal or seek to be so, but which nonetheless cause brokenness in the human community. Our search, then, is for what will renew or boost our innate acceptance of the one human community with all its positive aspects of diversity, and for what will divest the community of all that endangers its survival. In this search, no part of our human experience can be excluded by some *a priori* determined by a section of the community.

In Africa whole nations have successfully divested themselves of political colonialism and are actively evolving political institutions that they hope will result in justice, peace and stability for all. In the experiments all known forms, especially those considered to be particularly reflective of traditional African ideas and values, are being incorporated. The economic order that entered with colonialism has proved most intractable, but it is also a fact that none but the beneficiaries of the north-south economic imbalance are satisfied with the system. Young and old in Africa as elsewhere actively protest against the devaluation of their humanity on account of their colour. This protest is not new. The minute whites showed signs of arrogance based on thinking of themselves as a superior human-type, the blacks bristled. Bold protest, a sign of moral consciousness, is what preserved the black in Africa. The attempts to develop an alienated consciousness never succeeded. Deep in the consciousness of every human being is what Genesis has described as our special relation to God. Created in the image of God, we dare not succumb to life at an inferior level.[9] Never in Africa was it forgotten that the difference between black and white is but skin deep. If a white man is in dire need, he will speak the language of the African, goes a popular Ghanaian saying. To be human being is to be human, there is only one humanity.

The mission of the Church

Religion and ideology, factors which have a tendency to be missionary, are as fraught with the danger of being as disruptive as economic considerations, if not more. Both religion and ideology seek adherents among all peoples and in all climes. Further, while all ideologies have a tendency to ally themselves with particular economic systems, only some have built into them an anti-religious stance; others maintain a more or less neutral attitude to religion. Both Europeans and their African collaborators are beginning to realize that the ideological options hewed out in Europe do not seem to fit the African bill. Yet the super-powers continue to make Africa the battleground for their own favourite worldviews.

Realistic ideology for Africa would have to be one based on *survival* at a level and style that do not conflict with our self-esteem as children of God. This pragmatism and pro-life stance may be our hope for promoting community in Africa and, hopefully, universally.[10] The community building propensities of ideologies are limited, but religion does not seem to do any better. Those that operate in Africa seem designed to bring about division. Christianity vies with Islam and both are teamed up against the indigenous expressions of religion. Within Christianity and Islam is to be found an infinite variety of emphases.

The Church, if it has any mission at all, is to call all human beings into a faith-relation with God, a relationship which is the outcome of an absolute trust in the beneficient source of all life, including human life. It is to demonstrate the unity of the human community that has taken its origin from the one God who has many names. It is this mission that makes it mandatory that the Church demonstrate how diversity and variety may be handled in such a way that they become a blessing. I have indicated above how some community-building concepts which are present in both Christianity and traditional Akan worldview may be promoted.

On the level of ideas, the Church is rich with such as should revolutionalize the world of human relations, but somehow she is at her most unconvincing when she talks of unity. She is in the world to witness to the love of God and to demonstrate love among humanity, without which St John says we cannot honestly claim to love God. The love which resulted in the incarnation is meant to save us from a life without love. Practical acts of solidarity with those who suffer (and they are to be found all over the world) are expected of the Church. The Church has the duty to "accompany" those who suffer in their struggle for liberation, bearing with them the cross they bear and thus being a part of the constant combat against the chaos to which we threaten to return the earth. Poverty, ethnicity and racism are chaos generators that pollute community life in Africa and in relation to which the Church has demonstrated concern by performing acts of mercy towards the victims. The real problem, however, lies in the eradication of these forces that work against the solidarity of the human race. It is a challenge to build a reconciled human community in Africa, but reconciliation is not to be achieved without sacrifice. Human community continues to lack powerful symbols and signs of what such a reconciled community would look like. It is this that the Church based on the life of the triune God could become. The Church's self-image includes that of being a "sign of God's reconciling love for all humanity". We have to admit, however, that disunity has made her an inadequate sign.

In the worldview of the Akan, evil is a reality. Wrongs done, taboos broken and acts of beneficience left undone release a pollutant into the atmosphere which affects not only human community but also the rest of nature. A realistic attitude towards the power of evil is necessary since evil is cumulative and strong; evil materializes, takes body in structures of injustice and oppression and has to be *exorcized*. As there exist coalitions for evil, the Church and all who believe in humanity as being made in the image of God do have a duty to get into coalitions for good, that which alone combats the chaos of lovelessness.

The Church's professed unity

For the sake of the Church's mission, we cannot be over-critical concerning her own brokenness and disunity. In Africa the variety in the expressions of Christianity is more apparent than the ideal of the Church as being one. Visible unity, of course, will make the Church's claims more credible and her works of liberation and reconciliation more effective. She will be more believable in Africa. To proffer unity and community as viable without making any attempt to manifest even a semblance of it in one's own life will be to witness to a lie. Serving in a human community that is torn by so much variety, one would expect to see the Church operate in such a way that her own diversity becomes a blessing to herself so that it might become so to the continent. Her visible unity will strengthen in Africa the hope that the various dis-unifying principalities and powers will be conquered and that her people will reap the fruits of reconciliation. Unity is for the sake of faith. For the world to believe that God sent Christ, the Christian community must be united. The Church's claim to *de facto* unity is based on having Christ as the founder centre of the Church's preaching and life. But Christ comes alive to the African only as the Church becomes more of a living Christ in what she says and does and is.

Unity in diversity

As one Church with diversified structures and practices, as well as different emphases on aspects of doctrine, our life together could be a symbol of the unity of the human community and could even provide guide posts of actual community-building.

It is in this regard that I consider the doctrine of the Trinity rele-vant for our contemporary theological search. The metaphysics of it apart, it can be visualized as a way of be-ing and living in com-munity.

In the traditional religion of Akan, it is the very nature of God to delegate powers, though at the same time remaining actively involved in the workings of the cosmos. But human beings who lay claim to being specially related to God do not seem to know how to operate in this way. A study of some of the glimpses of God that Christians attempt to express in the doctrine of *communicatio idiomatum* may be relevant here. The element of mutual *perichoresis*, highlighted by Mar Osthathios at Bangalore, may enable us to break the chains of insularity and self-seeking which are a bane to our life together.

In the gospels, we find the teaching that it is in losing our lives that we find life. Jesus' faith, his perspective on life, precludes self-seeking. Here is a reassessment of the importance of self (the unit within the plurality) which demands a radical reinterpretation of salvation and security. When we are able to admit that others have something valid to contribute, we shall admit the necessity for a participatory style of life. We shall replace the struggle to succeed on one's own with cooperative efforts. What our doctrine of the Trinity demands is that we as a Church function in such a way that, while not being submerged as a unit within her, there will exist a concerted atmosphere in which one can live for all and all for one. In the doctrine we attempt to give an expression to how "several centres' consciousness are integrated with, and related to, one another".[11] We find the persons in constant and perfect mutual relationship, and we are reminded of the need for properly adjusted relationships in our human families, institutions and nations. Moreover, Leonard Hodgson asks us to see the doctrine of the Trinity as "a distinction of person with a closeness of unity characteristic of modes of existence".[12] In this way both the unity and diversity in a community will be seen as being equally important. In the doctrine is epitomized the shared responsibility repudiated by man (the male) in both the Akan and the Hebrew versions of the origin of sin. This demands that the Church's lifestyle be seen to approximate that of Jesus who was absolutely dependent upon God. His perspective was the outcome of a radical departure from the wisdom of this world. Store not treasures for yourself, the motive of your good works should not be directed towards obtaining public acclaim. Forgive. Living and dying is to be directed towards life for others. It is only then that we can turn "the world" upside down.

Jesus envisaged the Christian community as a microcosm of human life lived in faith, God's laboratory for the demonstration of the unity of human community.

Unity in action, towards and on behalf of the world, will be a necessary yardstick by which the Church's faith in her own unity will be judged. Just as the unity of the activities of the Godhead *ad extra* confirms for the Christian the unity of God, so it is hoped that, inspite of real "personalities", individual Christian communities will affect the world in such a way that oneness of the Church will become not only an article of faith for Christians but a factor of hope for the world.

A testimony

I have in this essay presented my belief in the presence of God in the culture and beliefs of my own people (the Akan of Ghana), not as a preparation for the gospel but as part of God's "religious education process" which has been confirmed and fulfilled by the living experience of those who actually experienced the Christ in those far-off days and lands. I have tried to give expression to my faith that the whole religious experience of Africa, including the Christian experience, is part of God's education of the whole of humanity. Finally, I have tried to present my faith in the importance of the Church not just for individual edification, not just for the sake of correcting the brokenness of humanity worldwide, but also as a sign that the innate feeling of dependence present in us is not just some hangover, and that our yearning for true community is not just a chimera but the reality towards which God directs the human spirit.

NOTES

[1] Basil Davidson, *Which Way Africa*, Penguin, 1971, p. 33; E.B. Idowu, *African Traditional Religion—a Definition*, London, SCM, 1973, pp. 103-106.

[2] I have dealt with this in some detail in a paper delivered at the intercultural Bible Study Forum of the 1979 meeting of United Presbyterian Women, Purdue, USA. See excerpts of "In the Image of God... a Theological Reflection from an African Perspective", in *Concern*, Spring 1980, p. 51.

[3] Basil Davidson, *op. cit.*, p. 32, quotes a Nigerian leader as saying in 1912: "I conceive that land belongs to a vast family of which many are dead, few are living, and countless members are unborn." This idea is attested throughout black Africa.

4 Harry Sawyer, *God: Ancestor or Creator?* London, Longmans, 1970, p. 105.

5 J.S. Mbiti, *The Prayers of African Religion*, London, SPCK, 1975, pp. 62-73, 107-108, e.g. p. 5 "O river, I beg leave to take fish in".

6 R.S. Ratray, *Ashanti Law and Constitution*, Oxford, OUP, 1929, p. 82.

7 The role of the Orthodox bishop sitting behind me, while I stood receiving the elements during the eucharist service held at the Nairobi assembly, is an experience that will not be easily rationalized. See also ed. Brian Hearne, CSSP (1980), *Living Worship in Africa Today*, Spearhead No. 62, Eldoret, Kenya, Gaba Publications, pp. 54-57.

8 E.B. Idowu, Olodumare, *God in Yoruba Belief*, London, Longmans, 1966, pp. 149-153.

9 F.L. Bartels, *Methodism in Ghana*, Ghana, CUP Methodist Book Dept. Ltd., 1965, p. 19, describes how at the death of Dunwell the Cape Coast Bible class resolved to remain in their new profession for "though the missionary was dead, God lives".

10 See the political philosophies of Nkrumah, Nyerere, Kaunda.

11 David Brown, *The Divine Trinity*, Sheldon Press, 1969, p. 60.

12 Leonard Hodgson, "The Doctrine of the Trinity: Some Further Thoughts", *Journal of Theological Studies*, New Series Vol. V, part I, 1954, p. 54.

The unity of the Church and the renewal of human community

JOHN DESCHNER

My task is to provide an introduction for our work here at Lima on the theme "The Unity of the Church and the Renewal of Human Community".

I should explain that I think I am a late substitute for Jan Lochman, who led our preparatory thinking on this theme. I have not personally been involved in it this time, but did know some of the historical background. I think that is why I was asked, and also why I was gently but explicitly instructed to give a practical and historical introduction, and not to theologize on my own.

My remarks will fall under three heads: (1) the proposed study here at Lima; (2) some lessons from the long history of our struggle with this theme in Faith and Order; and (3) some suggestions about the future role of this theme in Faith and Order and in the World Council.

The proposed study at Lima

The aim of the study is quite simply to ask us to pay more attention to the broader location of our Church unity work: not simply to our location among divided churches, but to the location of our churches in a divided world. From the beginning Faith and Order

• Prof. JOHN DESCHNER, United Methodist Church, is professor of theology at the Perkins School of Theology, Southern Methodist University, Dallas, Texas, USA.

has been asked far too often: Why are you so abstract? What is the relevance of your work? And, from the beginning, Faith and Order has struggled to formulate its answer in terms something like those of our theme.

But please note: the first and specific concern of Faith and Order, as of the World Council itself, is always "to call the churches to the goal of visible unity". We are not talking about a new basic concern, but about "a broader horizon" within which this Church unity concern remains our first and constitutive vocation. With that emphasis presupposed, we have a bi-polar theme: the unity of the Church *and* the renewal of human community.

Much has been said about method and process in this study. As far as I can see, there are two essential points here. The first is that the Church unity pole and the human community pole must be inter-related in such a way that each aspect is rightly respected and emphasized, and yet throws its distinctive light upon the other. Various terms have been used for this methodological principle in the past: "inter-contextual", "dialectical", "reciprocal" "double dynamic"; our preparatory paper calls it an "inter-relational method". Here, of course, our debates will strike fire; here lie the inescapable theological issues of the study.

The second methodological point is newer. The preparatory paper asks for a study which relates engagement and reflection—indeed local engagement and local reflection. The emphasis on *local* participation is emphatic. That obviously points beyond our work here at Lima. It looks towards the design of a continuing study in which theological reflection is permitted to grow in local "situational integrity".

For our actual work here at Lima, the preparatory paper organizes a kind of foretaste of that longer range study under five sub-topics. And, when you look at them, the preliminary character of our meeting is obvious, for these "sub-topics" appear to be very large indeed. So our real task here at Lima is not to *finish* but to *start* this study, to design its beginnings, to provide guidelines, and beyond that—perhaps—to initiate those Old Testament spies who returned with a sample of the grapes to be harvested in Canaan.

I have to confess that I myself got a better idea of the concreteness of the sub-topics from an earlier stage in our preparations. For whatever it may be worth to you, this is how I understood them:

1. *Creation:* The point here is the cosmological context of our Church unity concern. The focus is upon nature (e.g. ecological issues), and the inter-relations of Church unity, science and technology. I would say this theme asks about how Faith and Order work relates to the work of the MIT conference on "Faith, Science and the Future".

2. *History:* Here political and economic issues are focal. We are concerned with divisions between poor and rich, problems of power in human community, tensions between races, classes, nations—and all these as inter-related with our concern for Church unity. This is one place where I hope that Faith and Order can think about "the church of the poor".

3. *Culture:* Here our focus is the various diverse cultural and religious contexts of our concern for Church unity. Does not much (not all!) of our work on sexism and Church unity (the results of the Sheffield conference) also belong here?

4. *Alienation:* Here the sharp focus of our earlier discussion seems to have become somewhat blunted. Our original intention was to fix upon at least one quite specific context and see if it might not be as fruitful as the more general topics in other groups (as "the handicapped" proved to be at Louvain ten years ago), or even more so. Our idea was the quite specific topic of alienation *between the generations*, between parents and children, as exemplified by the squatters' movements in European cities, or in some of the counter-cultural movements. I hope this fairly specific focus will not be lost.

5. *Mission:* It was the challenge of the Melbourne conference and its theme "Thy Kingdom Come" which we wanted Faith and Order to look at here. Does the kingdom theme offer the most fruitful ground for inter-relating Church unity and human community?

So much for our work here at Lima. The result ten days from now should be some good guidelines for a continuation of this study, and perhaps a brief statement on the theme for the Vancouver assembly to use.

Some lessons from recent history

You have certainly realized by now that this is no new theme in Faith and Order. It is, in fact, one of our oldest themes. We have studied it many times and in many ways. In fact we published in late 1978 a 240-page book, *Unity in Today's World*, in which Geiko Müller-Fahrenholz sums up ten years of Faith and Order study on "The Unity of the Church and the Unity of Human-kind".

Why are we considering a new study? There are two reasons, I think. First, this study is not finished, indeed it may not be finishable. We have always acknowledged that. Moreover, the current situation is changing fast and full of new questions: an earlier, essentially western way of formulating the problem is being increasingly challenged by the Orthodox, by women and by the third world. The second reason is that the WCC's Central Committee has repeatedly asked us to pursue this study. The WCC has begun to hear a contribution from Faith and Order about which it wants to hear more. We have a new and expectant audience for our results.

So it becomes all the more important for us to review our past work and to learn the lessons hidden in it. Let me ask you, then, to use your memories a bit.

1. I would speak of three periods. The first is pre-Uppsala (1968). Here the topic we are studying was thematized again and again as the "Church-world" problem, and that was assumed to be primarily a problem for theological research and formulation. The roots go back to the 1920s as the Faith and Order and Life and Work movements parallelled each other and moved towards their unification at Amsterdam under the comprehensive theme "Man's Disorder and God's Design". Was it a unification? Or was it an institutionalization of the parallel? Hardly yet a unification. This was a time when Faith and Order spoke of the secular context as a source of "non-theological factors". The Church unity work moved ahead towards that remarkable New Delhi (1961) statement about the nature of the unity we seek, and the Montreal (1963) documents about Tradition and traditions. Meanwhile, the secular concern moved through "the responsible society" work of the forties and fifties to the Geneva conference on "Church and Society" in 1966, subtitled "Christians in the Technical and Social Revolutions of Our Time".

But there was obviously a gap, and there were earnest attempts to bridge it. The eschatological theme of the 1950s was the first such attempt. And then, the WCC sponsored a ponderous theological project in the mid-sixties on "The Finality of Jesus

Christ in the Age of Universal History". In Faith and Order itself, Montreal 1963 asked for a study on "Creation and Redemption" which would move beyond ecclesiology and christology to the question "How is Christ Lord of the world?", and which would bring theologians and scientists together in interdisciplinary discussion. This study never really took off. Two small groups of theologians (interdisciplinary dialogue with scientists never materialized!) produced two weighty theological documents on "God in Nature and History". Our Bristol Commission meeting in 1968 received them and immediately commissioned another study on "Man in Nature and History". Somehow it was felt that this would open up "a new area of enquiry". The initiating questions sound strangely familiar to us now: "What is the function of the Church in relation to the unifying purpose of God for the world?... What, then, is the relation of the churches' quest for unity among themselves to the hope for the unity of mankind?" [1]

It is worth remarking that the theological debate over natural theology dominated the entire discussion of the Church-world issue during this period, and not too fruitfully; there were two documents at Bristol because of two different approaches to *this* problem.

It is also important to note that although Roman Catholic participation in Faith and Order was still in the future, Vatican II had greatly enriched the discussion with its two constitutions: *Lumen gentium* on ecclesiology and *Gaudium et spes* on the Church in the modern world.

In general, in this pre-Uppsala period, Faith and Order faced our theme as a theological problem to be dealt with by international commissions producing theological documents on various aspects of the Church-world problem. The obvious question is: Is such a study procedure good enough?

2. The second period in Faith and Order's study of our theme is the decade 1968-1978. Bristol's proposal to study "Man in Nature and History" was transformed into our explicit study on "The Unity of the Church and the Unity of Humankind".

And then, the Uppsala assembly (1968) gave our work a decisive impulse (a good example of how necessary it is that Faith and Order belongs to the WCC). "We are in agreement with the decision of the Faith and Order Commission", it said, "... to pursue its study programme on the unity of the Church in the wider context of the study of the unity of mankind and of creation. We welcome at the same time the statement of the Faith and Order Commission that its task remains 'to proclaim the oneness of the Church of Jesus Christ'". And then, in its most famous single sentence, Uppsala gave us an important clue for our study: "The Church is bold", it said, "in speaking of itself as the sign of the coming unity of mankind".[2] That sentence may be a sign of Vatican II's influence upon the World Council, for *Lumen gentium*'s famous sentence had said: "The Church is a kind of sacrament or sign of intimate union with God, and of the unity of all mankind" (*Lumen gentium*, 1). Uppsala's accent was more eschatological ("the coming unity..."), but the agreement was profound.

The story of that decade-long study is instructive, both positively and negatively, for our task here. It began with the drafting of a rather substantial study guide dealing with biblical, historical, systematic, ecclesiological and ecumenical considerations. That took a year, and the Canterbury Standing Commission (1969) then approved its use with some interesting warnings against triumphalism, and against minimizing the diversity of situations, both ecclesiastical and secular. It also remarked that the most searching challenge to Church unity today may be the division between those who embody the priestly mission of reconciliation, on the one hand, and the prophetic mission of rebuking evil and making militant cause against it, on the other.[3] In that warning lay a hint of the agonizing ecumenical problem of polarization soon to come, a problem Faith and Order has done too little with.

Two main kinds of study then developed. First, a number of local study groups took up the study. Several attempts were also made to create interdisciplinary study groups. These groups produced a mass of material, and one of the serious weaknesses of the study was that this local work was never adequately used, and remains buried in Geneva archives. (Some was published in *Study Encounter*, and Geiko Müller-Fahrenholz made a sensitive review and appraisal of some of it several years later.) As far as I am aware, this local work never adequately entered into the mainstream of the Commission's study. There lies a warning to us.

The second main line of work was carried out internationally, in the Commission itself. The topic became the theme for the 1971

Commission meeting (Louvain). The groups in that meeting studied Church unity in five secular contexts, somewhat similar to our procedure here. These were: (1) the struggle for justice, (2) the encounter with living faiths, (3) the struggle against racism, (4) the handicapped in society, and (5) differences in culture. Almost no documentation came out of these discussions—that is doubtless a weakness—but it is nevertheless strangely true that these groups became a kind of high water-mark for the study and had a wide influence on Faith and Order's thinking. As for the general debate at Louvain, it emphasized the need for greater care and clarity in using the "intercontextual method", and asked for much more rigorous interdisciplinarity. But, in my memory, the most prophetic point made was José Miguez's question: "*Where* is the theologian placed who can think or write this theology?" Until then we had assumed that interconfessional commissions, although each member had a church "location", nevertheless could produce universally valid theological results. Miguez seriously questioned whether "universal" commissions could "transcend" class, nation, race, sex, and produce universally valid theology on this topic. He asked for a method which would take secular as well as ecclesial location seriously. That called our whole study procedure into question, though we didn't fully realize it at the time. And therein lies an important lesson for us.

After Louvain—that is, four years into the study—we began to work on a sort of consolidating phase: clarifying concepts, developing a theological document, publishing results. In fairness, it should be said that other studies—Account of Hope, Conciliar Fellowship—were claiming major attention. The Utrecht Standing Commission (1972) asked for a summary document. Zagorsk (1973) criticized an attempted summary and asked for clarification of several themes: the notions of "human interdependence" and "mankind", the concept of the Church as mystery and sign, the relation between the Church's unity and diversity, the bearing of our topic on the growing theme of conciliar fellowship. The most important emphasis at Zagorsk, though, was its protest against superficial notions of "the unity of humankind" or triumphalist claims about the Church as "sign". Zagorsk asked for sobriety and realism.

The next Plenary Commission at Accra (1974) attempted to conclude and appraise the study after six years of work. The documentary work was noted and remanded to Geiko Müller-Fahrenholz for a summary book. The main decision, though, was actually a creative step: that this study could continue fruitfully only by collaborative work with other units of the WCC, facing the Church unity questions in other agendas. Such concrete "intercontextual" work did continue and produced very fruitful results indeed. In late 1975 collaborative work with the Programme to Combat Racism produced a valuable booklet, *Racism in Theology and Theology Against Racism*. (Racism provided, from the beginning of the study, the clearest and most concrete "intercontextual" issue.) In 1978, from another collaborative effort, there appeared *Partners in Life: the Handicapped and the Church*. Valuable collaborative theological work has also been done with the sub-units on Dialogue, on Inter-Church Aid and on Church and Society. Certainly the most substantial collaborative outgrowth of our study, though, was the large study on "The Community of Women and Men in the Church" whose results are before us here in Lima. Thus, if one judges results in other ways than simple production of documents, the turn towards collaborative work at Accra produced much fruit. This theme flourishes best in concrete contexts.

There was one modest documentary outcome of Accra which has been too little noticed, I think. The Plenary Commission produced on the spot its own short statement entitled "Towards Unity in Tension" to be submitted as a contribution to the Nairobi assembly of the WCC. I am not aware that the statement ever appeared there (unless in preparatory materials)—and therein surely lies an admonition for us to use our channels with greater care. But that three-page statement deserves re-study. Its importance is twofold: (1) It develops a very necessary and useful set of distinctions for the term "humankind". There is, first, *human inter-relatedness*, a sheer fact of modern life with both positive and negative aspects. Satellite communications exemplify "inter-relatedness". There is, second, a more ideological term, "the just interdependence of free people", a positive secular, utopian vision of the human possibility. There is third an eschatological *unity* of humankind, the unity not of the Church simply, but of the kingdom to which all are called. Some such distinctions are needed in any study of this theme. (2) The second contribution is the attempt to speak of a Church unity which can include not simply diversity but conflict, a "unity in tension" and even a "fellowship in darkness" under the cross among those committed to human liberation. That realism about the theme was a growing emphasis as the study progressed. Naive optimism faded; there was readiness to see the Church as the sign of God's judgment as well as God's promise, and willingness to face what Canterbury in 1969 had already predicted as our deepest ecumenical problem: Christian polarization as we participate in the renewal of human community. That polarization was present at Uppsala and Nairobi and will be at Vancouver. The beginning made in Accra's short statement deserves development.

By Nairobi (1975) another Faith and Order theme, "conciliar fellowship", was our primary contribution. But the Church-humanity topic provided the principal concept and content for the middle part of the Section II report, "What Unity Requires", where Church unity is viewed in relation to the handicapped, the community of women and men, the problem of organization and personal community, political struggle, and cultural diversity. The paragraphs on political controversy as a Church unity issue are noteworthy today.

The formal end of our specific study came in 1978 with the publication of the summary book *Unity in Today's World*.

3. Why speak of a third period (1977-present)? Because the topic, though studied for ten years, was still very much alive in other studies and because by now the WCC as a whole was hearing it and asking for more.

This is not the place to recount the rise of the Baptism, Eucharist and Ministry (BEM) and Hope studies, although it can be noted that taken together they deal with the two aspects of our topic: BEM advancing the classic Church unity concern, and the Account of Hope study focused upon Christian witness in the many diverse secular situations. Both concerns draw inspiration from the Church-humankind study. Without it the Bangalore "Common Account of Hope" would have been impossible. And without the presence of this intercontextual theme, many in Faith and Order itself would have been reluctant to give so much hard work and thought to the BEM studies.

But that only makes it more appropriate to take up the topic quite explicitly again here. It has proved its power to integrate and inspire our work. It has been, more than most of us realize, a means of deepening the relation of Faith and Order to other units in the WCC and to the Council as a whole. Vancouver asks to hear more about it. And quite matter-of-factly, the present situation asks us quite fresh questions about it.

The future of this theme in Faith and Order

1. First, a modest, almost technical point: If there is to be a major new study, it needs a better design than the last one.

Unless we are careful, there is a traditional design which will assert itself. It has four points: a preparatory document, local study groups, a plenary commission meeting on the theme, and a summary book. Is that enough? Is that relevant?

In self-criticism, I think it could be said that our earlier study did not take adequate account of the long pre-history of the discussion. Again, it started up considerable local study but did not find ways to make full use of it. Again, the interdisciplinary aspect scarcely got off the ground. Or again, the aim and goal of the study was perhaps never sufficiently defined; it was clear that it aimed to enlarge the perspectives of Faith and Order's own thinking, but its aim for the life of the WCC, of the member churches, and of "humankind" was less clear.

Positively, it needs to be said that the study made a sort of initial breakthrough from Faith and Order theologizing to collaborative work with other WCC units. Further, although the documentary aspect was minimal, it did generate a good deal of interest and thinking beyond Faith and Order, locally and in the WCC: enough, certainly, to raise the question whether document production ought to be so central in Faith and Order work.

Finally—and this may be its greatest achievement—it did advance the claim that the Church unity concern is the heart of the entire WCC agenda.

So what can we learn from this for the future? Several things: the crucial importance of local study fully utilized, the necessity of collaborative work within the WCC, the need for interdisciplinary work, the importance of relating this theme integrally to other Faith and Order themes, the need for careful use of WCC channels in order to speak effectively within the Central Committee and the assembly. All that and more can be learned.

2. But that is not enough. We need to analyze where we are in the development of this theme in the WCC as a whole, for this

theme will compel us to face the fresh forms of the Church unity problem in the WCC. Let me over-simplify to make the point. From the 1920s to the 1940s there was a parallelism of the two parts of the theme, but a realization also that the inseparability of the two is the nerve of our ecumenical life. After Amsterdam, in the fifties and sixties there was continuing parallelism and grow-ing polarization, with massive efforts to find theological concepts which would bridge the gap—eschatology, christology, creation and history. In the 1970s there came Faith and Order's main explicit effort thus far to face the question in the Church-Humankind study. And this study actually broke in two parts: on the one hand, a continuation of the theologizing efforts of the fif-ties and sixties to find universally valid bridge-concepts ("sign"); on the other, collaborative work with other WCC units on Church unity issues in concrete contexts.

But the 1970s also saw a sharp increase in the polarization of the WCC itself. And Faith and Order responded with new ini-tiatives on both sides of our theme—BEM on the Church side, "Account of Hope" on the humankind side. Moreover, we began to develop "conciliar fellowship" as a new bridge theme—a "structural principle" and not simply a conceptual framework, as we said. Very important, incidentally, is that all three initiatives of the 1970s involved a quite new intensity of participation in Faith and Order work by non-Commission members. "Baptism, Eucharist and Ministry" became the first really thorough-going experiment in something like church "reception" of ecumenical thinking. "Conciliar fellowship" was developed with a quite new kind of participation by Central Committee and assembly. And the "Account of Hope" work was notable for the scores and even hundreds of local accounts which were seriously used in arriving at our "Common Account". There is an important practical lesson here: in a situation of growing polarization, growing par-ticipation.

My question is the following: In this ecumenical situation, what ought a new study of this theme to aim at? Not simply a new theological document, I think, nor simply a moving act of witness (as I would call our "Common Account of Hope") in contrast to a rigorous theological statement. And not simply, either, to generate more collaboration among the units of the World Coun-cil itself, polarized as the Council sometimes appears to be.

I don't yet see the concrete goal of a new study very clearly, but I think I can discern something of the new shape of this ecumenical problem in the WCC.

It remains a bi-polar problem. But the dynamics on both poles are changing.

On the Church unity side, there have been two basic developments in the last decade, symbolized for me (in terms that are very inadequate) by the Orthodox and the third world respectively. Let me rather call them developments A and B.

Development A has been a historical deepening of the Church unity problematic, involving the work on BEM, conciliar fellowship and now decisively on the apostolic faith. A Faith and Order which once understood its Church unity problem basically as inter-Protestant (much of the 50-year discussion in BEM was honestly that), has moved to a vision of conciliar fellowship which takes the relation with Rome and Orthodoxy with deep seriousness, and is now beginning to move into the unresolved issues of the Nicene period. We used to marvel at how contemporary the sixteenth century could be. But the agenda of Lima is finding the problems of the fourth century inescapable! That deepened historical problematic is basically new for the WCC. Though the Orthodox have always been in the WCC, and 1961 marks a new intensity of their presence, I think it is not wrong to see in the present Church unity situation a new profundity of Orthodox theological participation and presence.

Development B at the Church unity pole of our problem is the growing urgency of two liberation motifs: the notion of "the Church of the poor" as a way of thematizing how the third world views the *ecclesial* issue, and of "the community of women and men in the Church" as a no less clamant theme, especially, but by no means exclusively, in the west.

It is characteristic of both themes ultimately to ask for what the Roman Catholic bishops at Puebla called "a preferential option" for the victims of oppression, that option to be expressed in commitment not simply to compassion but to basic structural change. And about that option three things are claimed: (1) without that option, no Church unity, (2) that option must generate tension and even conflict within the churches as they presently exist, (3) therefore, Church unity profoundly understood must embrace such tension, controversy and polarization and make it fruitful.

I hardly need to say that under those challenges—the historical deepening and the contemporary polarizing of the problematic—the Church unity pole of our theme needs fresh work.

As for the humanity side of the theme, who can deny the rapid change in the past decade? And who can presume to describe it? Perhaps it is sufficient here to say that from this side comes not only an incredibly rich diversification, but also powerful new pressures towards polarization in the human community and among the churches. The human community is being divided as never before.

In the recent life of the World Council, these developments at both poles of our theme are tangled together. Not the least of the challenge to Faith and Order is to sort them out and say something helpful for the unity of the World Council itself. Perhaps we speak too easily of polarization. There is a wrong polarization which infects and divides our life and must be resisted. There is also a right demand for a "preferential option" which belongs to the quest for contemporary Church unity. The two must not be confused. Discerning that difference—and why the pressure for polarization is not the same as the demand for the "preferential option" which unity requires—is very near the heart of our challenge in designing a new study.

That study will require us to probe beyond, certainly to develop, the unifying principles and bridge concepts which have served us in the past.

Talk about the Church as the "sign" of the coming unity of humankind is profoundly right, but is very general and needs much development, as Bill Lazareth pointed out.[4] On the other hand, the demand for a "preferential option", necessary as it is to the quest for Church unity, is too particular to serve as a basis for unity. There is a Church unity problem among "the churches of the poor"; there is a Church unity problem among churches which claim to manifest "the community of women and men in the Church".

"Conciliar fellowship", as a basis for facing our growing polarization, seems to me worth developing, with two provisos: (1) this is no mere structural principle but an ecclesial principle with profound roots in the nature of the divine triune life in which we share, and profound implications for the future of our churches' life together; and (2) "conciliar fellowship" must be a fellowship of both ecclesial and situational integrity among churches which are facing and making the "preferential options" demanded by God in our time—and for whom controversy concerns not whether but how such options are to be actualized.

3. It remains only to remind us of the calendar, for we are undertaking a large task.

We have our initial study process here at Lima.

The next milestone is Vancouver, eighteen months from now. What do we contribute to Vancouver and how do we prepare it? What do we hope to receive from Vancouver for this study, and how do we propose to get it and make use of it?

Beyond that is the next Plenary Commission, probably in 1985. We need a study plan for this entire three-and-a-half year period which will help us accomplish a definite piece of work.

Beyond that, there has been talk of a possible Faith and Order Conference in the late 1980s—a larger gathering in the succession of Lausanne (1927), Edinburgh (1937) and Montreal (1963). Should we perhaps think in even longer range terms and design a study which could reach its climax in the call for such an occasion?

What would such a study concretely aim at? I don't yet see the goal very clearly, but I know what I would hope for as a provisional, not ultimate hope: for a result which would help the WCC in its still "pre-conciliar" life to make very explicit that the quest for the visible unity of the Church is at the heart of every item on its agenda.

NOTES

[1] *New Directions in Faith and Order*, Bristol, 1967, pp. 131-132.
[2] *The Uppsala Report*, pp. 223, 17.
[3] *Unity in Today's World*, Faith and Order Paper No. 88, p. 51.
[4] This address is included in Vol. I of the Official Report of the Faith and Order Commission meeting in Lima, 1982.

Working group reports

Creation

I

Introduction

In the outline for the programme for Vancouver, "Jesus Christ—the Life of the World", two sub-themes are mentioned which are closely related to the issue of creation:

1. Life, a gift of God: Life is inherited by all creation. We affirm this life as God-given through Christ to be nurtured among all people and in all creation. The Church is called to be the living body of Christ. Yet we confess that Christians share in the neglect and violation of creation. We must understand anew, and proclaim, God's purpose for the world and exercise a more responsible and reverend stewardship of its resources.

2. Life in unity: Christ prays that we may all be one. We affirm that God's purpose is to restore all things into unity in Christ. The Church is called to be a sign and foretaste of that unity. Yet we confess that in our world our communities and our churches remain divided. We must break down the barriers among ourselves and in our world.

God's purpose in creation

God's purpose in creation is that humanity may be one, that the whole creation may live in harmony, that all the richness of the created world should be shared by all people in a "just and participatory society". God created every race of human beings of one stock (Acts 17:26). God did not create people as rich and poor. "God created human beings in God's own image; in the image of God God created them; male and female God created them" (Gen. 1:27-28). God created male and female for a community of love and service which is the image of the *koinonia* within the triune God. God's purpose is a community of peace and service of love and sharing which includes all of humankind and the whole created cosmos.

Fall and restoration of creation

It is the fall and sin which bring distortions and tensions into God's creation, which lead to disintegration and, in our time, dangerously threaten the very existence of humankind and creation. Because of our sins and the sins of the world, we find ourselves under the judgment of God.

In spite of this, we affirm that God's purpose, as it is manifested in Jesus Christ, is to restore all things into unity in him. Everything was created in him (Col. 1:16) and all things, whether on earth or in heaven, are reconciled through him alone (Col. 1:20). As creation is aiming at its reconciliation in Christ, it has to be understood in dynamic terms of the "new creation" in Christ which is prevailing over the old creation. God the creator who sent God's Son that the world may be saved is at work through the Holy Spirit, the Giver of Life, counteracting the forces of disruption. "When thou breathest into them they recover; thou givest new life to the earth" (Ps. 104:30).

Since we are called as churches to be a sign and foretaste of new creation and of unity, we have to discover the forces of disintegration, to break their power and so break the barriers among ourselves and in our world, to renew our Christian community and to bring renewal and unity into the community at large. We have to be advocates of the life of the new age, of the life which was revealed to us in Christ and which is given to us in the eucharist so that all may have life abundantly.

Violations of creation

Creation is being violated and distorted in different ways. The community of men and women, which is at the root of all human community, is corrupted by the sin of domination; the right and the duty to work which is given to all human beings as the divine assignment (Gen. 2:15, 2 Thess. 3:10) is withdrawn from large numbers of people. Creation is violated by unjust distribution and accumulation of resources whereby humanity is divided into the poor and the rich, by exploitation of nature whereby resources which should serve all and be available for future generations are being wasted. Creation is threatened in the age of technology by nuclear destruction, misuse of genetic manipulation, ecological abuse... The list is growing.

These violations of creation are possible because the relation of faith to creation in many western churches is broken (as their relationship to the ecological movements indicates). As Dorothee Solle has written, there is "negligence and postponing of the issues, lack of creation spirituality, over-emphasis on (personal) salvation, lack of trust in God's promise and its symbol the rainbow, fear of principalities and powers, fear of the authority of the state, misunderstanding of Paul's teaching of obedience".

The violation of creation has very much to do with power. In the history of the Church, the doctrine of the Holy Trinity was often falsely understood in hierarchical terms of domination in close connection with political power.

Divisions within the churches

This situation of the world is reflected in the life of the churches. They live within these conflicts. "The Church must... bear the tension of conflicts within itself and so fulfil its ministry of reconciliation, in obedience to the Lord who chooses to sacrifice himself rather than to confer on the forces of division any ultimate authority. The Church accordingly is called to call for unity, through suffering, under the sign of the cross."[1]

In many places, the churches live in a sociological captivity of economic exploitation and cultural domination. They are not able to transcend divisions between the rich and the poor, the races and the sexes and so they are denying God's purpose of creation. The question of investment brings into the churches and into the ecumenical movement new divisions. The danger of war leads in many Christian circles to apocalyptic visions which weaken the responsibility for the preservation of the created world. Christians are not unanimous in the refusal of atomic weapons.

Overcoming the forces of disruption

The forces which lead to disintegration and destruction of creation have to be discovered and challenged on the basis of the biblical witness. In discussing these issues, and in taking a stand with regard to them in order to achieve unity, we are not following the goal of "general cosmopolitan or generally humanitarian unity" apart from Christ, nor are we dealing with secular questions in an ideological context.

In taking a stand on these issues, we are confessing our faith in God the Creator, our Christian hope that goodness and meaning in creation will prevail, and our faith in the resurrection by which we enter, through the Holy Spirit, into the realm of the new creation. The renewal of the Church and its true unity in the eucharistic fellowship cannot be achieved without overcoming these kinds of divisions. If we are dealing with these issues, we do not want to weaken the interest in traditional theological questions of unity and of confessing the apostolic faith. On the contrary, we discover the relevance of these traditional issues to our situation. In accepting the challenge of the situation of divisions within and outside the Church, we get deeper insight into theological issues.

The Church, in which conflicts of this world are being transcended in true reconciliation, is a sign of the new life which it manifests in its doxological and sacramental reality. But because the Church does know the mystery of God's plans as revealed in Christ, it has to announce the "wisdom of God in all its varied forms... to the rulers and authorities in the realm of heaven" (Eph. 3:10) in fulfilling its prophetic role.

God's ongoing work in creation

We are ashamed of our failures when we see that there are groups and movements outside the Church which were engaged in actions for justice, peace, and an end to ecological abuse before the churches were actively aware of these problems. Is it not a sign of God's ongoing creation? How is God working in his creation outside the Church? We were not able to find theological answers to these questions. But if we were to avoid these questions and link the activity of the Creator only with the Church, we could run the danger of becoming a countersign to God's reconciling love in the world.

Doxology to the Creator

"The earth is the Lord's and all that is in it" (Ps. 24). We are only stewards of God's creation. We have to praise God for the riches God gave to us. We have to develop a new spirituality in our relation to nature, a spirituality which shares in the growth of Christians into an even fuller, richer apprehension of the purpose of Christ in God's creation. Prayer shares in Christ's wholeness, is directed towards the wholeness of living and loving that he exemplified, and is already, this side of the final kingdom, an expression of a commitment that enhances the things of today into the horizon of eternity.

Community in love is God's purpose in creation.

> Human being...
> Why are man and woman created in God's creation?
> For the sake of being opposition and comparison?
> Or being an enemy to one another?
> Or being a manipulating-exploiting tool for one another?
> Human being...
> Woman-man exists for the truth of agape living
> Man-woman exists for the truth of power uniting
> Woman-man exists for the truth of being whole
> Man-woman exists for the truth of being one.[2]

II

In the second part of the discussion, further issues were identified for elaboration in future study.

1. God's ongoing work in the renewal of all things: This issue concerns several questions. Already at the Fourth Faith and Order Conference in 1963 in Montreal, the question was raised: How is Christ exercising his kingship outside the Church? This issue has to be clarified in a broader pneumatological and trinitarian context (the *filioque* discussion should not be forgotten in this connection). The function of the Spirit, the giver of life in creation, should be more developed. The issue also involves the problem of the relation between the kingdom of God and the Church, a problem which should be studied not only against the background of history but also against the background of creation.

The report of the Community Study helps us to see that there is a dynamic tension between our reflections on life in the perspective of creation and life in the christological framework of new creation. Although our contributions move in a pattern of creation-fall-redemption-new creation, they all include the tension of life-new life in Christ. Clarification of this dynamic tension needs to be given attention in the assembly work.

2. The need for a new spirituality in relation to nature and creation: This spirituality could be studied (1) in the biblical witness (e.g. in psalms), (2) in the old liturgies (e.g. in the baptismal liturgy of the sanctification of water), and (3) in other cultures in relation to the biblical understanding.

3. Corruption of the human community by power and the renewing and uniting power of the cross: This issue includes the question of different forms of domination (sexual, cultural, technological and economic) on one side and the reconciling power of the Cross in the eucharist on the other.

NOTES

[1] "Towards Unity in Tension", in *Uniting in Hope*, Accra 1974, Faith and Order Paper No. 72, p. 93.
[2] From "The Community of Women and Men in the Church", Sheffield report.

History

I

The word of God

The word of God goes forth in the history of God's revelation first of all as a prophetic word, summoning to exodus (cf. Gen. 12, Ex. 3, Matt. 19:16ff), to critical separation from the world. It warns of the need to be watchful in face of the enslaving powers of this world, and announces God's judgment on these powers. At the same time it promises peace and salvation for all humankind, and indeed for the whole creation. Again and again people were so deeply moved by this divine declaration regarding coming judgment and promise that they ardently advocated its obedient acceptance not only, it is true, by the witness of their preaching and example, but also by the use of methods of earthly power, often even "with fire and the sword". Their way of action in the name of God appears to us today to be ambivalent; these people were not only attached solely to obedience to the divine mission, they were conditioned by the historical circumstances of their age and by very arbitrary conceptions of God's rule. They often threatened and oppressed those they considered "God's enemies": people of a different faith as well as the "heretics" in their own midst (who, from our modern viewpoint, were sometimes the true prophets of their age). Examples of such intolerance are Elijah (1 Kings 18:40), the leaders of the people who condemned Jesus, the expansion of Christian rule in east and west, the Inquisition of the Catholic Church in the Middle Ages, and the attempts of some of the Reformers to establish God's rule on earth.

Very often, action for the word of God was at the same time a fight against the "images" of those pagan gods which are no gods, against the fascination of cosmic powers which captivate human beings, sometimes against the better judgment of their reason, through their hearts and their covetousness. Human emotional susceptibility to cosmic influences is, therefore, not only a precondition of vitality and self-possession, but also a latent ground of anxieties. In this way, commitment to the prophetic-critical word of God could be combined with an interpretation of alien religions as diabolical. Cosmic wisdom, the knowledge of the cosmic factors conditioning human psychosomatic wholeness, could be decried as superstition and magic. Sexism and racism also have their roots here.

The prophetic word

Correctly understood, the prophetic word is intended to free human beings from fear and, as a light in darkness, teach them the right way to deal with cosmic powers. The prophetic word is one of enlightenment, promoting objective, detached criticism of the powers of the cosmos, a liberating word which of course presupposes decisive conversion to the Lord of all powers, and abandonment of all sinful enslavement to them, but not an acosmic existence. For it is at the same time a word which promises a new cosmos, a word which directs history towards a future in which God himself will make all things new.

In Jesus Christ, this promise has become a reality. In him, history has received a reality in which the image (the "icon") of the renewed humanity, indeed of the renewed cosmos, has shone forth, and did so on the cross. It is the image of the Son, whose capacity to suffer is rooted in the fact that he remains in the Father's love (John 15:10). His message is that through his blood we have forgiveness of sins, and consequently share in his glory even now as children of God. We can and must walk in love, because God's love has made us free for that. It is through the experience of God's love that we become capable of accepting ourselves; the Son of God himself takes form in our hearts (cf. Gal. 4:19) through openness to God's liberating word.

Even as a member of the body of Christ, each of us remains in many ways conditioned by historical circumstances, necessities and pressures. In the midst of these conflicting powers and interests, and in the many insoluble antinomies of history, does the Church succeed in becoming effectively liberating and reconciling by representing its unity in Christ in a convincingly vital way?

The word made flesh

The word of God was made flesh. "He came to his own home" (John 1:11) in order to cause what had been created in the beginning by the word to shine in new glory. Christ is the renewing "Yes" to the whole cosmos. In him, the word of God caused the form of the new humanity to shine forth. That is why, on christological and soteriological grounds, the Second Council of Nicea declared the importance of images in relation to Christ. The image of the new humanity in Christ is an image intended to take form in all who accept the word of God. The message of this new reality is *eu-angelion*, "good news", intended to bear fruit in an "honest and good heart" (Luke 8:15), though indeed only according to the law of the grain of wheat (John 12:24) which must die if it is not to remain alone. To the extent that we carry the death of the Lord Jesus in our body, the life of the Lord Jesus will be manifested in our body (2 Cor. 4:10). The glory of the children of God is a reflection on their faces of God's goodness. The good news of Jesus' death and resurrection in us not only determine our actiont but also affect the conduct of our life in this world—in overcoming the consequences of sin, in healing all divisions and estrangements, all distortions of the human face. Only by representing and bearing witness to the image of the new humanity in whose heart God's glory has shone forth, can we as Christians credibly make our contribution to overcoming the divisions between poor and rich, men and women, people of different races and cultures (cf. Gal. 3:28).

A challenge to the Church

Nevertheless, even in the history of Christianity the word of God has often, and indeed increasingly, been preached in a one-sidedly intellectual way without sufficient attention to the cosmic reality in which it could have proved a transforming force. The history of the illumination which the word of God set in motion became more and more a history of secularized enlightenment, with all the consequences of destruction of the cosmos and human alienation with which the WCC conference on "Faith, Science and the Future" was concerned.

A critique of this rationalistic Enlightenment and its consequences has not been carried out, least of all by the Church. Since the nineteenth century there has been a demand for a critique of criticism, for enlightenment about the Enlightenment, and at the same time for a new, post-critical esthetics in quest of human wholeness, in the struggle for liberation and human rights—but too often without church support. However, protest against an acosmic, one-sidedly intellectualist and ethically oriented rationalism, for which the Judeo-Christian view of history is often made responsible, is appearing today, but in a different way: (1) in an irrational and destructive sub-culture among people who reproach Christianity with a rejection of the body, and (2) in a new gnosticism, among people who fail to find in Christianity a true wisdom regarding the cosmic laws governing the psycho-somatic wholeness of the human person.

All these phenomena constitute a challenge to the Church. In what way is it a historically formative force? Can it contribute to the saving welfare of the individual and of human society as a whole? The study on "The Unity of the Church and the Renewal of Human Community" ought, therefore, to promote new sensitive awareness of the expressions of the life of our churches. To what extent do they bear witness to the *eu-angelion*, to the power of the word of God to reshape the whole cosmos from within?

Towards unity and renewal

The ways in which the life of our churches finds expression are various. Often they have been an occasion for divisions, and they continue to be, as it were, consolidated grounds for division. Often such divisions resulted from historically necessary renewal movements. Often they reflect inherently different social situations. Certainly there are expressions of the life of our churches which have not yet been sufficiently clarified by the word of God, pre-critical manifestations of life which rightly provoke protest. There are, however, also in our churches, manifestations of life which are conditioned by an acosmic intellectualism or a one-sidedly ethical rationalism. Other churches are disturbed by contact with non-Christian religions. Others again see themselves quite newly threatened by confrontation with the challenges of secularized rationalism. All this is an obstacle to the unity of the Church.

On the one hand, the expressions of the Church's life cannot be a matter of indifference. On the other hand, there is a legitimate plurality. What are the criteria of truly incarnational forms of life which at the same time reflect Christ's cross and resurrection? That is the fundamental question of an ecumenical esthetics, the answer to which will provide the framework, for instance:

— for a fundamental appraisal of human experiences;
— for a renewal of the liturgy;
— for the relation with non-Christian religions and possible adoption of their wisdom and rites;
— for a new relation to the fine arts;
— for renewed language.

Very often Christians are not aware of the historical factors conditioning their own denominational attitude in these problems or of those of their brothers and sisters in the confessions separated from them. The study should therefore endeavour to make this known. We propose that, in the preparation for the WCC assembly in Vancouver in 1983, this process of education should be done in regard to the rites of baptism, eucharist and ordination, as well as to the Church's ministry itself. Undoubtedly, in this particular domain, there are distorting phenomena—for instance in bureaucratization, or in ritual forms and their language—which make it difficult for particular groups to recognize signs of their personal salvation in these important expressions of the Church's life.

The Faith and Order World Conference, proposed for 1987 on the 1200th anniversary of the Seventh Ecumenical Council, might serve as an occasion for achieving convergence of views on the basic questions of Christian conduct of life and, in this sense, on an ecumenical esthetics. An esthetics understood in that way is not a luxury but a consideration of the historical figure of the Church, of the question of how the Church must look in order to be an icon of salvation in a world in which many demonic powers estrange human beings from themselves (e.g. by awakening artificial needs through the images of seductive advertising).

Rediscovery

Our western history may be regarded as a dialectical juxtaposition and opposition of word and image, history and cosmos, enlightenment and gnosis. In the course of it, decisions have repeatedly been taken in favour of the word.

The studies on "Baptism, Eucharist and Ministry", "Community of Women and Men in the Church", and "Towards the Common Expression of the Apostolic Faith Today" are to be understood, in part, as attempts to rediscover dimensions lost in the course of history—that is to say, what we have suppressed and repressed in our own history and consequently have difficulty in accepting in others.

The endeavour to work out not only the socio-economic and political but also the philosophical, psychological and cultural conditions of our own history could make us more sensitive and open to discussion in regard to the history of others, and consequently more capable of ecumenism, and make us more aware and critical in regard to an all-too-uniform, liberal, enlightened civil religion, a religion of mediocrity.

Conflict

Confessional movements have set themselves against the unity of the Church in particular historical conflicts and have frequently been suppressed, thrust aside, declared heretical, by a prevailing ecclesiastical or secular power.

What part is played in such historical conflicts by the pursuit of unity and renewal? What role is played by power and authority? What do we lose, or suppress, in our endeavour to maintain or achieve unity? When does unity mean renouncing renewal? It might be useful to examine historical examples in regard to the tension between unity and renewal.

Language

Language exerts power. It separates and unites, frees and oppresses. Theology is involved in such oppression by language. For example, how do people in a church, in a particular theology, speak of men and women, war and peace, tradition and change? In what context do they speak, on what occasion, for what purpose? How are conflicts, ambivalences given expression? How is difference, plurality spoken about? And, above all, who speaks?

What does it mean that in the interpretation of events our western history is seen essentially as a history of men?

Ambivalence

Historical conditions are ambivalent. We live in diverging domains of responsibility, in unresolvable tensions. These tensions in themselves are also ambivalent, good and bad, destructive or productive. What do plurality, unity, renewal mean in face of such ambivalences (and antinomies)? How is such ambivalence to be judged theologically? Our (western) conception of history, despite (or because of?) the Enlightenment, bears the gnostic stamp: God's revelation is immutable. God does not really enter into history. The tension between creation and redemption, between "even now" and "not yet", is eliminated in favour of an imperative which is itself often timeless. Can we call our conception of history simply "Judeo-Christian"? What other elements has it incorporated? What, in this context, is the significance of dialogue with other religions and cultures?

In his paper, "Unity Between Hope and History—a 'Third World' Perspective on the Ecumenical Movement", delivered at the Faith and Order Commission in Lima, Miguez-Bonino described the Christian mission and ecumenism as a "capitalist bourgeois project". The attempt to see one's own history with another's eyes, to work it out jointly with others, is a possible chance to escape from imprisonment in one's own conception of history. We regard studies of this kind as necessary where unity and renewal are concerned.

Observations on the study

If we ask who determines history, it is clear that the powerful are obviously the masters of history. That means that the structures of the world and of the Church are not as they should be. The world and the Church must ask themselves how those who are not in power are to determine their history. We offer the following obervations:

1. The five concepts "creation, history, culture, alienation and mission" are, for the present study, undoubtedly very central, but they do not commend themselves as separable categories. Rather, for the sake of the study they might better function as perspectives cutting across the content of the whole. One such perspective might be furnished by the notion of an "ecumenical esthetics" (as elaborated in our group report). Another might be "the Church and the kingdom of God". Under this latter theme most of the ethical issues might be subsumed.

2. An important problem is the connection between creation and redemption. The gifts of "mother earth"—as well as the rich contributions of non-Christian religions, peoples and cultures—are from God.

Jesus found faith in the unlikeliest people. The Christian tradition is familiar with the notion of *anima naturaliter christiana*. On the other hand, there ought to be a standing warning against the misuse of this notion in such idolatries of the creaturely as the Nazis' "blood and soil". To what extent are some of the currently popular trends endangered by these idolizations? The basic problem is hardly new. Already, in the earlier history of Christian missions, there was the question whether the missionaries ought really to fell the sacred oaks of the pagans or rather to revere this latent praise of God's creation.

3. The proposed study should be particularly concerned with the extent to which the Church's proclamation (and indeed the study programme itself) is trapped by very time-conditioned trends. These trends often have their own agendas, their own programmatic concepts, which too easily serve to discredit and defame others who may not share these views. (For example, the "peace-movement" might imply that those who do not favour disarmament are opposed to peace.)

4. The Church must face the possibility of finding itself in *status confessionis*. Still, even in the circumstance of separation, the Christians, so divided, continue to intercede for one another, exemplifying thereby to the world the radical Christian power of "love of the enemy".

Culture

Introduction

In our quest for unity of the Church and renewal of the human community, we have increasingly realized that culture is the fundamental factor which affects our endeavour both positively and negatively. By "culture" we mean the total way of life of peoples which defines their corporate identity. Defined in this way, culture includes language, institutions of marriage and kinship, law, art, song and dance, politics, economics, religion and so on. Cultural identity includes the history in which that identity has been formed.

To say that in the contemporary world there is a great diversity of cultures is to say also that there is a great diversity of histories. The urgency of our quest for unity of the Church and renewal of human community is imposed upon us by our acknowledgment of the fact that until now the cultures of those nations which rule the world economically are imposed both directly and indirectly upon peoples in less powerful nations.

This imposition undermines our quest for unity in the Church. The endeavour to achieve unity in the Church is directly related to the quest for renewal of the human community. In turn, the quest for renewal of the human community includes a campaign against the cultural imperialism of powerful nations, and another campaign for the promotion of those cultures that have so far been downtrodden.

Our vision of the renewed human community is the vision of a community in which the peoples of all cultures appreciate mutual reciprocity towards one another, a community in which the individual members of every culture appreciate mutual enrichment by overcoming the barriers of race, sex, economic class and cultural heritage without underplaying the significance of these barriers.

The gospel is "Good News" for people of all cultures, and it challenges all cultures. However, the significance of that challenge in each culture should be determined by persons belonging to that culture, not by outsiders imposing what they think is best. All life comes from God. The ability of the human race to evolve cultures is an integral part of God's creation. We need, therefore, to affirm God's involvement in the creation and renewal of all cultures.

The cultural factor in our quest for unity of the Church and renewal of the human community may be viewed under the following themes: (1) diversity of cultures, (2) God's revelation in history, (3) the cultural mould of Christianity, (4) modern science and technology as pipelines of culture, and (5) towards a new approach for the cultural renewal of human community.

Diversity of cultures

The ecumenical situation in which we are living today encompasses all cultures of the world. The *oikoumene* of today extends far beyond the Greco-Roman, Mediterranean region in the context of which the classical creeds of the Christian faith were articulated. Today's *oikoumene* includes all continents, and its cultural orientation has been greatly influenced by the imperial powers which emerged during the last three centuries. The achievement of political independence in Africa, Asia and Latin America has brought about a new crisis within the Church because the churches which arose from the modern missionary movement have been rather slow in appreciating the cultural diversity among their members.

Cultural diversity underlies most of the conflicts which prevent peoples and churches from expressing a common and united identity as human beings and as Christians. Religion is lived and expressed within cultural contexts, and there is no authentic religious expression which is free from cultural conditioning.

The diversity of cultures in our world can produce positive ingredients for the renewal of the human community if there is mutual appreciation of the strengths and weaknesses of all cultures. No culture is perfect, but all cultures have positive values which should be affirmed. There is an ambiguity in every culture because the positive qualities of culture may promote renewal of the human community while the negative qualities may hinder such renewal.

When the heirs of one cultural heritage impose that heritage at the expense of others, such imposition militates against the renewal of human community and may produce the "worship" of that culture as an end in itself. Such idolatry produces tensions in the human community.

Since religion finds expression within cultural contexts, Christianity as a universal religion should reflect the culture of all the peoples who affirm it. However, in many places the churches are not rooted in the local cultures, but are superficial appendages which the local people find culturally alienating. This is especially so with regard to liturgical forms, the practice of baptism, eucharist and ministry and also in the cosmological and eschatological presuppositions underlying Christian theological expression. Cultural alienation in the expression of the Christian faith should be given priority in the study on unity and renewal of Church and community.

Culture is the basic factor that cements society. In our quest for unity and renewal of Church and community, we need to affirm and promote those aspects of culture which are socially integrative. For example, in Africa all social relationships are covenantal, so that every person bears responsibility towards others according to established custom. Marriage, for instance, is not just a union of wedding individuals, but a union of extended families. The individual personal identity is in terms of relations with others. Such integrative cultural values can enhance our quest for unity and renewal.

We need also to negate and campaign against those aspects of culture which undermine unity and renewal of Church and community. For example, we need to discourage those practices which hinder the participation of women and men as partners in Church and community, according to the gifts bestowed upon them by God. In our quest for unity and renewal, the study on "The Community of Women and Men in the Church" (particularly the Sheffield report) provides useful guidelines which should be followed up in the subsequent work of the Faith and Order Commission.

God's revelation in history

We have been accustomed to interpreting the Old Testament from the point of view of the Jews, without emphasizing the positive aspects of the relationship of the Jews to other peoples. How would the account of God's involvement in history be understood if it were told from the perspective of those people with whom the Jews interacted? The prophets occasionally emphasized that God is the Lord of all history and that nothing happens without God's direction.

If we affirm that the God whom we worship is the author of all history, then we have to affirm that God has been involved in the development of all cultures. This affirmation compels us to re-examine the doctrine of "election" from the perspective of those peoples about whom the Bible does not speak.

The New Testament records the faith of the early Christian community in the context of the cultural and historical challenges which the apostles faced. In particular, it reports how the tension between the Jews and Gentiles was resolved (Acts 15, Gal. 2 and 3): "In Christ there is neither Jew nor Gentile." It was not necessary for the Gentiles to undergo circumcision in order to become Christians. Thus they could affirm the lordship of Jesus, without subordinating themselves to Jewish culture. Unity in Christ transcended cultural identity without overlooking cultural distinction. Likewise, unity in Christ transcended the barriers of sex and social status without denying the existence of those barriers. In affirming unity in Christ, the early Christian community evolved a eucharistic fellowship which exemplified and heralded the renewal of humankind. What does our understanding of the apostolic Christian community in the context of Greco-Roman cultural variety mean to us today in our quest for unity of the Church and renewal of the human community?

Many of us have been accustomed to viewing Christianity as a culturally iconoclastic (destructive) religion. However, a critical rereading of church history from apostolic times to the present may reveal to us that the Church has been selectively culture-affirming. In the Epistles we find, for example, the acknowledgment of cultural variety, and the conscious endeavour to build a unified and renewed community transcending, but not ignoring, the cultural backgrounds of believers. Likewise, the Reformation in Europe was a process in which Christians endeavoured to root their faith firmly into their own national cultures.

In many places all over the world, the modern missionary movement adopted a *theology of cultural displacement*. In our quest for unity and renewal of Church and community we need to evolve a *theology of cultural reconstruction*. Christians whose cultures have been undermined in the name of mission, and those involved in the promotion of liberating and renewing theologies, should be in the vanguard of this reconstruction.

The cultural mould of Christianity

From the early Church fathers, we have inherited a common faith which we all share as Christians. We are obliged by our commitment as Christians to affirm this faith. At the same time, we are challenged to ask what that faith means for us today. Our ecumenical situation today includes a wider *oikoumene* than that which was presupposed in the early Church. Ours is an *oikoumene* in which many more cultures are in contact and conflict, in which many more languages are spoken and many more religious traditions are engaged with one another.

Our affirmation of the faith of the early Church fathers compels us to appreciate the doctrinal issues which they resolved in their time and cultural context, and honestly face the questions raised by the Christians of today, encompassing all six continents and all cultures. Our quest for unity of the Church and the renewal of human community will be greatly enhanced by a re-examination of the Christian faith from the perspective of those Christians who do not belong to this ancient cultural heritage.

Cultures come into being and after a time may be destroyed or transformed by historical factors. The extent to which a culture is able to renew itself depends on the ability of its people to absorb insights from other cultures while making an impact on those cultures. The dynamic of cultures is such that the more a culture contributes to others, the more it regenerates and transforms itself. In our quest for unity and renewal of Church and community, we believe that all cultures should have the opportunity to regenerate themselves by contributing towards the building of a universal community.

Modern science and technology as pipelines of culture

We live in an *oikoumene* where modern science and technology have become producers and pipelines of a culture that challenges both the Christian faith and the traditional cultures of all peoples. Science and technology have brought great blessings to all peoples. But at the same time their quantitative achievements have tended to overshadow qualitative renewal of the human community. Science and technology have made work easier, improved health, raised food production and offered the possibility of better housing and clothing. They have facilitated human communication on a global scale, thus facilitating interpretation of cultures at an unprecedented rate.

At the same time, however, science and technology have been abused in the production of weapons, in the manipulation of peoples through the mass communication media, and in the undermining of traditional cultural values.

Science and technology have a positive integrative quality (e.g. simultaneous translation, international telecommunications) but technological uniformity and automation can be culturally destructive. (Discussion on this topic may be stimulated by the published report of the MIT conference on "Faith, Science and the Future", as well as by subsequent consultations organized by the WCC Church and Society sub-unit.)

Reliance on science and technology has tended to replace faith in God, thereby producing a new idolatry. We need to continue investigating the theological implications of modern science and technology as producers and transmitters of a universal culture which is materially satisfying but spiritually empty. We need even to raise the question whether this universal technological "civilization" is not primarily the promotion of western cultural interests.

Towards a new approach for the cultural renewal of human community

When one culture is promoted all over the world as if it were the ideal culture for all peoples to adopt, the application of this approach can lead to competition of powerful cultures to dominate the world. In the process of this competition, the powerless peoples are culturally and economically subjugated in the interest of those who have the means to dominate.

Our quest for unity and renewal of Church and community should be based on the humble and voluntary acknowledgment that every culture has its shortcomings and stands to be corrected and enriched by other cultures. This reciprocal acknowledgment compels all human beings as a race to refrain from imposing themselves upon one another, and to seek the common affirmation of humanity on the basis of the intrinsic worth of all cultures.

All Christians should feel obliged to offer, for the unity and renewal of Church and community, the cultural values they have inherited. At the same time, they should feel obliged to consider critically the values offered from the heritage of other peoples.

In order to respond effectively to these obligations, it will be necessary for us to embark on educational programmes with the objective of incorporating cultural awareness in the life of the Church on the basis of cultural reciprocity.

Recommendations

1. Title of the study: we recommend that the study be titled "Unity and Renewal of Church and Community".

2. Theological focus: we recommend that the Faith and Order Commission accept the rationale contained in the "Bases and Outline" developed by the preliminary consultation in Geneva (June 1981).

3. Emphasis of the study: we recommend that in the study emphasis be placed on the effort to *relate* our quest for unity and renewal of Church and community to the global contexts of cultural pluralism.

4. Design of the study: we recommend that the proposed five themes (creation, history, culture, alienation, mission) be compressed into two main thrusts:

— theological interpretation and cultural pluralism;

— church practices and ecumenical consensus.

5. Processes of the study: we recommend that the study include the following processes:

— encourage informal local groups to discuss issues arising from the five group reports and send their reports and suggestions to the secretariat for wider dissemination;

— organize, in collaboration with the sub-unit on Dialogue with Peoples of Living Faiths and Ideologies, two world consultations before 1987 on "Religions and Cultures" and "The Christian Faith and Indigenous Cultures";

— prepare a presentation for the Vancouver assembly, using various audiovisual techniques, in order to stimulate discussion on the new thrusts of the Faith and Order Commission;

— promote collection and dissemination of folklore materials, oral history, cultural traditions, etc., as resources for a study on theology of cultures;

— encourage future theological study projects in non-European languages;

— cooperate with the Programme on Theological Education to promote the new emphasis on theology of culture in

theological colleges, especially in Africa, Asia, Latin America and the Pacific;
— initiate a study on the understanding of history and nature in the Bible and in other religious traditions;
— stimulate discussion on the function of culture in theologies of salvation and liberation;
— solicit case studies of situations that illustrate the role of culture in unity and renewal;
— undertake a study on modern science and technology as pipelines of culture.

Alienation

The theme "Unity of the Church and the Renewal of Human Community" has been divided in five sub-themes: creation, history, cultures, alienation, and mission. Of these five, the issue of alienation appears to be the most general, and the one least often addressed by Faith and Order.

Alienation—the loss of a common ground of meaning—is a universal phenomenon which can take various forms. There is racist alienation, sexist, tribal, cultural, and even linguistic alienation. Other striking examples of contemporary alienation include squatters' movements and anti-militarist crusaders, refugees and their families, and alienation between the generations. They all attest that the traditional Judeo-Christian belief that the deepest human need—to love and to be loved—is being displaced by a new vision of life concerned mainly with the individual's wellbeing. Individualism, and the attempt to make more of one's life—the compulsive drive to get, to own and to use—are increasingly seen as what gives life meaning. Other-centredness is transformed into self-centredness and the common ground of meaning is left behind.

This brokenness of the human community is God's concern, especially since it affects the Church as deeply as the human community. Realization of this fact challenges Christians to understand the role they play in the existence and perpetuation of alienation. It also challenges us to costly acts of repentance and renewal.

In this context, our concern to bring about the unity of the Church and the renewal of the human community implies the task of healing human alienation. Here the task of the Church reaches in two directions, towards both the churched and the unchurched, the alienated in both realms. With this in mind, we offer the following observations and recommendations:

1. We encourage the churches to address the situation of alienation within their own fellowship, all over the world. We recommend that meetings be arranged, under the auspices of Faith and Order, between representatives of various groups of alienated Christians—such as squatters, restless youths, members of anti-militaristic movements—with representatives of those they are fighting. Such meetings might help to discover new ways of healing alienation and, thus, to renew the human community.

2. Since Christians in the world are a minority, often alienated from secularized, materialistic or religious (non-Christian) societies, we recommend that Faith and Order consider studying the options open to the Church in its attempt, under such circumstances, to renew the human community. Should the Church, in such situations, accomplish its task by (a) fulfilling its "great commission" in terms of proclamation, instruction, and making disciples; (b) confining itself to its own membership; (c) fostering the Constantinian concept which envisions the Church, though a minority, as called of God to govern the human community; or (d) cooperating in these non-Christian societies, with those equally concerned with and engaged in their own programmes of human renewal?

3. We recommend that study be given to the relationship between the Church and alienation in third world situations. To many, the gospel which has been entrusted to Christians to lead people to the fullness of life in Jesus Christ appears instead to create alienation. Does the gospel, as brought from the first world, help indigenous believers to become integrated in their third world cultural communities, or does it encourage alienation? Why do some regard the Church, and the gospel it proclaims, as causes of alienation? Does the gospel, intended to make us whole, also beget alienation? Are these antithetical categories or are they compatible? Does the gospel alienate even in its attempt to relate faith to one's own local situation?

4. Work is basic to human life. It is essential to the meaning and fulfilment of human existence. Yet in many situations, and under diverse economic and social systems, the distribution and organization of work seems to contribute to alienation. In some instances, manual work, because of its routine and mechanical nature, appears to deprive people of an opportunity to fulfill their vocation to work. The same is true of intellectual activities, housework and other forms of human work. Such situations contribute to the disintegration of the common meaning of life. To some, such meaning seems to be available again only through involvement in voluntary work apart from the notion of wages. We recommend that, in the context of the study on "The Unity of the Church and the Renewal of Human Community", Faith and Order investigate what the Church has to say regarding the meaning of work, both to the individual and to the community.

5. In many instances, young people and young people's movements feel alienated from the activities of Faith and Order and the programmes it sponsors. We recommend that Faith and Order invite the participation of young people in various meetings which deal with its projects and documents (e.g. "Baptism, Eucharist and Ministry") in an attempt to arouse new interest in our ecumenical concerns and discover new patterns of relationships.

6. We recommend that Faith and Order consider undertaking a study of anthropology which would show what it means to become a whole human being who is able to find meaning in life in the context of a sinful world. Such an enquiry should enable us to address one of the undergirding causes of human brokenness and alienation.

7. With regard to methodology, we recommend that the studies and dialogues suggested above be pursued with the presupposition that the scriptures are regarded as the final criterion by which conclusions will be judged. Since these issues are closely related to concerns represented by other departments of the World Council of Churches, we recommend that such studies be pursued in close cooperation with other sub-units. Finally, such studies should take account of the Christian anthropological and cosmological vision that human suffering and alienation are rooted in sin, and should clearly state the Christian eschatological vision of complete healing and eradication of alienation.

Mission

Jesus Christ is the Life of the World. That is to say, he is living water which nourishes a dry and parched and thirsty world. Like an oasis, Christ's life among us brings forth fruit and green and living things. Therefore, we speak out of our own experience here in Lima.

Our concern for Christian unity arises from our conviction that God's purpose is to restore all things into unity in Christ, and thereby to bring together the children of God into a new world which restores God's design. Through Christ's life, death, and resurrection, and by sharing in the intimacy of the life of the Holy Trinity, the Church receives its calling. It is to be a sign and foretaste of the new humanity in which all become one, Christ having broken down "the dividing wall of hostility" (Eph. 2:14) between the races, sexes, classes, and castes, so that there is "neither Jew nor Greek, slave nor free, male nor female" (Gal. 3:28). In Christ, God's transforming power of re-creation and renewal is able to overcome the human sin which creates our disorder and brokenness. That power is able to restore goodness and wholeness and to make our diversities the blessings God intended in our creation.

No individual proclamation is sufficient to attest to the light of Christ's presence in the world, whereas the common witness of baptized believers, regularly fed at the one eucharistic table in becoming the body of Christ, provides the credibility of our proclamation. In confessing the apostolic faith as one people and in the mingling of our ministries, the power of the Holy Spirit is unleashed to disclose the presence of Christ for the unity of the Church and the renewal of human community.

Yet we confess that in our world our churches remain divided, even as our communities are divided. Instead of serving as "a sign and foretaste of unity", our churches often experience (and even erect) additional barriers, making our witness a lie. Too often we have celebrated the Lamb of God in our liturgy and yet have taken the part of those who slay him in our life in the world. Thus, our task is doubled: we must submit ourselves to God's renewal even as we participate in God's effort to renew the world in Jesus Christ.

For particular circumstances, this mission may take different forms or have different emphases. The scriptures themselves present the commission in a variety of ways:

1. In the "Great Commission" of Matthew 28:19-20, for example, mission is delineated chiefly in terms of proclamation of the message of salvation, instruction, and enlistment of converts. ("Go, therefore, and make disciples of all nations, baptizing them in the name of the Father and of the Son and of the Holy Spirit.")

2. In the sending out of the Twelve, according to Matthew 10:7-8, Jesus set forth the mission in terms both of proclamation of the reign of God and of compassionate service. ("And preach as you go, saying, 'The kingdom of heaven is at hand'. Heal the sick, raise the dead, cleanse the lepers, cast out demons.")

3. Jesus' so-called "inaugural" in Luke 4:18, using the words of Isaiah 61:1-2, represents the mission in terms of proclamation of good news, compassionate service, social justice, and human liberation. ("The Spirit of the Lord is upon me, because he has anointed me to preach good news to the poor. He has sent me to proclaim release to the captives and recovering of sight to the blind, to set at liberty those who are oppressed, to proclaim the acceptable year of the Lord.")

4. The Book of Acts and the Apostle Paul's writings likewise illustrate this diversity of emphases.

Everywhere there should be concern for proclamation, gathering in the eucharistic assembly as the one body of Christ, building the community of women and men, manifesting God's love for others in actions for justice, and seeking to increase among humankind the love of God and of neighbour which are the two great commandments (Mark 12:29-31). Nevertheless, given the diversity of human situations, Christians around the world today may interpret and attempt to discharge this mission in varied ways and with diverse emphases:

1. In a comfort, convenience, and consumption-oriented culture, such as that found in the United States where most persons are members of the churches, the mission emphasis may fall on resistance to over-consumption and waste, to the construction of deadly weapons' systems, to self-centred privatization and individualism, and to the disregard for other human beings, especially the poor.

2. Where Christians are a decided minority—such as in the Gambia, India, Sri Lanka, or the Middle East—emphasis may be placed on proclamation through the uniting of the churches, through witnessing as a pilgrim community, or through carrying on dialogue by listening to persons of other faiths (and by preparing the faithful for such dialogue or witness).

3. Where there are vast inequities and disparities in goods, services, and life-sustaining necessities, as well as poverty, disease and malnutrition—as, for example, in Peru, El Salvador and many other countries of Latin America—emphasis may rest upon presence and solidarity with the poor in their struggle to obtain justice and liberation from oppression.

4. Where religion is severely restricted, such as in the Soviet Union, emphasis may be placed on the witness of the faithful through gathering for eucharistic worship or through private celebration of faith in ways permitted.

5. Where all eucharistic services or public worship is difficult and where even private Christian gatherings occur at great risk, a situation which has obtained in China over the past thirty years, Christian witness takes place only by living the Christian faith in daily life by selfless love and service to neighbours beyond the call of patriotic duties, and sometimes by courageous witness regardless of the dangers to oneself by possible imprisonment or death.

6. In societies where racism manifests itself in apartheid, economic inequality, denial of human rights, and overt persecution, such as in South Africa, emphasis may have to be on the risk of open conflict and confrontation against powers and principalities in order for all people to achieve both individual dignity and mutual freedom.

Regardless of the style or the evident results of our proclamation, we will not let ourselves be overwhelmed by the magnitude of the mission, for we engage in it in active expectancy and living hope. Though we ourselves, acting with integrity in obedience to the word of God, labour to ensure the unity of the Church, our confidence rests ultimately in God's promised reign which brings the acknowledgment of human dignity, honouring of one another, justice in society, and peace in God's own world. Humans who seek to "be" will find that promise fulfilled as they in reality become one.

More specifically, as we look towards the assembly of the World Council of Churches in Vancouver, we understand that in Faith and Order's theme, "The Unity of the Church and the Renewal of Human Community", several aspects of Faith and Order's previous work on mission must be reflected:

1. The consultation on theology and racism: As long as race and class divisions give lie to our proclamation, neither Church unity nor the renewal of human community can be achieved.

2. The handicapped: New understanding of the meaning of wellbeing and wholeness, which are crucial to both Christian unity and human community, are being discovered.

3. The community of women and men in the Church: The pyramid of domination, as expressed in our relationships between the sexes, in the exploitation of third world women, and in the difficulties of achieving true partnership and mutuality in mission, weaves a continuing web of oppression which points to the integral connection between the unity of the Church and the renewal of the human community.

Unity

"I am come that they might have life—life in all its fullness."
"It is God's good purpose to bring all things together under Christ as head."

Life is hardly worth living without purpose and meaning. Christians believe we have been shown the truest meaning and the most worthwhile purpose of life in Jesus Christ. In him we have come to know God, Father, Son and Holy Spirit, as one God, God of life and God of love.

One God: Creator and ruler of all that is, God is bringing together in his kingdom every different hope, every different love in his creation. God gives us freedom so that we might respond in love, and in that freedom human sin raises barriers and enmities. But, on the cross, God in Christ reconciled the world to himself; by his Spirit he calls his Church to be a community of forgiven sinners, heralding the possibility of reconciliation beyond all rejection and all division.

God of life: God gives life to all that is and by his Spirit over-rules the history of the world in order that all may find the fullness of life when gathered into one around his throne. Life on this earth is limited by death, but, at Easter, God restored one dead man, Jesus, to a newer and richer life. This is the promise the Church holds out to all who live, not least as around the Lord's table it foreshadows and celebrates the heavenly banquet to which all humanity is invited.

God of love: Out of the love that flows before all worlds bet-ween Father, Son and Holy Spirit, God has created in love and for love a richly diverse family of human beings. The condition of love is openness, risk and vulnerability, and human beings con-stantly spurn love for greed, for power, for self. Yet in Jesus Christ God accepted the worst that humanity could do to one of its members, refusing to pass on the evil to others in the usual vicious spiral of hatred and death, and has called his Church into being as his body to show forth, in word and deed, that in God there is living water, springing up into life eternal in love.

As part of history's pilgrimage towards the kingdom, Chris-tians in this century have been led by the Spirit into a far-reaching "ecumenical" movement, the movement which seeks the proper renewal, unity and fullness of Christ's Church in her service of the proper renewal, unity and fullness of the human community. This embraces many different facets of vision and of obedience but it remains one movement under the Spirit. At its heart is the gift of faith—God making himself known and loved. On the basis of that gift, women and men then reach out

— for the integrity and wholeness of their own lives beyond all imperfection and contradiction;
— for mutual upbuilding and correction in each community of Christ's people;
— for the healing of all separation and rancour caused by breaches of fellowship in Christ's Church;
— for reconciliation beyond any human barriers that make Christians spurn and scorn each other;
— for mutual enrichment and fulfilment from within all the diverse cultures and inheritances of humanity;
— for the repentance and renewal that can overcome the sins of rejection because of race, sex or class;

— for the overcoming of fear and hatred between the nations, the powers and the ideologies;
— for the witness of people of all convictions and faiths to each other, that we may together discover and respond to the will of the one true God.

In this pilgrimage there is always for Christians a double command—to search for what God wants for his Church and to search for what he intends for the whole inhabited creation, the *oikoumene*. These can never be separated, for the Church exists as a human community called in and for the world as a whole. They are not the same command; in some situations what is necessary and appropriate for the renewal of the Church may not appear to have much to do with the most pressing needs for renewal and reconciliation in the human community as a whole. Yet, in every situation, the search for the oneness and wholeness of the human community has much to contribute to the search for the oneness and wholeness of Christ's Church; it is also always true that obedience in the search for the oneness and wholeness of the Church, in her specific calling to be the body of Christ, will sooner or later contribute to the search for true human community. There are negative as well as positive lessons to be learned, pitfalls to be avoided as well as possibilities to be seized. The dynamism of this inter-relatedness is the leading of the Holy Spirit, restlessly guiding his people through all limitations and all sin towards the kingdom.

In the reconciliation of churches which has moved on a long way in this century, we have learned that the pilgrimage moves through a variety of stages, of which the following are examples:
— the stage where churches are in open rivalry with one another (competition);
— the stage where they begin to admit that the others are also in some sense churches, in a "live and let live" attitude (coexistence);
— the stage where they are prepared to let some of their members and leaders work together on certain aspects of their task as churches (collaboration);
— the stage where they enter into a general and binding partnership to work together over a large number of central concerns (commitment);

— the stage where that partnership has issued in such a fulness of understanding and such full mutual acceptance that they reach the goal of a single body gathered around a single eucharistic table (communion).

Of course this is an oversimplified schema; in any one actual story of church union there will be all sorts of complexities and paradoxical eddies in the total movement. Nor is the progression from one stage to another in any way automatic. Councils of churches are generally established by pioneers at the stage of "coexistence" in order to help the churches move into "collaboration" and then further towards "commitment", when they have to be replaced by a more binding form of common decision-making. But they can easily get stuck at the stage of "collaboration" as a convenient but optional extra to the central life of the Church and, thus, serve as an excuse for a lack of movement. So also bilateral conversations at the international level run the risk of being used to prevent forward movement among all the churches at the local level, and covenants between certain churches can harden the barriers between them and others. Any such structures need to be reviewed from time to time, from outside as well as from inside, to test if they are genuinely serving the pilgrimage under the Holy Spirit. A scheme like this will be helpful for such review.

Similarly, we have learned from the search for Church unity that there are always several different levels which need to be held in dynamic complementarity:

— the local, where previously separated groups come to know each other, to worship, witness and work together as one in direct personal contact;

— the area/district/diocese/synod, where church leaders can meet in mutual trust and plan together their churches' outreach and renewal in common episcopé;

— the national, where so many crucial acts of witness to secular authorities and vital internal decisions are made in conferences and assemblies;

— the international, where Christians are gradually learning to inspire and correct one another's worship and witness beyond the limitations of language, culture and political systems;

— the universal, where, in the communion of the multitude of fellow-saints of every time and place, Christians are learning to look to the "reasonable service" of a "genuinely ecumenical council" that can enable the true freedom-in-partnership of all the churches.

All purpose in human life is grounded in a vision of what may be, of what ought to be. Any such vision of a renewed world has a central criterion. Christians are inspired by the teaching, the example and above all the suffering and resurrection of Jesus, to set their hope on a new *oikoumene* of peace and justice growing out of vulnerable love, reflecting here on earth the fullness of life that God has shown us in Christ and has by his Spirit laid up for his people in his kingdom. Yet this vision, this hope, is mere vain dreaming if there is no community to show, however fragmentarily, that it can be achieved in this frustrating and sinful world. The achievement of each new unity in the Church, however ambiguous and limited, even if it must always lead us beyond further repentance and forgiveness to yet other unities, is nothing less than a witness to the actuality of God's promise of reconciliation. To spurn the possibilities that the Spirit is holding out in our time, whether because of laziness or of over-attention to detail, is in practice to suggest that God wants us as we are—which in a fragmented Church and a world of oppression is nothing short of blasphemy. The biblical vision is of a promise grounded in the life, death and rising of one who gathered his followers into a single body and who prayed that they might be one "as you Father are in me and I in you, that the world may believe".

Notes for a study on "The unity of the Church and the renewal of human community"

1. The theme of the renewal of human community, as a crucial area for exploration of the means of Church unity, continues to be key for the Faith and Order Commission in deepening its relationship to the other units of the World Council of Churches and in responding to the needs of member churches.

2. Both the theme and style of the study are needed to complete the continuing work on reception of "Baptism, Eucharist and Ministry" and "Towards the Common Expression of the Apostolic Faith Today". They have contextual aspects built into the next stage of their design but need this study on "unity and renewal" to remind them of the seriousness of contextualization. This study should also raise significant questions about the importance of "culture" on credal formulations and of "community" on eucharist and ministry. At the same time, "unity and renewal" includes a serious component for inductive research into theological issues, yet needs to be reminded of the depth of the work and challenged by new insights into the barriers or opportunities for Church unity coming from the other two study processes.

3. Faith and Order needs to explore new theological methods in the promotion of unity, methods which seek to move beyond

● These notes and recommendations, drafted by a small working group, were received in plenary by the Faith and Order Commission in Lima.

the dichotomies of universities-churches, deductive-inductive, doctrinal-historical, etc. The search for a "third way", and the reflection on what we are learning about methodology and hermeneutics, is an important part of the intended design for the study.

4. Along these lines, we are convinced that the study needs a "second level" methodology which seeks to deepen and expand the findings and insights of previous studies. The study will continue to be rooted in concrete *situations of engagement*. In seeking to clarify and narrow the focus of the study, the first step seems to be to begin with theological insights that have already emerged in other studies which present opportunities for further research, action and reflection. This would thus represent the second level of a continuing "hermeneutical circulation" in which the initial action/reflection materials, and the initial theological work (as in the Community Study), would be subject to further critical reflection and theological development, as well as further "situational testing" through already existing local and regional networks and programmes.

5. Faith and Order needs to learn how to utilize the gifts of all its members and to incorporate styles of theological reflection arising out of a wealth of cultures, spiritualities and pastoral responsibilities.

Specific recommendations

1. That the Faith and Order Commission in Lima recognize the study on "The Unity of the Church and Renewal of Human Community" as one of its major studies in the period from Lima to 1987.

2. That the Faith and Order Commission in Lima appoint the nucleus of a Steering Committee that would, along with the staff, guide future work on the study.

3. That the Faith and Order Commission, through the Steering Committee, initiate reflection on the theme and methodology of this study in order to prepare a full prospectus to be submitted to the Commission at the earliest appropriate opportunity.